SOLO

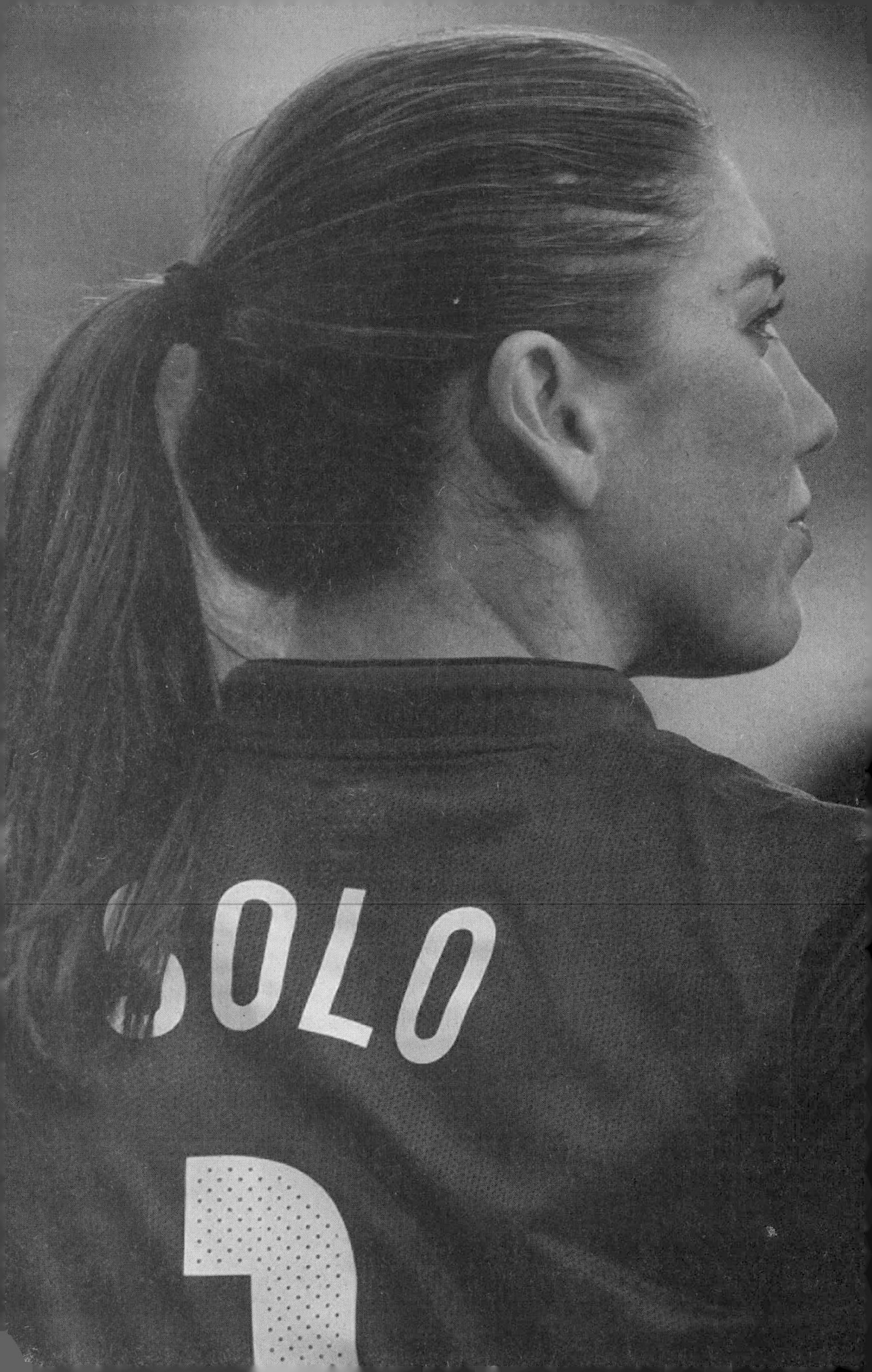
SOLO

SOLO

A Memoir of Hope

HOPE SOLO

WITH ANN KILLION

HARPER

NEW YORK · LONDON · TORONTO · SYDNEY

HARPER

A hardcover edition of this book was published in 2012 by HarperCollins Publishers.

HarperCollins books may be purchased for educational, business, or sales promotional use. For information please e-mail the Special Markets Department at SPsales@harpercollins.com.

All photographs courtesy of the author unless otherwise noted.

First Harper paperback published 2013.

Designed by Renato Stanisic

Library of Congress Cataloging-in-Publication Data has been applied for.

ISBN 978-0-06-213675-6 (pbk.)

13 14 15 16 17   OV/RRD   10 9 8 7 6 5 4 3 2 1

To my mom, the true champion

CONTENTS

AUTHOR'S NOTE

When I was young and things in my life got crazy, I would think to myself, "I'm going to write a book someday." This book is my story, one I've waited years to tell. It is my opportunity to share my life, in my own words, from my own perspective. The events and people I describe to you in the book are portrayed the way I experienced them. The conversations in the book all come from my clear recollections of them, but as a general rule they should not be taken as word-for-word recitations. In all instances, though, I have remained true to the essence, mood, and spirit of the exchanges.

—*Hope Solo, June 2012*

PROLOGUE

I don't believe in happy endings, but maybe my mother did back when I was born. She had known a popular older girl in high school named Hope who had been nice to her; for her the name was imbued with a sense of friendship and belonging. My father said he viewed my birth as a fresh start, a chance for him to leave something good in a world that had brought him mostly trouble and bad luck.

Hope.

But my family doesn't do happy endings. We do sad endings or frustrating endings or no endings at all. We are hardwired to expect the next interruption or disappearance or broken promise.

Case in point: September 27, 2007. I sat on the bench in China, at the Women's World Cup. I had been the starting goalkeeper for the U.S. national soccer team for three years. We needed to win the most important tournament in soccer to reclaim our international dominance and prove to ourselves that we were of the same mettle as the 1999 World Cup champions—the greatest women's team in American sports history. We were incessantly compared to them, the team that had changed women's sports forever during the summer following my high school graduation. Not just a great athletic team, those players had molded a reputation of overwhelming goodness, the girls next door who kicked butt on the soccer field. They projected an image of best friends—their closeness mythologized by a Nike ad campaign in which all team members announced to their dentist that they "will have two fillings," in support of a cavity-prone teammate. The '99ers cast a long shadow, one we couldn't escape.

My father had died unexpectedly two months before the World Cup. I was emotionally fragile, even though I was strong between the posts. We won our group and trounced England in the quarter-finals. I dedicated my growing string of shutouts to my dad: three consecutive World Cup games without allowing a goal.

Yet for the semifinal game against talented Brazil, I lost my job. My coach, Greg Ryan, called me into a meeting two nights before the game. He wanted to replace me with a popular former starter, Briana Scurry—a '99er who had been in goal for that championship and who had also shut down Brazil in the 2004 Olympic gold-medal game. But that was the past; Bri had barely played for three years, while I had ascended to the top spot. Yet Greg decided she would do better against Brazil based on those long-ago results.

Only a few of the old guard remained, but Greg claimed that one of those legends, Kristine Lilly, along with Abby Wambach, a younger player who had allied herself with the '99ers, had suggested the change. I felt betrayed, especially by Abby. It was a bitter disappointment, but not a complete shock.

II.

Fate, like some coaches, plays favorites. On the soccer field, I expected to be judged by my hard work and performance. Soccer made me a star in my hometown. It insulated me from hurts and harsh judgments. It lifted me out of eastern Washington and set me on a trajectory that only a few ever get to experience. It gave an anchor and order to my life, which too often had been defined by drama and chaos. But even the wins on the field, the growing success, couldn't overcome my fatalism, the sense that life was beyond my control. My father's sudden death—after he had finally found a calm place in his life after years of erratic, self-destructive behavior—was all the evidence I needed.

Being benched in Hangzhou was still more proof that hard work and talent might not be enough. Devastated, I thought of my father: I had spread a little of his ashes inside the goal at every game until this one. He had planned to be here, watching his youngest child. He always called me his Baby Hope.

I thought of my family—my mother and brother, my grand-parents and aunt, my best friend's parents, my boyfriend, and my brother's fiancée—who were sitting in the stadium. They had trav-eled around the world to support me. They were wearing black armbands in memory of my father. I had wanted to be strong and courageous for them, but now that chance was gone.

The game was a disaster almost from the start. Bri looked rusty, colliding with Brazilian forward Formiga as she came out on a free kick. In the twentieth minute, U.S. defender Leslie Osborne dove to head away a corner kick and ended up knocking the ball past Bri and into the net.

An own goal, the most demoralizing play in soccer. We were trailing 1–0.

Seven minutes later, Marta—the most feared player in the world—dribbled down the right flank and was fouled by one of our defenders, who grabbed her shorts. Marta wriggled out of the grasp and blasted a shot into the lower right corner of the net. Bri dove and got a hand on it, but couldn't keep the ball from slipping past her. On the television broadcast, former U.S. women's coach Tony DiCicco told viewers at home that it was exactly the kind of shot Bri had once always stopped. "If she's on her game, she makes this save," he said.

We were down 2–0, and it was about to get worse. In stoppage time of the first half, Shannon Boxx received her second yellow card of the game for taking down Brazilian forward Cristiane.

It was a questionable call, but there's no appealing the referee's decision. Boxx was sent off, and our team was going to have to play the entire second half a player short—ten versus eleven, for forty-five minutes.

I didn't feel vindicated by what was happening. I was distraught. I couldn't believe how poorly our team was playing—at every position. I knew we were so much better than this.

Watching from the bench in the second half, I witnessed the complete collapse of my team and our four-year dream. Eleven minutes into the second half, our defense was out of position and Cristiane flicked in another goal. Brazil 3, U.S. 0.

I sat at the end of the bench, stunned and pissed, and my face broadcast those emotions to everyone watching. It usually does. I don't try to sugarcoat bad news. At that point—in the midst of the worst loss in our team's history—smiling happily seemed pointless and fake.

At one point, my teammate Natasha Kai leaned over and nudged me. "Hey," she said. "The cameras are on you."

"I don't care," I told her. Was I supposed to act pleased as our dream derailed?

The last blow came in the seventy-ninth minute with one of the most beautiful goals in World Cup history, a dazzling play by Marta who flicked the ball over her shoulder, caught up with it, and spun past our defense to make it 4–0.

An eternity later, the whistle finally blew. The Brazilian players celebrated wildly at midfield. I had just one mission—to make my way over to where my family was sitting in the stands, to thank them for their support. As I crossed the field, Abby Wambach approached me. She looked me straight in the eye. "Hope," she said, "I was wrong."

I looked down and nodded. What could I say? The hard evidence was lit up on the scoreboard. Abby gave me a quick, hard embrace, and we walked away in separate directions.

At international soccer games, players exit the stadium through the "mixed zone," an area where reporters gather for postgame interviews. They line up on one side of metal barricades and the players walk through on the other side. Our press officer, Aaron Heifetz, stuck next to me. When someone reached out to me across the barrier, Heifetz announced in a loud voice, "She didn't play. You only want to talk to people who played the game."

One thing I've learned in my life is that I can speak for myself, that I can fight my own battles. I don't like anyone telling me how I'm supposed to feel or think or what I'm supposed to say. If I had meekly accepted what others told me, my life would be radically different: I would have gone to a different school. I never would have reconnected with my father. I would be estranged from my mother. I would have viewed myself as a failure.

I turned to Aaron. "Heif, this is *my* decision."

I stepped toward the microphone and, in an instant, broke an unwritten code that decrees female athletes don't make waves. We don't criticize. We don't dare wander beyond political correctness. Our hard competitive edges are always smoothed down for public display. "It was the wrong decision," I said, my voice shaking with emotion. "And I think anybody who knows anything about the game knows that."

I was speaking into a microphone, but I was talking directly to Greg Ryan. "There's no doubt in my mind I would have made those saves," I said. "And the fact of the matter is, it's not 2004 anymore. It's not 2004. It's 2007, and I think you have to live in the present. And you can't live by big names. You can't live in the past. It doesn't matter what somebody did in an Olympic gold medal game three years ago. *Now* is what matters, and that's what I think."

I turned and walked away, an angry Heifetz on my heels. He reprimanded me harshly for speaking out as we boarded the team bus. I told him that if he didn't want me to answer questions, he shouldn't have taken me past reporters.

I got on the bus and went to my usual spot in the back, where I always sat with my closest friends on the team. The mood was grim; everyone was in shock. We hadn't lost a game in more than three years. The conversation was muted.

"You guys," I told them, "I just did an interview."

They asked what I had said.

"I said I believed I would have made those saves."

Someone said, "Uh oh, Hope," but it was in kind of a joking way. Carli Lloyd said, "Hope, I'm sure it's fine." Other teammates had no reaction. The bus started up, taking us back to our hotel. I thought that was that, the end of a bad day in U.S. soccer history.

But it was only the beginning.

CHAPTER ONE

Life Behind the Smiley Face

My first memories are a kaleidoscope of happiness: A small red house surrounded by a wooden fence; my free-spirited mother, Judy; my big, outgoing father, Gerry; my older brother, Marcus; and me, Baby Hope.

On the outside of the fence, for everyone passing by to see, was a giant yellow smiley face. On the other side was a yard with a sand-box and a jungle gym. An English sheepdog named Charlotte. Rabbits and turtles and kittens. Out back we played Red Light! Green Light! and had Easter-egg hunts and birthday parties. Inside the house, my mother, a budding photographer, set up a darkroom to develop film, as well as a workout room where she practiced karate. I snuggled with my parents in their bed and watched TV. The cozy kitchen was where we had family spaghetti dinners.

Smiley face on the fence, happy people in the house.

But as with so much of my life, the truth is a little more compli-cated. Clutter—plastic toys, yard equipment, bikes, an old jalopy—filled up our side yard. The neighbors complained, so my parents were forced to put up a fence to hide all our crap. My mom didn't like thinking the neighbors had won some kind of victory, so she painted that garish yellow happy face as tall and as wide as the fence would allow. The smiley face wasn't a reflection of internal happiness. It was a big "Fuck you" to our neighbors.

II.

How did we all arrive there, in a tract house on Marshall Street in Richland, Washington?

My mother came for the same reason most people settled in Richland: because of the nuclear reactors. Richland, Washington, looks like a normal American town, with neat rows of streets along the banks of the Columbia River. But behind that unremarkable facade is a complex history, a town created in the dark shadows of the American dream. During World War II, the U.S. government searched for an isolated swath of land with an abundant water supply and plenty of electrical power where it could hide a highly classified extension of the Manhattan Project. They found what they were looking for in an arid stretch of emptiness two hundred miles southeast of Seattle. Hanford is in the high desert, on the confluence of the Columbia and Yakima Rivers, not far from the Grand Coulee and Bonneville Dams. It had water, electricity, and not much else. It was the perfect place to build the world's first plutonium production reactors.

The U.S. government forced the relocation of about 1,500 residents from the small farming community of Hanford, which became the 586-square-mile site of the nuclear campus. Workers were imported and housed in tent barracks, and later, in small tract houses in nearby Richland. Within a few months, the workforce swelled to 51,000, and three nuclear reactors were producing the plutonium that, once shipped to Los Alamos, was used to build some of the first atomic bombs. Most workers had no idea what they were helping develop. No one was allowed to speak of it: husbands and wives weren't even permitted to tell each other what their jobs were at Hanford. Residents had phony mailing addresses in Seattle, hung blackout curtains at night, and spoke in whispers inside their own homes. There were signs posted in public places: CARELESS TALK COSTS LIVES.

Old-timers tell stories that have been handed down over the years, of neighbors seen chatting in public before abruptly disappearing without so much as a good-bye. The secretive origins of Richland seem to have filtered down into the dusty riverbanks of the Columbia and infiltrated our ordinary lives.

Ours was a patriotic place. In 1944, every employee of the Hanford Works donated one day's pay to buy a bomber—a B-17 that was christened *Day's Pay* and flew more than sixty missions over Germany. There's a huge mural of the aircraft on an exterior wall at my high school. we are the Richland High Bombers. The bomb dropped on Nagasaki, Japan, on August 9, 1945, was filled with Hanford plutonium. Six days later, the Japanese surrendered and World War II ended. Around most of the globe, that victory, manufactured on the banks of the Columbia River, is viewed as an apocalyptic moment for mankind. But in my hometown, that incineration is still celebrated. The logo of my high school is the nuclear mushroom cloud—it's painted on the floor of our basketball court, emblazoned on T-shirts and the backs of varsity jackets and defended vigorously by Richland citizens against periodic attempts to change it to something more politically correct. The Richland motto is "Proud of the cloud."

We don't do politically correct in Richland. When I was in high school, one of our school cheers was "Nuke 'em, nuke 'em, nuke 'em till they glow!"

My family didn't help manufacture the annihilation of Nagasaki. My grandfather, Pete Shaw, was in the navy during World War II and went on to become an electrical engineer in the nuclear industry in Southern California during the 1950s and '60s. But Hanford stayed busy throughout the Cold War, so in 1969 Grandpa Pete and Grandma Alice moved to Washington with their four children. Their oldest daughter, my aunt Kathy, lasted only a few weeks. She left Richland as soon as she turned eighteen. My mother, the second oldest at sixteen and about to start her senior year of high school, was so distraught about the move that she had tried to run away beforehand, concocting an adolescent fantasy of escaping with a boyfriend. But the plan only lasted a few hours—the boyfriend was interested in someone else. When Judy Lynn Shaw looked out the plane window at the brown barren landscape below her, she groaned in despair, "What is this place?"

III.

How did my father come to Richland? I wish I knew the entire answer to that question.

Here's part of the answer: my mother, who had moved to Everett, Washington, as a young woman, married my father and became pregnant with me during a conjugal visit while my father was serving a prison sentence in Washington. My brother, Marcus, was a toddler at the time. Overwhelmed, my mother had no choice but to move in with her parents in Richland. My father followed after his release. He and my mother eventually set up house behind the smiley-face fence, a few blocks from my grandparents.

I was born on a hot, dry day in the middle of summer: July 30, 1981. My father chose that day to bring his other two children from his first marriage to Richland from the Seattle area for a visit. My half brother, David, was twelve, and my half sister, Terry, was nine. My mother brought me, her new baby—Hope Amelia Solo—home from the hospital to a chaotic house with three young children. Things never really got any calmer.

David and Terry lived in Kirkland, Washington—just outside of Seattle, on the other side of the mountains—with their mother, whose name was also, oddly, Judy Lynn Solo. My father had the name tattooed on his forearm. Once, when my mother went to visit my father in prison, she was denied entrance because a Judy Lynn Solo—David and Terry's mother—had already been there to visit him. Though we had different mothers, the four of us shared my father's DNA: piercing eyes, Italian coloring, intense emotions. David and Terry came to visit every summer, and sometimes went camping with us. They learned to call my grandparents Grandma and Grandpa. I didn't realize until I was much older how unusual it was that both Judy Solos managed to work out travel plans and schedules and invitations so that the four or us could, at brief moments, resemble a nuclear family.

David and Terry and the other Judy Solo were my first indications that my father had a past that didn't include my mother or me and Marcus, that our life wasn't as simple as four people and a sheepdog inside a tract house. Terry adored me. She liked to dress me up and curl my hair, but as I got older, I resisted. I was an active, grubby little kid. I didn't want to wear dresses. I didn't like dolls. I liked to play outside, wear an oversize Orange Crush hat and do whatever Marcus was doing, which was usually something athletic.

If he ran, I ran. If he played baseball, I played baseball. If he rode his skateboard, I wanted to ride his skateboard—not mine, *his*, because mine was hot pink and girly and his wasn't compromised by frills. Even as a little girl, I was tough and strong. One day I took Marcus's skateboard to the top of the little hill across from our house and rode down. I smashed into our bikes, which were lying in the driveway. A pedal gashed my chin and blood splashed everywhere. I was running in circles to distract myself from the pain as the blood gushed through my fingers. I had to go to the emergency room and get stitched up.

Marcus and his friends would challenge me to pull them in a wagon. And I could do it, all three of them. When my mom went on a bike ride, I would run alongside her chatting, never getting winded. I wanted so badly to play basketball with Marcus and David—my father and I would play against them, and he would have to lift me up toward the hoop so I could shoot. I loved to play whiffle ball and hated losing, determined to play until I won.

Luckily for me, I was growing up in a time when active little girls could finally turn to organized sports. That wasn't the case for my grandma, who had loved speed skating while she was a girl in Duluth, Minnesota. Or for my mother—a wiry, athletic woman—who turned to karate, and later waterskiing, for her sports fix. In the early 1980s, youth soccer was growing fast everywhere. It was my first organized sport, starting in kindergarten. I had no problem scoring goals, even as a five-year-old. We were the Pink Panthers, my dad was the coach, and I always played forward. I would dribble through all the other kids, who seemed to lack my skill or coordination, and I'd score. It was easy for me, and fun.

We played on soccer fields along the banks of the Columbia. The river dominated our lives. My mother's teenage depression over moving to eastern Washington disappeared once she discovered the river and the fun-loving community that it sustained. The river snaked through every aspect of Richland experience: we jumped in to cool off after soccer practice; we spent weekends on one another's family boats; we hung out with friends on the river docks, gossiping and tanning; we tied rafts together to create giant flotation parties; we jumped off bridges into deep, cool pools. My grandparents had a yacht and hosted large parties on the river. My mom had a small boat, and we would head upriver to the sand dunes every weekend, staying there all day, hanging out in the heat. The adults barbecued and drank, and the kids shot skeet guns, rode kneeboards down the dunes, and went inner-tubing.

My mother was working at Hanford by then, testing plutonium samples on rotating shifts, which meant a week of day shifts, a week of swing shifts, and a week of graveyards. She was exhausted a lot of the time. My father stayed home, taking care of Marcus and me. He worked sporadically, sometimes doing counseling for troubled youth. My early memories of my father are of a loving, loud, larger-than-life man—six-foot-three with a huge belly and a big laugh. He had jet-black hair and tattooed arms—a skull and crossbones on one biceps, a mermaid on one forearm, and JUDY LYNN SOLO on the other.

To him, I was always Baby Hope. We had a special bond. I remember riding on his shoulders and stroking his thick black hair.

I remember wrestling on the floor with him—his big round belly shaking with laughter. He helped teach me to read. On Christmas he dressed up as Santa. He was a popular youth coach—my soccer teammates loved him. He also coached all my brother's sports teams—baseball, basketball, soccer—and all the kids adored Coach Gerry. Sports were his passion: in our house we loved the Oakland Raiders, the Red Sox, and the University of Washington football teams, which made us outliers in an area loyal to the Seahawks, Mariners, and Washington State.

When my dad was around, we would share tubs of Neapolitan ice cream—although he ate all the strawberry—while we watched TV. We'd go to 7-Eleven and get white powdered donuts and Slurpees, mixing up all the different flavors into a sweet, soothing concoction. But as I got older, I started to see the cracks in my idyllic life. One spring, when I was a Brownie, the Girl Scout Cookie money went missing. Sometimes my father went missing. One morning, my mother went out to get her car and it was gone: repossessed for lack of payment.

When I was about five or six, my parents and grandfather stood outside in our driveway having an animated conversation one afternoon. "Come inside, Hope," Grandma said. "Come on, Marcus."

We sat at the kitchen table, with an Etch A Sketch between us. "What else can you draw on that?" Grandma asked as soon as we finished a picture. She was trying to distract us from what was going on outside, but I could hear the angry voices. I knew something bad was happening. Grandpa Pete was very upset as he talked to my parents in front of the smiley face.

Later I learned that my father had taken my grandfather's checkbook out of my grandparents' home and stolen $1,800 by writing checks to himself. He told my grandfather he had been poking around in his private office because he wanted to take his guns, but they were all locked up. He found the checkbook instead.

My father moved out the day after the Etch A Sketch marathon. I didn't get to say good-bye—he asked my mother if he could pick me up from school, but I was going to a friend's house, so he said good-bye only to Marcus. My brother wanted to give Dad something to make him feel better, so he gave him the baseball he had hit for his first home run. Marcus signed it and added the date, the inning, and the ball-and-strike count of his home run. I felt guilty for years that I didn't say good-bye to my father that day.

A short time later, we were evicted from the smiley-face house. We came home to find a sheriff standing in our front yard, saying we had to move. My father had never paid the mortgage, even though he told my mother that he had. She deposited money in their bank account, and he was supposed to pay the bills with it. To this day, she doesn't know where the money went.

IV.

There was a lot we didn't know about Gerry Solo. For one thing, that wasn't his name. I found out later, through police reports, that his name was Jeffrey John Solo. Maybe. He had other names. One time, he hinted that his last name was really DeMatteo. Or was it really Beyers? In a police investigation, years later, we learned he had two social security numbers. He said he was from New York. He said his parents were from Italy and came over in the 1880s. He was born sometime before World War II. He said he had an aunt but grew up in an orphanage in the Bronx. He had a brother named Marcus, who, he said, died in a parachuting accident in Vietnam. He may have been a loan shark in Boston. He may have had another family in Michigan.

How he got to Washington is also a mystery. He liked to hint that he had a criminal past, that he had been in the Mob. Maybe. Or maybe he wanted everyone to think he had. Maybe he was in the Witness Protection Program. He said he'd been a boxer and a semipro football player. He said he'd been in the navy and alluded to a tour of duty in Vietnam.

We did know this: he was tall and gregarious and loud. As a young man, he was extremely handsome, with classic Italian looks and a distinctive style, wearing leather loafers without socks. He oozed charisma. He had met his first Judy in the 1960s, while they were both working at Boeing, which pretty much rules out that tour in Vietnam. David was born in 1969 and Terry a few years later. Thanks to help from the first Judy's parents, they lived on twenty acres in Carnation, Washington. They had horses, sheep, goats, chickens, ducks, and German shepherds. They lived in a little cabin while they had a house built, which was finished in 1976.

Around that time, he met the second Judy. My mom had been married briefly and was on the rebound. She was living in Everett, Washington, going to community college and teaching karate. She was a black belt, and that wasn't the only tough thing about her back then: she also worked as the first female corrections officer in a men's prison in Monroe. My dad met her in a karate class. They went out for drinks. She thought he was fun. He thought she was cute. Pretty soon she was pregnant with Marcus, and they bought a house in Marysville with big bay windows overlooking Puget Sound. So now he had two families and there might have been others.

The two Judys found out about each other when the first Judy found pictures of my mom and Marcus in the glove compartment of their car. My mom got a phone call from the other Judy. When it was all out in the open, my dad brought David and Terry to the Woodland Park Zoo in Seattle to meet my mom and Marcus. Terry was thrilled to have a little brother. David was confused. Both Judys were intertwined—to my father and each other—forever because of their children.

And then my father was arrested for embezzlement. David and Terry and their mother were living in a house built with funds stolen from Lockheed-Martin, where my dad was working at the time. They were tossed out, their furniture was confiscated as restitution, and my father was sent to Walla Walla State Penitentiary.

David and Terry and their mother moved to Kirkland, where she got a job that paid $6 an hour while she filed for divorce.

My mom lost the house on Puget Sound, also part of the restitution, and moved home to Richland, and toward the end of my father's sentence, she married him and became pregnant with me. Not long after I was born, my father started an affair with the wife of a minister. My mother found out about that when the credit-card bills for Seattle hotel rooms came to our house.

It's a complicated thing, knowing how much pain my father caused in my life and the lives of others whom I love, yet still holding love for him in my heart. No matter what he did, he was my father. He helped create the person I am. He showered me with love; he just didn't know how to be a husband or a father or a responsible member of society. Yes, he was a con man. Yes, he was a ladies man. Yes, he was unreliable at best and a criminal at worst.

If I hadn't made peace with him later in my life, I'd still be bitter and angry.

V.

After we got evicted, and moved into a duplex in a low-rent part of Richland, we still had occasional contact with my father. My mother didn't bar him from our lives because she knew how much we loved him. He would promise to come and take us out for ice cream or come to our soccer games, and then he wouldn't show. I remember waiting hours for him. Sometimes he would give me a card with a check inside, and I would ask my mother if the check was any good. Even as a little girl, I was learning not to take things at face value.

One afternoon I came home from school. My mom was at work as usual. My dog, Charlotte, wasn't rushing to the door to greet me. Something seemed odd. Then I heard a noise down in the unfinished basement. "Come downstairs and see me, Baby Hope," my dad called.

To my delight, my father was in our unfinished basement. Marcus came home, and we all hung out down there: the kids, Dad, and our sheepdog, Charlotte. We wrestled and laughed. It was a great treat. But we knew to keep it a secret from my mother. We knew he wasn't supposed to be there: he had broken in and was crashing on our old couch at night. Eventually, of course, my mother found out. But instead of immediately tossing him out, she let him stay until he found another place to sleep.

Looking back, I realize my mother was pretty remarkable. She put up with a lot because my brother and I idolized our dad. Though she harbored her own demons, she had a kind heart. But there was only so much she could take. The breaking point came in July 1989.

My mother had already moved on: there was a new man in her life, Glenn Burnett. That created more tension in our household—Marcus and I weren't ready for a new parent—and my father's behavior was becoming more and more erratic. One weekend he took Marcus to Seattle without permission and had an accident—a car crash at an intersection. Marcus wasn't wearing a seatbelt and hit the windshield. He was OK, but the crack in the windshield was clear evidence of my father's recklessness. My father phoned in bomb threats to the Richland credit union and was arrested, a swat team kicking down his door and his name printed in the local paper. He wasn't particularly good at covering his tracks, whether it was leaving photos in the car glove compartment or having his phone number traced. My mother thinks the bomb-threat stunt was a ploy to distract from the fact that he was siphoning money out of her account.

After that arrest, my father was allowed to see us one night a week at the Bali Hi Motel, where he was living. But after awhile, he couldn't afford the motel and started living in the office of Chilly Willy, a packaged-food processing plant where he had a part-time job. When my mother found out that that was where her children were staying when he took them out, she put her foot down. She had just married Glenn and was trying to create a stable home. She wasn't going to have her children sleeping on the floor of Chilly Willy, even though we thought grabbing food out of the giant freezer and unrolling sleeping bags on the office floor was a treat.

One afternoon when I was seven, while my mother was at work, my dad picked up Marcus and me to take us to the Little League All-Star game in Yakima. Marcus was eleven and was upset that he hadn't made the all-star team, and my dad wanted him to experience the game. But we never stopped in Yakima. We kept going, all the way to Seattle.

We were excited, going to the big city with our dad. He made sure it was a special trip. We had ice cream and Chinese food and went to the Space Needle and the Pacific Science Center. We stayed in a hotel. It was like a vacation.

But back in Richland, it was the beginning of a nightmare. As my mom waited and waited and the hours ticked by, she realized her children had been kidnapped by their unreliable father. She didn't know if we even knew our phone number or the address of the new house we lived in with Glenn. She borrowed my grandpa's truck and drove all the way to Seattle on what she knew was a futile mission, circling around places she thought we might be. It was useless. She ended up driving back over the Cascades and contacting the Richland police.

I knew in my heart that my father was hurting my mother and grandparents, yet I was just happy to be spending time with him. I wasn't happy with my new life with Glenn, and the changes made me angry. I knew my dad and brother would keep me safe. I didn't want to think about the consequences.

BUT AFTER A day or two, the fun started to wear off. One morning in the hotel, I woke up and my dad sat down on the bed. "Baby Hope, you just missed your mom," he said. "She just called and said you could stay another couple of days."

I hadn't heard the phone ring. I hadn't heard him talking. I knew something wasn't right.

In the middle of another night, a woman came to our hotel room. My dad opened the door a crack and let her slip in, thinking Marcus and I were sleeping. I remember waking up and seeing her naked at the foot of the bed with my father. He was on top of her, and then they slowly slipped down to the floor. I squeezed my eyes shut tight, trying to erase what I had seen, but I was scared and confused and ashamed. In the morning, I pretended to be asleep until the strange woman left and then made a deliberate show of waking up. I was angry with my father and didn't speak to him but refused to tell him why. As the "vacation" continued, I was more and more sure that what we were doing was very wrong.

Then, on July 26—I know because of the police records—my father took us to a bank in downtown Seattle to cash a check. The police, guns drawn, quickly surrounded him when we walked in the door. He was handcuffed and pushed into the back of a police car as my brother and I watched in horror. He was driven away, and Marcus and I were all alone on the sidewalk in a big city, abandoned and terrified.

How did my father get caught? It was a setup. I was told that the naked woman in our hotel room had a love-hate relationship with him—she sometimes gave him money; her daughter may have been *his* daughter, but he didn't claim her. That woman wanted to hurt him, so she gave him a check to cash and then called my mother to let her know where he'd be. My mother called the Richland police, who alerted the Seattle authorities.

Marcus and I were taken to the police station. My father was allowed to see us. He was crying, tears running down his big face. "I fucked up," he said. "I'm sorry."

He pulled two hundred-dollar bills out of his pocket and offered them to Marcus. "Go buy something," he said. "Buy something for yourself and Baby Hope."

Marcus pushed the money back. "You're going to need this more than we do," he said.

In that moment, my brother seemed very grown up.

Child Protective Services took us out of the jail and to an office, where we were watched over by social workers and given a childish coloring book. I pushed it away, overcome with anger at the attempt to placate me. The grownups were trying to fool me into thinking everything would be OK if I colored a happy picture.

The other Judy Solo finally picked us up and took us to her house in Kirkland. There we were with our parallel lives: moms named Judy, older sons, younger daughters, and all those seemingly happy lives blown apart by the same man.

That afternoon, the other Judy drove us to Ellensburg, midway between Seattle and Richland. My mother met us there. As we drove back to Richland, I boiled with anger. I was mad at my mother for taking us home. Mad at my father for lying to us. Mad at myself for doing something wrong. I was mad at the world.

A few days after I got home to Richland, I turned eight. And I didn't see my father again for a very long time.

CHAPTER TWO

God's Second Paradise

The whimpers and howls drifted skyward in the night air, snaking through my bedroom window and under my covers. Wails of suffering and fear and loneliness. I couldn't bear it anymore. I pulled on a sweatshirt and flip-flops and pushed open my bedroom window, climbed out onto the deck and crept down into the backyard to where Charlotte, our massive English sheepdog, was dying.

We had just returned home from a family vacation in Priest Lake, Idaho, a state park in the northern tip of the Idaho panhandle. We had driven there and back—my mom, Marcus, and my new stepdad, Glenn Burnett—towing our boat behind us. Charlotte was too big and too old to come along. We had left her under the care of a neighbor, but when we got back, we discovered that Charlotte had been in the same spot in the backyard the entire time we'd been gone. Unable to stand up, she was matted and weak and covered in her own waste.

I was nine. Charlotte had been my lifelong companion. I learned to stand by pulling myself up on her curly white fur. She had been my playmate, my protector, my pillow for as long as I could remember, always there. She had moved with us—from the smiley-face house to the low-rent duplex we lived in after my parents split up to the house we now lived in with Glenn.

The move to Hoxie Avenue hadn't been easy for her. Glenn was a hunter and had two Chesapeake Bay retrievers; sharp-witted, protective dogs that I thought were mean to Charlotte. She seemed distressed to be sharing her home and her people with outsiders. Now Charlotte was about to die. She weighed close to one hundred pounds and couldn't move. My mother couldn't get her in the car to take her to the vet; she could only manage to clean her up as she lay outside. The vet suggested my mother give her some potent painkillers, strong enough to allow Charlotte to slip away in her sleep. Marcus and I hugged our dog and cried, saying good-bye. My mother got the painkillers down Charlotte's throat, and we had left her alone to fall asleep.

But the painkillers weren't working. She was moaning and yelping, alone and scared. Outside in the dark night, I crawled onto her blanket under a tree and lay down beside her, inhaling her familiar musty scent. "Good girl, Charlotte," I whispered. "You're a good girl."

I kept my arm around her and we breathed together. She stopped whimpering. We both fell asleep.

Hours later, my mother came out and found me in Charlotte's bed. She made me go back up to my room and get into my own bed.

The next morning, when I woke up, Charlotte wasn't there. Glenn had disposed of her body. The big dog that had played with me and my father in the yard of the smiley-face house was dead. One more part of my family was gone. *I* felt like whimpering and howling, but at least I could take comfort in knowing I had eased her pain in her final hours. Many years later, when I was an adult, I found out that Charlotte had not died in her sleep. The painkillers had never taken hold. Glenn had finally taken his gun and shot Charlotte in the head.

When I learned that, I burst into tears. My poor sweet dog.

II.

My mother and Glenn met while boating on the Columbia River. They were both river enthusiasts, both Richland natives, both

Hanford employees. I'm sure my mom—after the chaos of life with my father—was attracted to Glenn's steady, authoritative personality.

They were married on the Columbia River on a beautiful March day in 1989. I was wearing a polka-dot dress that matched the one worn by my new stepsister, Connie. She was Glenn's daughter from his first marriage, three years older than me. Two boats were tethered together, bobbing on the current. The wedding party—including Connie, Marcus, and me—walked from the bow of one to the other, where the marriage was performed. Other boats pulled up alongside, and the occupants cheered and clapped for the newlyweds. I stood rocking gently on the calm water, proud and happy to be part of the ceremony.

But the calm didn't make it ashore. Glenn inherited two angry, traumatized stepchildren, who didn't have boundaries. He tried to instill order—I know now he was trying to do the right thing, but Marcus and I weren't interested in a new father, or new rules. And we didn't have a vote in the matter. Glenn was a no-nonsense man—six foot six, more than three hundred pounds, with a voice as rumbly as the truck engines he worked on. He could usually be found in the garage, dressed in Carhartt coveralls, cleaning guns or sharpening knives with his buddies. He had a fondness for racing dirt bikes and speedboats and hunting deer. His presence filled up the split-level house on Hoxie. He barked orders at Marcus and me, made up rules, occasionally even tried to spank us. We had never been treated like that. Before Glenn came along, we had been free to do what we pleased, latchkey kids dependent only on each other, with a mother constantly working to support us. Now we had more order, more stability, but tension and anger pulsed through our home.

When my mother first started dating Glenn, my father was still living in Richland. He mocked Glenn and said mean things about his stoic personality, his size, his intellect. Marcus and I happily mimicked his disdain. When Glenn arrived, our opportunities to spend time with our father became more and more restricted and our mother less and less willing to leave us in his care. We didn't understand that my father was creating the situation by having nowhere to live and becoming increasingly unpredictable: we could only see that since Glenn had entered our lives things had changed.

My father kidnapped us four months after the wedding. To Marcus and me, it wasn't a crime. We viewed it as a desperate attempt by a loving father to connect with his children, who were living with another man.

Not every interaction with Glenn was a fight. He took me to hunter safety lessons, where I learned how to shoot a gun, clean a duck, build a blind. We went boating up to the sand dunes and inner-tubing on the river. I did my homework in the living room sitting next to him. We had family dinners in the kitchen—my mom's tacos were everyone's favorite. Glenn bought Marcus his first hunting dog, Hank. One day, Glenn took me to get Rex, a yellow lab that was being given away by a hunter because he wasn't a good hunting dog—he was too goofy and uncoordinated. He quickly became my new best friend.

But after his arrest in Seattle, my father dropped out of our lives. He simply vanished, leaving behind a gaping hole.

Our resentment of Glenn quickly filled the void.

III.

My best friend, Cheryl, and I braced against my bedroom door, pushing as hard as we could, trying to keep Marcus out. He was pounding and screaming on the other side. I'm not sure what he was furious about, but Marcus was frequently mad. He wanted to hurt us or at least scare us, and we were desperate—panicked, really—to keep him out.

Marcus tried to get us to back off. Through the crack underneath the door, he poked sharp arrows, trying to pierce whatever body part we had wedged against the door—our butts, our feet.

When this storm passed and Cheryl and I tried to leave the

house, the situation wasn't any safer. My room was at the end of the hall, and to escape we had to go past Marcus's room. He sat by his door and took aim at us with arrows or darts. Once, trying to dash to the front door, I took a dart in my ass. Sometimes, Marcus shot me with a BB gun leaving welts on my body.

The house on Hoxie was a battlefield, a war zone of screaming, swearing, and disrespect. Chaos was the norm. Glenn was mad. I was angry. My mother started drinking heavily. And my brother was in a rage.

The day our father was shoved into the back of a police car in Seattle, Marcus was eleven, on the cusp of adolescence. We were both scarred by the experience, but Marcus's wounds ran deeper. He was becoming an angry, volatile teenage boy.

Around the time that my dad vanished, our oldest brother, David, distanced himself. After high school, he had played football at a community college in nearby Walla Walla, and we saw him frequently. Marcus idolized him. But now David was off playing football at Willamette College in Oregon. He had his own falling out with our father, and his way of dealing with the pain was to move on. From all of us.

Marcus took after my father—dark-haired, dark-eyed, and big. As a child, one boy teased him relentlessly. When Marcus was in seventh grade, he beat the crap out of the kid, bad enough to send him to the hospital.

With that fight, Marcus was branded. He was a tough guy, a target of local police, viewed as a threat by teachers and parents. There was another side of him too: he was a good athlete and had lots of friends in the popular crowd. He had a kind heart and would defend kids who were outcasts; every morning he gave a mentally challenged neighbor a ride to school. But Marcus never backed down from a confrontation, and by the time he got to high school, his reputation was firmly established all over town. You didn't mess with Marcus Solo.

The violence extended into our house. I learned to fight from my battles with Marcus. We would joke that we had normal brother and sister fights, but in truth there was nothing normal about them. We pushed and punched and kicked and scratched and screamed insults into each other's faces. He hurt me; he hurt things I loved. He would take my pet rat, Stinker, and throw him in the street or drop him from the second story onto the trampoline. I'd laugh and then scream, running to save my pet.

War was waged on physical and emotional levels. Marcus knew exactly what to say to hurt me. He called me selfish, ugly, a stuck-up bitch. He once told me I was mentally retarded, explaining that mom hadn't ever wanted to tell me. His nicknames for me and Cheryl were Nasty and Nappy. He called us dykes, even though we were too young to know what that meant. Even though the insults were rude, I still craved the attention. Yet I tried to hurt him back. With words and with my fists. I called him fat and stupid and whatever cruel things I could think of. Marcus claims I gave worse than I got and that he simply got in trouble for retaliating. That was true, at times.

And like Marcus, I was gaining a reputation. When I was in fourth grade—the same year that Marcus pummeled the boy who had teased him—I saw a bully picking on a classmate, a nerdy kid who couldn't defend himself. I was furious. I pushed the bully off his bike and punched him in the face. The school principal called my mother, and I was suspended from after-school sports for a few days. The boy's family was outraged that a girl had beaten up their son.

That was the first time I remember getting in real trouble at school, the first time I remember using my fists outside my own house. But it wasn't the last time. I was trying to prove myself to Marcus. He was not only my tormentor; he was my closest family member and my protector. He walked me home from school, kept me company, made me laugh. We were welded together, the only ones who understood the crazy shit we'd been through. We could fight each other, but pity the outsider who tried to mess with us. And the outsider in our house was Glenn.

IV.

Every time we went to Priest Lake on vacation, we returned home to some sort of disaster and drama.

One summer we got home late, the day before school was to start. I woke up to the sound of my mother screaming. Our house was on fire and she was trying to find Marcus, whose room was engulfed in flames. But Marcus was in my room: for some reason he had fallen asleep there. My mother was about to throw herself into the inferno to pull out her son when we burst out of my bedroom. I think that was a bonding moment for us, when Marcus escaped what seemed like a sure death. We made our way out of the house, wrapped in sleeping bags and trying to make sure all our animals were safe. We stood in the street and watched the house burn as firefighters tried to keep the flames away from the garage, where Glenn's engine fuel and ammunition could have caused an explosion. The top level of the house—where my bedroom was—burned up, along with all my recently purchased school supplies and clothes.

On the first day of school, I wore one of my grandmother's oversize T-shirts, tied up on the side. I was humiliated. The four of us moved into a horrible cheap motel room, increasing the tension exponentially.

Usually, when things got too tense, Marcus and I escaped to our grandparents' house. Grandma Alice and Grandpa Pete lived just a few blocks away from our house on Hoxie. They had a sign by their front door: GRANDKIDS WELCOME. And they meant it. When we showed up at the front door, we were always let in, no questions asked. We could get a snack or play a board game or just tip back in one of their big recliners and watch TV. It was calm at my grandparents. They loved us unconditionally.

Grandpa Pete was brilliant; he'd earned his electrical engineering degree from USC after serving in the navy. He managed the engineering unit at Hanford until he retired in 1988. Grandma said she married him because he was the only man she'd met who was smarter than she was. He always seemed happiest when he was out on the river, at the wheel of his yacht. Every Christmas Grandpa would decorate the boat for the parade of lights with a lighted tree, a star, and a cross he had welded together. He would let me steer the boat and get on the intercom to say, "Ho, ho, ho—Merrrrrrry Christmas!" We liked to walk down to the river together with his black lab, Maggie, and throw the rubber dummy into the water for her. And Grandpa could always make me laugh with one of his jokes, even if I had been in tears just moments before.

Grandma Alice was the rock of the family, making sure we all went to Sunday school, that we had enough pocket money, and that we had a place to stay if we needed to get away from home. My grandparents were spiritual people—they pastored at a church in nearby Mabton. Grandpa sang in the choir, Grandma gave sermons, and we helped clean up after the services; it felt like our own little family church. I went with Grandma to deliver flowers to nursing homes and to funerals. I walked up to caskets with her to say good-bye—I was never afraid of dead bodies because Grandma seemed so at peace with them. My grandparents set an example for how to treat others and withhold judgment; they cared for disabled adults, opened their home to those in need. They loved to travel: to Germany for the Passion play in Oberammergau and to the Holy Land for pilgrimages. Grandma Alice called Richland "God's second paradise" because the stark desert plateau reminded her of Israel.

Grandma explained that every stress and strain in life was the Lord's will. She peppered her conversation with bits of scripture and Christian thoughts. She told me, "Don't let the devil steal your joy." She loved my name and once told me, "Hope is, by definition, defiant. It is only when everything is hopeless that hope begins to be a strength."

Grandma and Grandpa showed up for all our sporting events and school activities. They took me to soccer tournaments in their camper, setting up chairs and playing cards while they waited between games. Their house was our shelter—a place to escape Glenn, and our mother's drinking. We'd stay there until my mother could convince us to come home, promising that Glenn would be cool. We'd go home for a while, and then the chaos would start again, and we'd run the four blocks back to Grandma and Grandpa.

V.

My mother was working full-time at Hanford. By the time I was in middle school, Hanford had shifted into cleanup mode. The government had to deal with the massive amounts of contamination and hazardous waste left behind from the nuclear buildup of the Cold War. The new emphasis kept Richland citizens employed. Mom was working to clean up what has been called the most toxic site in the world. The environment after work was pretty toxic too.

My mom had always been a social drinker, partying with her river friends. But for whatever reason—the trauma caused by my father, the tension at home—her drinking escalated. As I got older, I noticed the signs more and more. I learned to detect the plummy smell on her breath. I saw her passed out at night. I was ashamed.

Battles became our primary means of interaction. If she tried to discipline me or offer advice, I would throw her failures back in her face. I felt like the outsider in my own house. My mother seemed more concerned with Marcus than with me. He demanded more attention: he was in constant trouble as he got older, requiring my mother's intervention. She seemed to believe that Marcus needed her more—because of childhood illness, Marcus was deaf in one ear, and because of an inner-tubing accident when a rope snapped, he was almost blind in one eye. He had almost died in the house fire. I was lower-maintenance: younger, a good student, busy with sports and my social life. But I felt neglected and driven away by my mother's drinking. I didn't have my father. I rebelled against my stepfather. And I couldn't depend on my mother.

At night, lying in bed, I made up stories about running away to Seattle to find my dad. We'd eat Neapolitan ice cream—he could have all the strawberry—and watch sports and maybe even get a new sheepdog.

VI.

My sister, Terry, decided I needed a female influence. Ten years older than me, she was a young woman with her own busy life, but she stayed connected, driving over the mountains to visit whenever she could. When she went to New York, she sent me fashionable gifts, like a pink Swatch watch. One day she picked me up and took me back to Seattle for a girls' weekend. I was thrilled.

Terry is beautiful, dark-haired and stylish. When I was young, I was in awe of her looks and fashion sense. On that weekend in Seattle, she tried to spoil me and smooth down my rough country edges. She had always liked to dress me up and do my hair when I was a baby, but as I got older, I spurned her efforts and took pride in being a grubby tomboy.

But this weekend I loved the attention. She took me shopping at Nordstrom's department store and bought me a green dress covered in little white flowers, along with green suede shoes. I twirled in front of the mirror and admired the way I looked: I hadn't had on a dress in years—since my mother's wedding to Glenn. I usually just wore a dirty old Raiders hoodie, with my hair pulled back in a ponytail, my thick, dark eyebrows slashing a line across my face.

But in that fancy downtown Seattle department store, I liked what I saw in the mirror. I felt beautiful.

"Let me do your eyebrows, Hope," Terry said.

We went to a skin-care salon where I got a facial. Terry shaped and tweezed my brows. Then, all dressed up and made over, we went to the Space Needle Restaurant for dinner. The Space Needle was like our Eiffel Tower. Being there meant you were someplace important and sophisticated, high above everything else. When my father took Marcus and me there in the summer of 1989, the visit signaled that our trip to Seattle was a special event. Dinner with my sister was also a memorable night.

From high atop the Space Needle, I looked out over the city and felt like a princess, like Dorothy in the Emerald City. I felt so lucky to have a big sister who was so kind. While the rest of the Solo children inherited our father's hot temper and short fuse, Terry was a peacemaker and a caretaker. She knew that things were difficult for me at home, that I needed to feel safe and beautiful.

When I got back to Richland, I was teased because my eyebrows looked too perfect. Back then adolescent girls didn't shape their brows. But I didn't care.

And, besides, my best friend, Cheryl, told me I looked pretty.

VII.

When I was in third grade, just a few months after the kidnapping, I'd started playing on a new recreation-league soccer team. On the first day of practice, I'd met a little blond girl named Cheryl Gies. Pretty soon we were inseparable. Cheryl and Hope, Hope and Cheryl—for the next ten years.

Cheryl was one of the only people I let get close. She was allowed into my house, inside my crazy life, an eyewitness to the turmoil. She saw it all—the screaming fights with my mother, with Glenn, with Marcus. She didn't pass judgment or criticize. I think she knew things were weird in my house, but she didn't want to hurt my feelings. She remained my friend, no matter what she witnessed. When I didn't feel like a normal kid, I took solace in having a normal best friend and in her normal life. So that was something, even if it was a step removed.

Cheryl lived on the other side of town, in a new development of large homes set back from streets with equestrian names that evoked rich leather saddles and patrician roots. Many of the homes had horse pastures and sweeping views out over the Columbia Plateau. At Cheryl's house, on Appaloosa Way, no one was screaming or fighting. Cheryl's older brothers didn't torment her. There were framed pictures of her family on the walls, pleasant-smelling candles in the bathroom, no darts shooting out from behind bedroom doors, and there was no clutter in the hallway or on the stairs. Even their garage was neatly organized. Being at Cheryl's was like traveling into an opposite universe. I started to spend almost as much time there as at my home.

Cheryl's parents, Mary and Dick, were kind and generous. They invited me to spend the night all the time. They could see past my tough front. They could tell I was a good kid. Their biggest concern was my risk-taking: I was always the first one to jump off a cliff into the river, to try to swim out to an island, to leap between balconies at a motel where we were staying with our soccer team. I urged Cheryl to keep up with me, to try something new.

The truth, however, is that I'm not completely fearless. When I was a small child, I had dreams that my stomach was sliced open by pirates, and I would cry and crawl into my father's arms upon waking. I'm scared of flying, a difficult fear to deal with, considering my job and lifestyle. And I'm terrified of sharks, so I get nervous in the ocean.

But in general, Mary and Dick were right. I took risks; I wasn't intimidated by much. Why should I have been? I was coping with risk and threat on a daily basis at home.

VIII.

In middle school, I was assigned to write a paper about what I wanted to be when I grew up. It was then that I decided: *I am going to be a professional soccer player.*

I was dreaming for something that didn't even exist. This was years before the 1996 Summer Olympics, when the U.S. women's soccer team first entered the nation's consciousness. This was long before any kind of professional women's league had been established. I didn't even know the names Mia Hamm or Michelle Akers. I didn't have any role models. But I knew how soccer made me feel, and I knew I wanted to hold on to that feeling for the rest of my life.

Life was calm and ordered on the soccer field. I was special. My strength and aggression were a plus—I dominated as a forward. Back then, no coach would have ever dreamed of taking me off the field and sticking me in goal. I was a playmaker. Sure, if our team needed a goalkeeper, I was perfectly willing to fill in for a half—some kids didn't have the stomach for it, but I didn't care. I was fearless. But I was too good an athlete to be stuck in goal. That was where the slow, overweight girls played, the uncoordinated ones who couldn't run or score. I was a goal-scoring machine, always leading the attack. I felt free and unburdened when I was on the soccer field.

In middle school, our soccer team jumped up to another level. The core group had been together for years—pretty much since the day I met Cheryl—with our coach, Carl Wheeler. We became a "select" team, which meant a higher level of competition and commitment. We were expected to travel to tournaments. And there were costs involved, which made it difficult for my family. I was fortunate that Cheryl was my teammate. Mary and Dick drove me to games and tournaments, took me out to eat, and never made me feel as though I didn't have enough. My coaches, Carl and later Tim Atencio, gave me rides and helped me out, buying snacks and Gatorade if I didn't have anything with me. Of course my mom and Glenn and my grandparents contributed, but I was getting help from others as well, though I was too young to realize it.

Our team traveled around the state to play. We loved going over the mountains and beating the top teams in Seattle. They were the big-city kids who were supposed to win. We were the scrappy country kids, who showed up with garish blue eye shadow and T-shirts with numbers instead of fancy jerseys. When we beat the rich-kid Seattle teams, it was especially gratifying.

One autumn Sunday, we were on the other side of the mountains for a game. It was a dark, rainy Seattle day. Cheryl and I had carpooled with another player's family. We pulled up in the parking lot next to the field, which was located in the middle of a park, surrounded by woods and dripping trees. I got out of the car and looked around for our coach. I saw a large man, limping through the parking lot in a rumpled trench coat.

I dropped my bag. "Cheryl," I said, "I think that's my dad."

CHAPTER THREE

A Double Identity

My heart thudded as I walked across the parking lot. There was no doubt in my mind who this man was, even though the last time I had seen him was about five years earlier and he'd been in a holding cell at a Seattle police station. He was stamped on my brain forever, a figure constantly invading my thoughts and daydreams.

He stopped walking. We looked at each other and—for a beat—I wondered if he would even recognize me. I had been a small girl the last time he had seen me, but now I was on the cusp of becoming a young woman. "Baby Hope," he said and opened his arms to wrap me in a hug.

I stepped forward, into his embrace. Of course my father recognized me. Of course I was still his Baby Hope. It didn't matter how much time had passed. I wanted to ask him a thousand questions, tell him a million things. But I didn't know where to start. I felt shy and nervous, and I also had a game to play.

"Cheryl," I said. "This is my dad."

"My dad." The words tasted funny in my mouth.

During our warm-ups, Cheryl and I tried to impress him. Our ongoing goal was to break the team record for number of times heading the ball—usually we could get around seventy headers back and forth without letting the ball touch the ground. That day, heading to each other across a little path that led into the woods while my father watched, we broke the record, keeping the ball in the air for eighty-eight touches.

I wanted to play the game of my life on that muddy field in Seattle. I wanted to show my very first soccer coach what a strong player I was. My father loved sports. I wanted him to see what kind of athlete I was becoming. I was like a puppy, amped up and eager to show off, and once the game began, I channeled that onto the field. In the first half, I scored on a header, and then scored two more times. In the second half, we had a healthy lead, so we rotated goalkeepers, and I went into goal. I slipped going for a ball, and my opponent chipped it over my head and into the net. My dad never let me forget that: the first time he ever saw me play in goal, I let in a sky ball.

Happy and sweating, I went over to my father when the game ended. I wasn't sure what would happen next.

"Would you like to see where I live, Baby Hope?" my father asked.

Absolutely. I motioned for Cheryl to come with me, and we followed my father as he limped down the path that led into the woods. It was wet and dark, and our footsteps were quiet on the damp earth. I wasn't scared, just curious. To the right of the path we spotted a blue tarp set up like a tent, covering some belongings. My father stopped in front of the makeshift shelter. "This is where I live," he said.

My father was homeless. His few possessions were inside a duffel bag, stuck under the blue tarp to stay dry. There was no one else around; just one man's lonely spot in the rain-soaked woods. I hadn't had much experience with homeless people, yet I wasn't completely shocked. My father was such a mystery, he could have flown us to the moon and told me he lived there and I would have believed him.

Cheryl was more unnerved than I was. I think that was the moment she fully realized how different my life was from hers, that no matter what direction I turned, I wouldn't find a normal life.

It was time to go—we had a long drive back to Richland and even though I wanted to stay and spend more time with my father, I was just a kid. I wasn't in control. My father promised to keep in touch.

"Dad, come see me play basketball sometime," I begged.

"I will, Baby Hope," he said. "I'll send you some money."

We hugged good-bye, and I got into the car. I can't remember anything about the ride back home, except that I was shaking and numb.

How did my father end up at the same field where I was playing? I never found out. Maybe he saw that a Tri-Cities soccer team was scheduled for a game and thought there was a chance I'd be there. Maybe it was happenstance; perhaps one of the reasons my father had settled by that playing field was that he took joy in seeing young people play sports. Maybe it was just fate.

II.

That sky ball I let in while my dad was watching didn't bother me. I wasn't a goalkeeper. I was just goofing around, doing my coach a favor when he wanted to let the regular keeper out to play in the field after we had established a healthy lead. And that lead was usually because of my goal-scoring. I was a standout field player. When I was thirteen, I went an hour north to Moses Lake for tryouts for the Eastern Washington Olympic Development Program. Olympic development programs target the top young soccer players in each age group by area. The road to the women's national team begins in youth ODP. But that road can be an expensive one: ODP costs a lot of money—for travel, uniforms, and coaching. But I wasn't thinking about any of that when I went to Moses Lake. All the best players from the east side of the Cascades were there, their registration numbers written in black Sharpie on their arms and legs. Looking around, I realized how many strong players were in my age group, and I started to get a little worried that I might not make the team. For one of the first times in my life, I felt insecure on the soccer field.

There was a shortage of goalkeepers—there almost always is. Talented athletes—the kind who make up the ODP programs—are reluctant to commit to the position. Goalkeeping isn't glamorous. It's tough and stressful and thankless. And in youth soccer, players see that the less athletic kids are stuck in goal, creating a stigma about goalkeeping. But some of the coaches evaluating the ODP players had already seen me play the position. At a club tournament in Oregon when our regular goalkeeper was injured, I had filled in, and I was good at it. I was a strong athlete, and playing basketball had honed my hand-eye coordination and leaping skills—traits that not all soccer players possessed.

"Hope Solo," a coach called.

I came over to him. "We'd like to take a look at you with the goalkeepers."

I was game—I just wanted to make the team. I batted away shots, dove to make saves, and easily made my team. But then an older team—three levels up—decided they wanted me for a backup goalkeeper and cherry-picked me off my age-group team. That was flattering. So there I was, a scrawny little thirteen-year-old, playing on an under-sixteen team with girls who were much more mature than I was. Amy Allmann, a former national team goalkeeper who was the coach of the regional ODP team, didn't think I was anything special the first time she saw me play. Then she realized I was playing against girls who were three years older. All of a sudden, she was intrigued.

The older players were sweet to me. They did my hair and made me wear lip gloss, and we listened to Shania Twain's "Any Man of Mine" over and over and over again on the CD player. I was their baby sister, just a lanky little thing among the tall trees. I liked the status of playing above my age group, and I was good in goal because I was athletic and fearless. But still, I didn't want to be a goalkeeper. I wanted to touch the ball, to attack. Now I stood in the net, watching the action running away from me, waiting for my turn to do something.

My family hated watching me play goalkeeper and let everyone—coaches, players, other parents—know it, complaining loudly. My mother and grandmother thought I was being robbed of my true talent. They were also convinced I was going to get hurt in a collision with girls who had already reached their full maturity.

Their concern was valid. The first time I played with my new ODP team, I replaced the starting goalkeeper, who had just suffered a concussion in a collision in the net. As she was carted away in an ambulance I pulled on my oversize goalkeeper jersey and giant gloves and went into battle. My mother and grandmother covered their eyes. I was nervous, but I prided myself on my toughness and ability to rise to a challenge. And I did.

After that, I started living a dual soccer life. For my club and eventually my high school teams, I was always a forward, a goal scorer my teammates relied upon to win the game. But at the ODP level, I was always a goalkeeper, the one my teammates needed to save the game. The two roles kept me interested and challenged and also helped my soccer development. I learned both ends of the field. Knowing how a forward attacks is an advantage for a goalkeeper. It was as if I had a double identity—my Richland life and my expanding outside world as a successful goalkeeper.

III.

I wasn't the only one surprised to see my father at a game. Marcus went to Yakima one summer to play in a summer-league baseball tournament. He looked in the stands, and there was Dad. It was the first time Marcus had seen him in several years.

My father invited Marcus to spend the night with him in a hotel, and Marcus's best friend, Dominic Woody, came along. My dad had been Dominic's Little League coach, and Dominic loved him.

In those rainy woods in Seattle, my father had told me that

he would try to stay in touch. And he attempted to be true to his word. He called on our birthdays. Once or twice a year, we'd get an envelope in the mail stuffed with cash—$400 for each of us, an enormous amount of money for teenagers. One fall, he came to town to watch Marcus play football every weekend and stayed in a hotel. On one of his visits to Richland, Cheryl and I met him at the Holiday Inn. That was a big deal: the Holiday Inn was the tallest building in Richland at the time, and its nicest hotel. He treated us to lunch. He took us shopping at the mall and bought us matching brown-and-black-checked fedoras. He was generous, peeling twenties off a wad of bills to give to us.

My dad loved talking to Cheryl and me about soccer. He was enthusiastic—he called Cheryl "Bulldog" for her play on the field. And Cheryl learned to love him. "He makes me feel like a champion," she told me. I understood what she meant. My dad was charismatic, especially with young people. He made you believe you were capable of anything. My brother's Little League teammates always spoke fondly of him. The Richland adults were suspicious of my dad, but not the Richland kids. It made my mother crazy; seeing my father trying to impress us and act as though he had money. Any time he was around, we were ecstatic. Still, she didn't try to stop us from seeing him.

The source of my father's money remained a mystery. He was no longer in a tent or on the streets but seemed to be living with the same woman we had seen in the hotel in Seattle when he kidnapped us. She was well-off and appeared to be supporting him. One Christmas Marcus and I went to Seattle to see him at that lady's fancy house. The visit was awkward. The woman had a daughter who wanted to play board games with us. She called my father Dad, which made me furious. She didn't look like us: she had red hair and wasn't athletic, and I refused to believe she could possibly be related to us. I just wanted her to leave and let us be alone with our dad.

Eventually that woman must have kicked my father out, because one day he showed up at Terry's door in Kirkland. He was clearly living back on the streets and in need of a shower. Terry, who was married by then to her husband, Jeff, let Dad in, gave him something to eat, and allowed him to stay a few days. Then one morning he was gone.

From then on, he appeared at Terry's door sporadically, staying for a week or two, leaving his duffel bag of belongings at her house. Sometimes I visited him there. But we never knew when he'd show up or where he was the rest of the time.

IV.

By the time I got to Richland High, I already had a target on my back. I was a standout soccer player. I was a Solo. I wasn't going to blend in. As a freshman starter on the varsity soccer team, I scored seventeen goals and got attention from reporters who loved making puns out of my name: I was trying to win games "solo" or was giving my team "hope."

One afternoon, we were playing Eisenhower High. It was a nasty, physical game, and our opponents were double- and triple-teaming me, pushing and elbowing. A girl punched me, I pushed back, and a brawl erupted. I was on the ground being pummeled, and no one—not the referee or the coaches—did anything to stop it. My mother ran onto the field, screaming, "Stop it, stop it."

Our athletic director, Mr. Potter, stepped in front of her. "Judy, get off the field," he demanded.

"If you were doing your goddamn job, I wouldn't have to do it for you," my mother screamed at him.

"Get off," Potter shouted.

"Hey," shouted Marcus, coming up behind them, "don't you talk to my mother like that."

The athletic director kicked them off the field. I was ejected from the game, along with the girls who were hitting me. Marcus had to go to the principal's office for shouting at the athletic director.

The Solos had a reputation.

Marcus was a senior when I was a freshman. He'd been in trouble a lot through high school—fighting, drinking, driving under the influence. His coaches and some of the teachers at Richland loved him, but others hated and feared him. The same was true for the students—there was no middle ground with Marcus. When I got to Richland High, I sensed teachers and administrators eyeing me, thinking, *Oh no, here comes another Solo.* I, too, split people into camps: they either loved me or hated me, even though I wasn't a troublemaker. I got good grades. I made the honor roll every semester of high school and kept my grade point average at 3.8 for four years.

But Marcus's reputation was unavoidable. Guys wouldn't ask me to dance at school dances because they were afraid of my brother. One night, I tried to sneak out of my house to meet an older boy. Marcus found out, and he and Glenn ambushed the boy with baseball bats, trying to intimidate him. It was a bonding moment. Another time, down by the boat dock, Marcus beat the shit out of an older boy who was calling my grandparents' house in the middle of the night, looking for me.

Marcus was my protector, but we still battled. As I got older, his insults got worse. He used my soccer prowess as a weapon against me, calling me a "golden child," a selfish bitch who thought I was better than everyone else. Our fighting didn't let up. Still, we were a team. At the homecoming dance in my freshman year, my brother asked me to dance. I was so proud, a little freshman dancing with my cool senior brother.

V.

My mother's drinking was getting worse. I suspected she was drunk when she showed up at my basketball and soccer games. Once, cops found her passed out in her truck. She blacked out all the time, never remembering what had happened the night before. One day Marcus and I broke our grandparents' Ping-Pong table; the next day, when my mother asked what had happened, we told her she had done it. Her face dropped—she couldn't remember whether or not that was true. We were being cruel, but I wanted to hurt her: I thought that maybe if she were embarrassed enough, she would stop drinking.

I always knew where to get booze for a high school party. I could just steal a bottle of rotgut vodka from underneath the front seat of my mother's truck. It didn't matter how many times I stole one; another bottle always appeared.

Our fighting escalated. I had little respect for my mother or Glenn, so I refused to acknowledge their rules. One day Glenn had enough of my defiance. "If you don't like it, get the hell out," he shouted at me.

"I will," I screamed.

And I did. First I went to my grandparents for a few weeks. Then—encouraged by my forgiving Grandma to give Mom and Glenn another shot—I went back home. But it was still unbearable.

"Cheryl," I cried, "I don't know what to do. I can't live with them."

"Why don't you come stay with me?" Cheryl said.

She checked with Mary and Dick, who, as always, welcomed me into their home. At the time, Mary and Cheryl's middle brother had moved to Iowa for a few months for Mary's work, and her oldest brother was in college. So it was just me and Dick and Cheryl. Cheryl was sad that her mother was gone and was more than happy to have my company. So was Dick.

In those months that I lived on Appaloosa Way, Dick made us breakfast every day. Those mornings were sweet: Cheryl and I listened to music while we got dressed and did our makeup for school, like two normal sisters in a normal family, singing along to Sheryl Crow.

All I wanna do is have some fun.
I've got a feeling I'm not the only one.

After school, we did our homework in the den while Dick puttered around in the kitchen. When he asked us to be home by a certain time, we complied without argument. When he asked us to help with the dishes, we didn't complain. No one was drinking. No one was fighting. The police didn't come to the door. It was a vacation from my real life.

But eventually I went home. I knew who my family was. I knew where I belonged.

VI.

The night before Marcus graduated from high school, my father came to Richland. He and Marcus stayed up all night talking. He told Marcus a long story about working for a loan shark in Massachusetts and being involved in a shootout while trying to collect money, and having a friend who was able to get him a driver's license under another name and a plane ticket to Seattle. He said that he had two sons in Michigan. He hinted that his last name was really DeMatteo. When Marcus relayed all this new information to me, I was more confused than ever.

"I don't even know what my name is," I cried to Cheryl one night while I was staying at her house. "It might not even be Solo. I don't even know who I am."

I was a teenager. I was self-conscious. I was embarrassed that my father was homeless, that my mother was a drunk, that my brother was in constant trouble with the police, that I wasn't even sure of my last name. I didn't talk about it to anyone, except sometimes to Cheryl.

But inside, I told myself that all this bullshit was making me tougher. I was perversely proud of all these challenges, fiercely protective of my strange family tree. I was a survivor.

CHAPTER FOUR

Somewhere—Anywhere—Far Away

One evening, my mom and Glenn called me into the living room and told me to sit down.

Oh shit. What had I done this time?

"Hope, we don't think you can play ODP this year," Glenn said.

I stared at him in shock. I was in high school and I'd already been playing in the Olympic Development Program for years. I was in the regional pool. I was being scouted by top college coaches.

"It's just very expensive," my mother said. She looked unhappy. My mother had been laid off from Hanford. The economy in Richland rose and fell with every election cycle and federal budget fight, and Hanford was dependent on government funding, leading to a seesaw of hirings and layoffs. My mother was a victim of the latest round of job eliminations, and Glenn was on disability. They were about to file for bankruptcy.

I understood that finances were a strain. What I didn't understand was how they could think about taking away the most important part of my life. Soccer was my way out, how I was going to make it in the world. Between club soccer and high school soccer, I played seven days a week, and as soon as the fall soccer season ended, I played varsity basketball. In the spring and summer, there were ODP tournaments. I was working hard with a goal in sight—a college, one far away. The recruiting letters were filling up our mailbox. I loved counting them, eager to accumulate more and more. They validated all my sweat. I kept the letters in two big binders—one black and one white—and I often shut my bedroom door and flipped through them, envisioning my escape. I imagined what the schools were like, what I'd look like in the team uniform, how it would feel walking across campus somewhere far, far away, like North Carolina or California. I would leave Richland behind.

And now they wanted to take it away from me. "You can't do this to me," I shouted. "This is my life. This is how I'm going to go to college."

Glenn and my mom looked at each other but didn't say anything. I think they were surprised at the intensity of my reaction and realized, maybe for the first time, the depth of my passion and commitment. I ran into my room, slammed the door, and sobbed. If I couldn't play ODP, if I couldn't get a college scholarship, I was going to be stuck in Richland my entire life. I was probably going to end up working at Hanford, cleaning up nuclear waste.

My fears were unfounded. I lived in a community that was proud of its athletes. Without my even knowing, several people in the community had already helped me out financially, chipping in over the years to make sure I could play soccer for the Three Rivers Soccer Club, pay the tournament fees, stay in hotels, and travel to away games. My first coach, Carl Wheeler, helped out. So did Tim Atencio, who aided me in raising money to play ODP. After that conversation with my mother and Glenn, I set about fund-raising. It was humbling—soliciting money at local tournaments and asking my club for help. But people seemed to take pride in giving me a hand; my Richland neighbors were invested in my athletic success.

I was able to keep playing. And, eventually, the state and regional programs found money for me. My soccer career wasn't going to end.

II.

It was a good time to be a female athlete. The summer before my sophomore year, the Atlanta Olympics were dubbed the Women's Games. American female athletes—including the U.S. women's soccer team—stole the show. This success showed how well Title IX—the federal law passed nine years before I was born and that I was only vaguely aware of—had worked. Title IX, enacted in 1972, bans gender discrimination in institutions receiving federal funds, which opened up collegiate and high school athletics to girls. Now the first generation to grow up under Title IX was winning fistfuls of gold medals.

The U.S. soccer team drew capacity crowds that summer as they made their gold-medal run. That was the first time most people had ever heard of players like Mia Hamm, Julie Foudy, and Michelle Akers, and their popularity was rooted in soccer-playing kids like me all over the country.

But Title IX didn't make things easier inside my house. Money continued to be a touchy subject; I felt like my soccer was making things harder on my family.

After being laid off, my mother started her own business as a handywoman, doing fix-it jobs around town. Her best clients were older men and single women who didn't want to let a stranger in their homes. But her drinking got in the way, and she lost customers. It was the first in her string of odd jobs: working at a health club, running a secondhand store.

Marcus had been a good defensive lineman in high school and was planning to play football at Walla Walla Community College, just as our older brother, David, had. But he got in a car accident, breaking his ribs and suffering a contusion to his liver. So instead of playing football, he spent his first full year out of high school partying and raising hell. One night he borrowed our mother's tricked-out red Nissan Maxima and went to a friend's house to get loaded. Coming home the next morning—still drunk—he took a turn too fast and totaled the car. He tried to run away but was arrested. Because he had a suspended license, he was facing jail time. He pleaded guilty and was sentenced to two months in jail plus forty-five days of house arrest, during which time he had to wear an ankle bracelet tracking device.

Marcus was released from jail in time for football training camp at Walla Walla, but because Walla Walla is in a different county, he couldn't live there while he wore the bracelet. So my grandma and grandpa drove him there and back, ninety minutes each way, every day for forty-five days—a round-trip trek of unconditional love.

III.

My first serious boyfriend was a guy I'll call Tom. I'd had a boyfriend when I was younger—his parents were friends with Mom and Glenn, and we camped and snorkeled and played sports together. I had also dated some older guys—I never had a problem getting a date or earning the attention of boys I liked. But Tom was special. He was a year ahead of me. Tom was handsome and he played football and basketball. He was the new guy and all the girls were interested. He quickly became attached to the popular group, but was dating me. He was my first love, although I wasn't ready to sleep with him.

I didn't hang out with the popular girls. I was too busy playing sports to play their social games. I couldn't keep track: friends one day and backstabbers the next, who was wearing the right clothes, who was on the outs. I was good friends with the athletes in the group, the ones who knew me as a teammate, but a lot of the popular girls saw me as a threat. They didn't like the fact that the boys they liked liked me. And dating a guy like Tom made them hate me even more.

I was traveling a lot for soccer, missing parties, dances, and weekend outings. After I got back from one trip, I heard that Tom had cheated on me with a cheerleader, one of the popular girls. I was devastated. Late in the summer, a few weeks later, Cheryl and I walked through the dusty entrance of the county fair in Kennewick. Coming out the exit was the cheerleader who had slept with Tom. Cheryl prayed I wouldn't notice her, but I did. I made a beeline toward the girl, cutting through the stream of carnival goers.

"Hey," I said, stepping in front of her. "You're a fucking slut."

She smirked at me. "Tom's pretty good," she said. "You should give him a try."

I punched her in the face. Cheryl grabbed me. "Come on, Hope," she said. "We've got to get out of here."

We fled into the county fair, trying to lose ourselves in the crowd. I was shaking and furious. Like Marcus, she had sliced into my tender spot, and my instinct was to fight back as hard as I could.

The fallout was huge. Her parents wanted to press charges. I spent every morning in the counselor's office for weeks when we got back to school in the fall. Her parents also called my mom, who—in her blunt way—asked if they knew why I had punched their little darling.

Just another incident for the Solo family file.

Liz Duncan was my other best friend. Cheryl and I had been children when we became friends, but Liz and I had a friendship that had grown out of mutual interests. She was a year older than me and also played both basketball and soccer. Liz was also an amazing track athlete. She was fiercely competitive but dorky and funny off the court. She was beautiful and dated the best football player at our high school, but like me she wasn't locked into the popular group. I looked up to her and was happy when she went out of her way to befriend me.

Liz was a midfielder and assisted on many of my goals. Off the field, we were a team as well—two jocks dating football players that all the popular girls wanted. We were both nominated every year for Homecoming princess but seemed destined to never win. It was our standby joke—we thought the hoopla and banquets were stupid—we'd rather have been running suicide drills at practice than parading around in plastic tiaras. But, her senior year, Liz won. A year later, I did too.

Cheryl and Liz and I weren't angels. We did regular teenage stuff. I sneaked out with my mom's car before I got my driver's license. We would party down by the river—often with my mother's horrible vodka. But we weren't troublemakers, and I was just as happy kicking the ball around with Cheryl on a Saturday night or shooting hoops with Liz as going to the in-crowd party.

Cheryl and I went to soccer tournaments together. Mary and Dick drove us to Colorado for one and to Long Beach, California, for another. In Long Beach, Cheryl and I went for a walk in search of Snoop Dogg—we knew he was from Long Beach and that the "Gin and Juice" video was filmed there, so we wanted to find the house. We found ourselves in the ghetto, and Mary and Dick were not pleased when we came back to the hotel escorted by the police, who had let us know we were in the wrong place. As usual, I was blamed for orchestrating the outing. "You are the fake angel," I told Cheryl. "You do everything I do, but you never get caught."

Our high school soccer team had become a force. We made it to the state championships twice, losing in the semifinals my sophomore year and winning it all my senior year. I finished my high school soccer career with 109 goals, 38 scored in my senior year. As our soccer team became more successful, our games became events. The parents and players helped construct a new soccer field next to Richland High, so we didn't have to travel across town to play. The football players dragged couches from Goodwill out to the field and sat on them, wearing matching yellow shirts, proclaiming themselves the Bleacher Bums. When we made it to the state finals, it seemed that our whole town drove over the mountains to Seattle to attend, caravanning in buses and cars. Students were allowed to miss school for those two days.

In basketball, Richland went from having a losing program to being a regional contender while I was playing. We had a two-story gym—with that mushroom cloud painted on the middle of the court—and our games were packed with fans, some hanging over the top balcony. We made it to the state semifinals my junior year—and I had my nose broken in the process. I was an aggressive basketball player, stealing the ball at will and snatching rebounds.

All the state semifinals and championships were played on the other side of the mountains, just outside Seattle. My father came to those games. Marcus picked him up in downtown Seattle, drove him to the games, and then dropped him back off on the streets afterward.

IV.

In the winter of my junior year, I was named a *Parade* magazine All-American as a goalkeeper. I made the under-seventeen national team, which was coached by April Heinrichs. She had been a national team assistant coach when the United States won gold in Atlanta. I went to train with the team in Chula Vista, California, and played a tournament in Florida. April told me I was the top goalkeeper in camp. All around the country, coaches were noticing me: the up-and-coming goalkeeper who only trained at the position half the time.

The recruiting letters started to get serious. And I was beginning to understand that goalkeeping was going to be my ticket. Some coaches promised I could also be a field player, and others dangled playing basketball as an incentive as well. But it was clear that my major selling point was my ability in the net.

I didn't know what I wanted out of college. When asked by local reporters, one day I would say, "It's been a lifelong dream to go to Portland or North Carolina." Another day, I'd say, "It's my dream to play at Stanford, but Santa Clara is very interested." What did I know? I just wanted to go to college: somewhere—anywhere—far away. All I knew about North Carolina was that it was really good at women's soccer: the Tar Heels had won fourteen national championships, and the school put players like Mia Hamm on the national team.

Other schools were interested in me. Portland was a perennially good team that was the pride of the Northwest. Stanford was a top program and was flooding my mailbox with letters. April Heinrichs was the head coach at Virginia and was recruiting me hard. And then there was Lesle Gallimore at the University of Washington.

I knew Lesle, and I was scared to death of her. For years she had been a regional ODP coach—one of those frightening people sitting in a chair on the sideline with a clipboard, evaluating every player on the field. I think that every time I talked to her I started crying.

One summer we were at a regional ODP camp in Laramie, Wyoming. I was selected for the national pool of players, which meant I had to stay for another week. I started to cry—I was just a kid and sick of being in Wyoming. I wanted to go home. Lesle walked over to me. "Hey, Hope," she barked. "The bus is warming up, but it hasn't left yet. Go ahead and get on it if you don't want to be here."

I stopped crying right away. Lesle was intimidating.

Oh my God, I thought. *She hates me.*

Her goalkeeping coach at Washington was Amy Allmann, another one of the ODP regional coaches. She was scary and blunt, and I was pretty sure she hated me. Of course, it didn't really matter. Lesle and Amy were coaching at Washington, which was about the last place on earth I was planning to go to college. I was going somewhere far from my family.

College coaches could finally contact me directly the summer between my junior and senior years. When the restrictions were off and they were allowed to call, my phone rang constantly. Even Anson Dorrance called. Though I had expected that to be a big moment—after all, he was the most famous soccer coach in the country—it was a letdown. He made me feel that I'd be lucky to go to North Carolina, and he said something about not usually offering goalkeepers full-ride scholarships. That bothered me; it made me wonder if he respected the position. Maybe every other player in America wanted to go to North Carolina, but after that phone call, I didn't.

I started to get sick of the phone calls from recruiters. I just wanted to find a school, make a decision, and get on with my new life. And then the phone rang again. It was Lesle.

"I thought you guys hated me," I told her.

Back in Seattle, Lesle and Amy had flipped a coin to see who would call me. I was intimidated by them, and now they were intimidated by me. They thought it would be a difficult conversation because they knew I had no interest in staying in Washington. But they also knew they'd be crazy not to call a kid in their backyard, one they'd been coaching for years. "Well, we thought you hated us," Lesle said with a laugh. "But we'd like you to come to take a recruiting visit."

I knew that Cheryl really wanted to go to Washington, which was her father's alma mater. She didn't have any expectations about getting a scholarship to play Division I soccer, but she was a good player and might be able to make the team.

"OK," I said. "Do you think Cheryl Gies has a chance of making the team?"

Lesle said that she would absolutely have a chance to walk onto the team. That made me happy and I decided I would visit.

I didn't want to go to the University of Washington. But at least I was going to get a cool trip to Seattle.

CHAPTER FIVE

Bare-Branched, but Ready to Bloom

From Richland, head west, out of the dry desert of the Tri-Cities, down through the vineyards of the Yakima Valley and across the apple-covered belly of Washington State. Then up into the snow-dusted Cascades and finally down through the pine forests and into the Emerald City.

I was taking my recruiting trip to the University of Washington on a clear, cold weekend, the sky a clean blue slate above Puget Sound. I had a full itinerary: a team breakfast, lunch with Washington's head coach, Lesle Gallimore, a team dinner, and a soccer game to watch. My main goal was to have fun, hang out with a boy I knew from Richland, and go to a fraternity party or two. I would humor Lesle by showing interest in the soccer team, but I wasn't going to college at Washington.

The Huskies pulled out a close match against USC, winning 3–2. They had a defender playing goalkeeper because their regular keeper had been injured in the previous game and they didn't have a backup. It didn't matter. There was no way I was going to college there.

I liked the team's determination and the way Lesle coached them. I liked the rowdy support they got from their fans—surprising considering their relatively low profile in the sport. The enthusiastic

Huskies fans reminded me of our boisterous Richland fans. And I liked the fact that Lesle and her assistant, Amy, weren't trying to bullshit me—they didn't even promise me a starting spot. They said that maybe I could play forward at times but that I belonged between the posts.

I was the top goalkeeper prospect in the country, one of the top ten recruits overall. But Lesle and Amy were as blunt and honest as they had been back when they had coached me in the Olympic Development Program when I was fourteen and an unknown. They hadn't changed. They weren't fake. I felt I could trust them. I also liked the fact that they had experience on a national level. Lesle had been part of the talent pool in the early years of the U.S. women's national team but had never played in a match. Amy was a goalkeeper on the national team from 1987 to 1991 and was on the roster in the very first women's World Cup in 1991, which the United States won. They knew the history of the sport. I didn't.

"Hope," Lesle told me, "I can see you on the gold medal podium for the World Cup."

It was nice to hear that kind of stuff. But really, I had other plans. UW wasn't even considered much of a soccer school. It definitely wasn't a powerhouse like North Carolina. It didn't place players on the national team the way Stanford or Santa Clara did. I knew I could get a full ride at the school of my choice.

On the last day of my UW recruiting trip, a Monday, I took a walk across campus. I saw students just hanging out, enjoying the sunshine. It was an eclectic crowd by ethnicity, age, fashion sense, and social stratum. I felt comfortable. Unscrutinized. I stopped by the university's music building at the top of the steps leading down into the main quad. The campus spilled out in front of me, the Gothic-style redbrick buildings arranged in a rectangle, the bare cherry trees that would blossom in clouds of pink the following spring. In the distance, Portage Bay glistened. Beyond it, snow-capped Mount Rainier, the jewel of the Northwest, sat on the horizon like a scoop of ice cream.

I suddenly realized that this was *my* corner of the country, where I belonged. I felt a rush of emotion and a click of recognition so strong that it forced me to sit down hard on the stairs. I wanted to be more than a one-dimensional athlete, a number on a jersey, a prize to be attained by some coach. I wanted more—from my college, from my family, from myself. I was like the cherry trees on the quad—bare-branched but ready to bloom.

There on the steps, my future was abruptly rearranged. I wasn't going to UW, and then suddenly I was. I could see myself here. I could be a normal college kid, without having to flee from my roots. I could be far enough away to have independence, yet maybe my family could participate in my success and be proud. Maybe my mother and I could build a relationship. My father could even watch me play. I almost started to weep from the force of my sudden conviction. I looked out at Mount Rainier, the smooth white crust covering the volcano below and knew I should be here.

Grandma would have said God was speaking to me.

II.

By the time I got back to Richland, I knew I was going to be a Husky. But I told Lesle and Amy that I didn't want to announce it yet. I wanted to keep my private business private and be 100 percent sure of my decision, so other coaches were still recruiting me. April kept up the hard sell from Virginia. I knew that April—who had been one of the main assistants to national team head coach Tony DiCicco—could be my ticket into the national team pool. She kept nagging me to take my official visit to Charlottesville, so I finally scheduled it.

Somehow Lesle found out. My phone rang again. "Hope, don't go, don't get on the plane," she said. "You're good enough that no national team coach is going to pick you based on where you go to college. You'll end up getting picked for the national team on merit."

We were on the phone for more than two hours. "If you're just going because of the national team, that's the wrong reason," Lesle said. "That's not fair to Virginia. That's not what the college experience is all about. Don't get on the plane."

I didn't get on the plane. To this day, I've never been to the University of Virginia.

III.

With college still in the murky future, I concentrated on enjoying the present, my final year of high school. On November 21, we capped our undefeated soccer season by winning the state title, the first-ever championship for Richland High. I scored two goals in the game to bring my four-year total to 109. Within a couple of weeks, I was back on the basketball court, determined to enjoy my last season of competitive hoops. The year before, we finished third in the state, but we'd lost some key players to graduation, including Liz, who was playing soccer at Washington State. Our basketball team wasn't as strong in my senior year, but I was having fun. I was key to our man-to-man defense. I loved shutting down the other team's best player, and I was our second-leading scorer.

Senior year was going well. Glenn and I were getting along better—he even used a chunk of money from his disability checks to buy me a white Nissan Maxima. I felt special, that he wanted to invest in me. Marcus was away at college, so the house was calmer. There were a lot of parties with the other seniors—we were getting sentimental about going our separate ways, leaving old friends behind. The weekend before national signing day, our basketball team played Walla Walla. Afterward, there was a big party. My entire team was there, and everyone was drinking and telling stories, laughing about old times. I was a few days away from signing my national letter of intent with UW. Cheryl and her boyfriend were there, and I was with a date who went to a different school. In fact, my date was the designated driver for the evening. When

Cheryl and her boyfriend left, my guy was eager to leave too—he didn't know anyone, and he wasn't drinking, so we left, while the party—and my teammates—raged on.

We headed home. Suddenly the car filled with red light. I turned around and saw a police car behind us, pulling us over. Thank God my date hadn't been drinking. The officer shined his flashlight in the car.

"Hugging the line there a little tight," the officer said. Then he shined the light over toward the passenger seat, on my face.

"Hope Solo?" he asked. Then, "Have you been drinking?"

There was no point in lying. I was kind of buzzed and I was a minor. It probably didn't help that I was also a Solo. He gave us both a Breathalyzer test. It proved what we already knew: my date hadn't been drinking, and I had. But the cop let us go. He just used the opportunity to give me a lecture. "You know you're a role model to a lot of people," he said. "You should be making better choices."

I was just a seventeen-year-old kid. And I thought my choice about leaving with a designated driver had been a pretty good one, but ours was a small town. Somehow our athletic director, Mr. Potter, got wind that I'd been pulled over and that I'd been drinking. He started digging around. Though I had great relationships with most of my teachers and coaches, I didn't have one with Mr. Potter. He had had run-ins with my family. Even though I was one of our school's best athletes—something I thought should make our athletic director proud—I never got the sense that Mr. Potter was on my side.

And this time was no exception.

He suspended me from the basketball team for violating team rules. Even worse, the news came out in the paper on February 3, 1999, the same day as the big news that I had signed with UW. Letter-of-intent day is a proud moment, when you get to tell the world that you're going to be a college athlete. But my day was sullied by the suspension. There was news that two of my Admiral club teammates and one of my Richland High teammates had also signed letters of intent to play college soccer, Bradee Fitzpatrick signed with Idaho, Megan Maxwell with Utah, and Jessie DeLucchi with Montana.

Further down in the story, behind a few basketball scores, was this line:

> The Bombers will be without Solo for this weekend's games as she serves an indefinite suspension for violating the school's athletic code.

My teammates told Potter and our coach that they'd also been at the party. They knew that they would have a tough road in the playoffs without me. In the hallways of Richland, students and teachers expressed outrage over the decision. Even the principal and vice principal gave me a word of support.

But a week later, the suspension was made permanent. I was kicked off the team for the season. I was very hurt—I had made a bad decision, but so had others on my team. I was being made an example of. It was the first time I realized that by excelling I could become a target. I thought about appealing the decision. Glenn went down to the school and fought hard for me. It made me realize that, in many ways, he was my dad. But the season was almost over, and I knew that basketball wasn't my ticket out of Richland. So I let it drop. I never played organized basketball again.

IV.

We graduated in June. My cap and gown were shimmering gold, and I wore a white Hawaiian lei around my neck. When I looked out at the audience, there was my father. Terry had made sure he was there—picking him up, getting him cleaned up, putting him in a nice blue shirt and driving him out to Richland with her son, Christian, who was just a toddler. I was thrilled to see my father, but his presence made anxiety bubble up inside of me. I would be going to college in the same city where he lived. Would I see him on a regular basis? Would it be embarrassing? Would my new teammates and friends judge me because of my dad?

We went out to dinner that night with both my family and Cheryl's. It was awkward trying to share my attention among my mom, Glenn, my grandparents, and my dad. I felt divided, trying to please everyone. I wasn't concerned just about my dad. I didn't know how things would be with my mom when I got to Washington. Our relationship was still tense. It was hard to imagine how we could change our deep-rooted habits of arguing and accusation.

That summer was a very cool time to be a soccer player. The Women's World Cup was taking place, and everyone in the country seemed to be talking about women's soccer. A few weeks before my graduation, the U.S. team had played in Portland, and some of my soccer teammates and I made the trip down to see the game. The players signed autographs afterward, and my teammates pushed me toward Briana Scurry. "You should meet the goalkeeper," they said. But the player I really wanted to meet was Michelle Akers. She was from Washington state and was a strong, physical player. She seemed to stand apart from the others, with her bushy hair and powerful game.

I watched every minute of the World Cup games, some of them with my grandparents and some at Cheryl's while we were making plans for our big move to UW. America's penalty-kick victory in the championship over China was thrilling. Scurry made a save that helped set up the game-winning penalty kick by Brandi Chastain. I was captivated by the effort of Akers, the aging lioness of the team who gave so much that day that she had to take an IV to rehydrate and wasn't available for penalty kicks. I loved her power, her ability to impose her will on opponents. I was still thinking like a forward.

I didn't watch the World Cup games as a fan. I didn't have a poster of Mia Hamm on my wall. I watched like a player—I was planning to someday be on that roster. And a few weeks after the World Cup, I contributed in a small way to what was dubbed the Summer of Soccer.

In late July, the U-18 national team reported for the Pan-American Games in Winnipeg, the first-ever inclusion of women's soccer in the Pan-Am Games. Soccer was becoming more than just a distraction from my home life. For the first time, it felt like a full-time job.

I allowed only two goals in the Pan-American games, had shutouts in the semifinal and final matches, and my team won the gold medal. It was a great experience: the U.S. men's team was full of up-and-coming young stars like Landon Donovan and DaMarcus Beasley. Goalkeeper coach Peter Muehler worked with both the men's and women's goalkeepers and had us train together. I trained with Tim Howard and Adin Brown, and Tim and I clicked on the field. After the final, Peter told me that my performance was the best he had seen by any goalkeeper of any gender. It meant a lot for me to hear his words of praise. He was so well respected in the U.S. Soccer hierarchy, and I knew he'd pass along his high opinion of me.

I flew through Seattle on my way home to Richland. My dad came and met me at Sea-Tac Airport, and waited with me for my connecting flight. He was thrilled to see my medal and stopped total strangers at the airport to tell them what I had accomplished. "My blond Italian goddess," he said over and over. "You're the greatest, Baby Hope. Never sell yourself short."

V.

It was time to move to Seattle. I was finally leaving Richland—and my family—behind. My mother drove me over the mountains to help me move into my preseason dorm. We went early because soccer training camp was starting, so there weren't a lot of other students around. I already felt lonely.

We pulled the boxes out of the back of the truck and started hauling them up in the dorm elevator. While my mom was upstairs, I pulled more stuff out of the truck and carried up a load, leaving some of my other possessions on the curb. When I came back down, I saw a man walking away with my small television. I stared after him in shock. "Mom!" I shouted to her as she came out of the dorm. "That man stole my TV."

"Relax," my mother said and she chased him down the street and got it back.

I felt like a country mouse! How was I going to function in a big city without Mom to rescue me? I felt very young and very dumb.

We rushed to unpack because I had to hurry off for the team's preseason physicals. It was time to say good-bye, the moment I'd been waiting for my whole life. My mother looked at me and her eyes welled up with tears. To my surprise, I started crying too. I had never said good-bye to my mother in my whole life. It was my father who was always disappearing; our relationship was a never-ending good-bye. Mom was the one who had always been there. She was the one who had been left with two kids, the one who had to support us and deal with all our shit. She made sure we got to school, that we were fed, that we had the best basketball shoes and a way to get around. She wasn't perfect, but she had tried her hardest. Despite all the harsh words and fights between us, she was my touchstone, the one I knew I could lash out at without fear of her walking out. I had been so obsessed with my father's drama, had idolized and romanticized him so much, that I had taken my mother for granted. Now that I was saying good-bye, I realized I had never needed her more.

"I love you, Hope," she said, hugging me.

"I love you, Mom," I said.

It was true. I did love her.

VI.

Before my first UW game, my goalkeeper coach, Amy, and I headed out to the field early to warm up. My dad, hands shoved into the pockets of his rumpled trench coat, was waiting outside the gate to the stadium. "Hi, Dad," I said and gave him a hug.

"Hi, Baby Hope," he said. "You look good."

"Thanks," I said, awkwardly. "Well, gotta get to work."

I went back to Amy.

"Who's that?" she asked.

"Uh, that's my dad," I said, and left it at that.

When the game started, my dad went to sit high in the upper-most corner of the bleachers, as close to one goal as he could get. When my mother and grandparents arrived, they sat in the "family and friends" section at midfield.

And that's pretty much how it went for my entire UW ca-reer—my family split into two sides, sitting in different places. My dad would come to games early; often waiting outside the fence when I arrived. He sat at the top of the stands, removed from every-one else. He would watch me intently and sometimes call out, "Let's go, Baby Hope" at a quiet moment. He wanted to make me laugh, but I was determined to keep my serious game face. He wouldn't mingle with the rest of my family—he knew how much animosity they still carried for him. He waited awkwardly for me after games while I visited with the others. I always felt pulled between the two halves of my family.

A big group from Richland made the trek over the mountains for every home game: Mom, Grandma Alice and Grandpa Pete, Aunt Susie, sometimes Marcus. Mary and Dick came to watch Cheryl, who had indeed made the team. Terry made the quick drive from Kirkland. My Richland family was unconditionally supportive, but they still hated the fact that I was a goalkeeper. They were sure that I was being punished in some way and that my true talents were being denied. Grandma Alice often wore a T-shirt with my photo on it, covered with buttons with soccer photos of me dating back to grade school. She responded to a fund-raising solicitation from our coaching staff with the following note: "I will only donate a penny for every shutout Hope registers, but I will donate $100 for every goal she scores."

But Leslie and Amy couldn't be bribed. They were thrilled to have a dominant goalkeeper. Still, they remained true to their word. I wasn't handed the starting position. I had to earn it. I split time with a junior, Leslie Weeks. I started twelve games and quickly learned that playing against twenty-one-year-old girls was a huge leap from what I'd been doing. The speed of play was so much faster; the contact going up for a cross was brutal. The pressure was intense.

In my twelve games, I made seventy-seven saves, the fourth-highest total in school history. Against BYU, I made thirteen saves, one short of the school regular-season record. But for the first time in a very long time, I learned what it was like to lose. Our team wasn't great. We finished fifth in the Pac-10 conference that year and didn't make the playoffs. I've always enjoyed challenges, and I never regretted my decision to be at Washington, not once. When my grandparents celebrated their golden fiftieth wedding anniversary, I was able to be there—heading home for a quick trip with Cheryl. And I liked taking my own path, helping to build something new.

That fall was a period of huge adjustments. When I got to UW, I started weight training for the first time. I was living in the dorms and eating dorm food. I was no longer the skinny kid who graduated from Richland High. My body was changing. I did what I was told by the trainers. I always prided myself in being first in fitness, first in sprints, first in weight training. I was great at drills: I could go up and down, diving for balls a million times and never getting tired. I wanted to work hard, harder, the hardest. But it was a shock to see how quickly my body could change. I was self-conscious of my new muscles. I thought I looked ugly in dresses.

That wasn't the only adjustment. That young, naive feeling I had while I watched a stranger carry off my television never fully went away. Back in Richland, I felt pretty savvy, but now my high-school rebellions seemed like childish stuff. At UW everyone seemed more comfortable socially and more stylish. Though I was still a good student, I was more self-conscious in class. I stopped speaking up. I was shocked by the constant partying, the random sex in the bedrooms at fraternity parties, the illegal drugs being exchanged— and the apparent ability of everyone to go crazy at night and then get up and go to class. My roommate was far more adept than I at juggling sports, studies, and men. I really liked her—she was fun to hang with—but I was uncomfortable with her habits. It seemed there was always a man in our room. Sometimes I'd wake up in the middle of the night to the sounds of her having sex in the next bed. I'd lie in bed squeezing my eyes shut, pushing away memories of my father in that hotel room with the strange woman. I felt like a little child again, in a situation beyond my control. I was put off by my roommate's lack of modesty and her disregard for privacy, but it seemed normal, so I never spoke up.

I just rolled over and pretended to be asleep.

VII.

The team activity for the week was to feed the homeless at the Union Gospel Mission Men's Shelter in Seattle's Pioneer Square. Lesle made sure we were involved in our community with regular activities, such as visiting kids at the Children's Hospital and conducting soccer clinics at schools. I knew the community projects were important, but I just couldn't do this outing. I'd seen those homeless men lining up outside Union Gospel, in rumpled coats and worn-out shoes. I knew I was probably the only one on my team who was willing to make contact with a homeless person without being forced by the team.

Plus, I was afraid of running into my father. So I just didn't show up. They all got on the bus, and I stayed behind in my dorm and studied.

The next day, Lesle called me aside. "Hey, Hope," she said. "That wasn't an optional activity. Where were you?"

I swallowed hard. "I couldn't go," I said. "I didn't want to see my dad."

Lesle looked surprised. She and Amy had seen my dad at our games, had even exchanged brief hellos. But they had no idea that he was homeless. With my secret out in the open, I let the rest out. I told Lesle the whole story, the kidnapping, the erratic contact, his blue tarp in the woods. She listened. She let me talk, without interruption or judgment. "OK, Hope," she said. "Next time we go to Union Gospel, you don't have to go."

The next time the team went down to Pioneer Square, I went to the library. My teammates thought I was getting a special privilege, that I thought I was too good to feed homeless people.

They didn't know the truth. And Lesle didn't explain.

CHAPTER SIX

The '99ers

A horde of squealing Mia Hamm fans swarmed around me. They had signs. They had posters. They wielded sharpies like switchblades. I was trying to get into the lobby of our hotel in Portland without my USA warm-ups being torn off my body. Hotel security was no match for the passion of those prepubescent girl soccer players, who pulled at us with their sticky hands. Some of my teammates and I formed a wedge and made it from the bus and through the revolving door into the lobby, which was cordoned off from the fans. Once inside the elevator, I exhaled. Safe at last. I was starting to get it. This U.S. women's national team was a big deal.

I knew, of course, that winning the World Cup seven months earlier had elevated women's soccer into the mainstream. I knew that Mia Hamm and Brandi Chastain had become household names. But what I didn't know was that their rock-star aura had generated Beatles-level hysteria.

April Heinrichs, who knew me well from having recruited me at Virginia, had been named head coach of the national team in January 2000 after Tony DiCicco retired. Lesle had been right: I was going to be a national-team candidate no matter where I went to college. April called me in to her first training camp, and I joined the national-team players as they prepared for the Algarve Cup, an annual tournament played in Portugal. Though I didn't make the squad that traveled there, she nevertheless invited me to join the team in Chula Vista, California, where we would live and train for the 2000 Olympics.

I was excited. Less than a year ago, during the World Cup, I had hoped to be on the national team. And now I was in the player pool. I withdrew from school for the spring quarter, with Lesle and Amy's support—even though I would miss spring practice and possibly the fall season if I made the Olympic team. They knew how important this was. Back in Richland, a rumor was going around that I had withdrawn from school because I was pregnant.

I was one of the youngest players of the thirty in that camp. I roomed with another young player, Aly Wagner, who was from Santa Clara and a year older. Aly was good friends with veteran Tiffeny Milbrett, so I got to know Millie a little. I was full of confidence coming into camp. I didn't idolize the national team players. I just wanted to compete with them. But when I got to Chula Vista, I was hit in the face by what a big deal the team was. Reporters and television crews were hovering. Fans crowded outside the training camp fence. And the skill and confidence level of the top players was daunting.

In one of my first practices, Brandi Chastain turned around and barked at me, "That's your ball."

Oh fuck, I thought. *Brandi Chastain is yelling at me.*

Brandi was always yelling. She had made the winning penalty kick at the World Cup and had triggered a national debate about how women athletes should behave with her bra-baring celebration that made the cover of every newspaper and magazine in the country. She had posed nude in *Gear* magazine. Her teammates called her Hollywood, for her skill at grabbing the spotlight, and I could tell it wasn't always a term of endearment. I liked Brandi, but she intimidated me. She had a lot of opinions and a lot of advice—whether you asked for them or not.

When we were on the road, I roomed with Brandi, but I rarely saw her. She was so busy, rising early, coming back to the room late, locking herself in the bathroom to talk on the phone to her husband while I sat on my bed and studied for my UW independent-study classes.

As much as Brandi talked and yelled on the field and off, Joy Fawcett was the real leader of the defense. She was the smartest defender I ever played behind. She was very even-keeled and didn't try to intimidate the young players, as I felt Brandi did. I loved playing with Joy.

Michelle Akers had helped me get ready for camp. She was also from Washington, and she came out to UW and did drills with me after I got my camp invitation from April. When I arrived at camp, Michelle was my partner in fitness tests. I was honored and in awe of her. I knew that she suffered from chronic fatigue syndrome and that every physical activity was a challenge for her.

Julie Foudy was the team leader off the field. She would meet with the media; she was the team voice. The quietest veteran was Kristine Lilly. The other players were always trying to set her up on dates and give her a makeover—her hair was too big and bushy. The team's most famous player, Mia Hamm, was also pretty quiet—that is, unless she wanted to get her point across. In one practice game, I was playing with Mia, and I ran out at the top of the box to punt the ball: it went straight up in the air. Mia stopped playing and looked at me. "Do you want me to fucking head the ball? Then you need to fucking learn how to drop-kick it."

Oh God, I thought. *Now Mia Hamm is yelling at me.*

I stayed behind after practice that day to work on my drop-kick. If I was going to play at that level, I couldn't rely every time on my booming punt—I needed to perfect a lower-trajectory dropkick.

The veterans clearly felt invincible. They were taking full advantage of the success they'd had the summer before. Around the time I joined the team, they had successfully negotiated a new contract from the U.S. Soccer Federation, putting them on equal footing with the men's national team and gaining more control over things like their victory tour. They had just helped found a new league—the Women's United Soccer Association—that was scheduled to debut in the spring of 2001. They had fought a lot of battles together. I was just a kid, an outsider, and was kept out of the inner circle. The veterans were making decisions for the group on things like the new league and our contract. They didn't seem interested in the younger players' opinions—they just told us what had been decided.

The enduring image of the team was of best friends who would have two fillings for each other, but I quickly learned that there were cliques and jealousies. For the younger players, it felt like joining a sorority, as though we were going through some sort of initiation process. There was tension surrounding Michelle's chronic-fatigue issues, which prevented her from practicing all the time. I figured she was a star and deserved accommodations: not every top-level athlete should be treated exactly the same.

I just wanted to compete. April had only a few months to figure out her goalkeeper situation. When I joined the team in Chula Vista, I was surprised to see that Briana Scurry—one of the heroines of the '99 team—wasn't in championship form. Her uniform was tight on her. She exhausted easily. She had gained significant weight and as a consequence was suffering from terrible shin splints.

In the aftermath of the World Cup, all the '99 players were awash in new opportunities: they were shooting commercials, endorsing products, making appearances, basking in their new fame. Mia had written a book. Brandi was in a Nike commercial with basketball star Kevin Garnett. Bri made appearances. Everyone agreed that this was great exposure for women's soccer, uncharted territory for women athletes. But Bri had relaxed a little too much. She had, by her own admission, gone home and celebrated. She was confident that she could get her form back quickly, but she couldn't. Diving for balls, running sprints, doing fitness tests—I was kicking her ass. So were the other two relatively inexperienced goalkeepers, Siri Mullinix and Jen Branam. We were all outperforming the legendary Briana Scurry.

I was shocked. I didn't understand how you could relax so close to the Olympics—risking missing out on one of the great opportunities in sport. "We have a problem in that we have four good goalkeepers," April told reporters. "We have one with a wealth of experience and three with little experience. . . . Hope knows we don't guarantee playing time. But, at the same time, I have confidence in her."

April was going to cut twelve players before she named the final Olympic roster. She would keep two goalkeepers and make one an alternate. I felt I had a decent shot. I got my first start for the national team on April 5, 2000, against Iceland at Davidson College in North Carolina. The game was closed to the public. In a scheduling quirk, U.S. Soccer wanted back-to-back games with Iceland but felt it could only market one game, so the other was closed. At least I didn't have to deal with the screaming throngs of Mia fans in my debut. A player from North Carolina who was on the Iceland roster lifted a ball right over me that could have been a disaster, but fortunately it bounced wide right of the goal. That was about the only threat. On offense, our team was ridiculously dominant, scoring 8 goals. I had my first appearance for the national team—known in soccer parlance as a *cap*—and my first shutout, even if no one saw it.

II.

The hotel in Portland was the nicest I'd ever been in. Security kept fans out of the lobby. It wasn't just kids begging for autographs now. Professional autograph seekers were lined up trying to get signatures they would turn around and sell. Because I was wearing USA warm-ups, I was asked for my signature. But I knew I hadn't done anything to earn the attention—I was just surfing in the wake of the '99ers.

I was scheduled to play against Mexico in the Nike Cup on Cinco de Mayo. My family drove down from Washington for the game and attended a family dinner in a banquet room at the hotel. Well-dressed mothers and square-jawed fathers stood in groups and chatted about real estate and the Internet boom. My family stood out: Grandma Alice wearing her Hope shirt, my mother tasting every dessert and then asking for a doggie bag. They stood around awkwardly. Few of the other parents came up and introduced themselves. *My family*, I thought, *does not fit in here.* I fought the urge to hide.

For the game against Mexico, fans filled the stands at Portland's Civic Stadium. I subbed for Siri in the second half, with a 4–0 lead. We were firmly in control, but in one sequence, Brandi let a ball through the back line, and I had to dive to make a save. Brandi turned around and yelled at me—"Come on, Hope!"—blaming me for not coming out for the ball.

It hadn't been my mistake, but I didn't argue. That was my mistake.

After the game, April called me in for a conversation about my status. She wanted to talk about the ball Brandi had missed, and our interaction. "That tells me that you're not ready, Hope," she said. "We all knew Brandi made a mistake. Yet you didn't have the courage to call her out and yell back at her. You're not ready to lead this defense."

I knew then I wasn't going to make the final cut. When the team went to Australia for a pre-Olympic tournament a few weeks later, I wasn't on the traveling roster. I stayed behind in California to train. I was disappointed, but I understood April's decision. I was gifted, competitive, fit, and determined. But I was still learning. I wasn't polished. There was still a lot of work ahead of me.

After the final cutdowns, I went directly to the U-21 team. In Germany, a few days after my nineteenth birthday, we won the Nordic Cup.

Shortly after I was cut from the team, I received a letter from my dad.

Dear Baby Hope,
   It is always so nice to hear from you, you make my day. I miss and love you. Well, Baby Hope, you are the greatest soccer player

in the world! Pele comes second to you. Sorry you didn't make the
soccer team—that's their fault. Now you get back to school—you
lost a year. . . . You know you can hang with anyone in soccer
now. We always knew Baby Hope was the best.

I have an idea, let's have our own soccer team. You be the
goalie. Cheryl will be our defender, she has bulldog in her.
Marcus, Dave, and I will be strikers—we all have lead in our
legs. Your mom will be a defender, she has bulldog too. She
knows how to protect you in more ways than one. Teresa will
be the cheerleader; she wouldn't want to get dirty. Jeff can be a
midfielder too and Christian has to play. When you are playing
striker, Christian will be with you and you can set him up and
he will score! Family team—wow.

I hope you don't feel bad, Baby Hope. Just know you are
loved and we all know you are the greatest. I miss you and don't
worry—you made our dream team in soccer.

Smile and be happy. Take care of your mom. Tell Marcus I
love him.

Baby Hope, my thoughts and prayers are with you every day
and night. I love you so much.

Dad

I laughed at the image my dad created—our family all playing
soccer together. I knew he wanted me to remember who my lifelong teammates are.

As the Olympics drew closer, Michelle Akers retired. Based
on the tension in camp between her and the other veterans, I suspected it wasn't entirely her decision. And April made her choice on
the goalkeeper: Siri Mullinix—fresh out of North Carolina—was
named the starter over Bri. It was the most controversial decision
April had to make, but Bri's lack of fitness made it easier.

On September 28, I was back in Seattle when the United States
lost in the Olympic final to Norway on a controversial goal in overtime. A shot bounced off a Norwegian player's arm—normally, a

play-stopping infraction—before she punched it in past Siri. The U.S. women had to settle for the silver medal. Bri admitted she was bitter over being benched. Later, she would tell reporters, "I personally still feel that if I was playing in the goal in the final we would have won it. I'm just a big-game player. When it's on the line, I've been very successful."

She was applauded for her fire and competitive drive.

III.

Back in Seattle, I felt like an outsider. While I'd been off pursuing my soccer dreams, college had gone on without me. My teammates had gotten closer to each other, bonding in the second half of freshman year. It seemed that a new social order had formed and everyone had been issued the organizational chart except me. Even Cheryl—now tight with our teammates Megan and Suz—had a personal life that didn't include me. It hurt. I think some of the estrangement probably stemmed from jealousy. I knew other girls thought I was arrogant because of my national-team experience. I couldn't even grab a clean T-shirt out of my drawer without hearing people talking about me behind my back. "Oh my God, she has to wear her national-team gear all the time. She thinks she's so great."

Wow, I thought. *Be careful what you wish for. Once you reach a certain level, everything you do will be critiqued.*

I didn't feel like a different person. Through my experience with the national team, I'd been exposed to a lot, learned some lessons, and been challenged. I felt I'd grown up. But when I got back to school, I felt that I was behind and that everyone else had moved on without me. Even Cheryl. That was the most painful part. We were still like sisters—we always had been and always would be. Lesle and Amy still relied on Cheryl to find out what was going on with me in my personal life, but she had branched out and formed new relationships. I had new friends, too, like my teammate Malia

Arrant, who was two years ahead of me. She and I were both tomboys, not interested in the sorority scene. But I was hurt by the growing distance between me and Cheryl. She wouldn't tell me about certain things—a party she'd been to that I had missed. I know she was trying to protect my feelings, but it stung, because Cheryl was the one person I could always count on to tell me the truth.

I think Cheryl saw that soccer was becoming a career for me, and in many ways it was. I was working hard at it, and I was getting paid for my work. I suddenly had money—not just my college scholarship but per diem money from U.S. Soccer and grants from the U.S. Olympic Committee, which didn't compromise my amateur status. I bought a Chevy Blazer, and now I could afford to go on spring break trips or snowboarding weekends like other UW kids. I felt rich, thanks to soccer.

Maybe Cheryl was right: I was more businesslike. I didn't goof around and gossip as much as some of my teammates. I felt at the time that they didn't take soccer as seriously as I did, didn't view it as a potential career. Despite all that, we were functioning well as a team on the field. I started all twenty-one games for UW my sophomore year and set a school record for fewest goals allowed in a season. We won eighteen games and our first-ever Pac-10 championship, and made it all the way to the Sweet Sixteen of the NCAA Tournament. Lesle was named the Pac-10 Coach of the Year.

My father was still a fixture in the stands, one that by now everyone on the team accepted. Having unburdened myself to Lesle and Amy, I was less self-conscious about him. There even seemed to be a slight thawing in the relationship between the two sides of my family. Though my father remained ostracized by my other relatives, sometimes my mother would climb to the top of the stands and give him cookies or a cup of cocoa. She knew he was hungry. She understood that I needed my father in my life.

Once I got my own car, I gave him rides. He usually asked me to just drop him off by the side of the highway, near a freeway exit west of UW. But eventually he let me see the small tent that he lived in, deep in the woods. I learned that I needn't have worried about running into him at the Union Gospel Men's Shelter—he avoided the large homeless population downtown that filled the shelters, spilled out under freeway overpasses, and lined up outside the soup kitchens. Instead he survived on his monthly $67 social security check and by shoplifting at grocery stores. He said he preferred being out in the woods alone. Sometimes, after my games, I brought macaroni and cheese or picked up hero sandwiches and sat in a park with him, eating and talking about sports. I was finding I really enjoyed his company. I knew that I hated being judged by others, so I did my very best not to judge him but simply appreciate him. It wasn't always easy, but I learned to embrace who he was.

My father's behavior could still be troubling. Cheryl would sometimes give him a ride. Once, when Cheryl and I had to make a quick stop at our dorm, we left him in the car, and on our way back out, I saw him going through the console, pocketing her spare change. I was mortified, but Cheryl didn't care. She figured it was the least she could do for him.

My dad doted on me and was interested in hearing about everything in my life—the national team, UW, my Husky teammates. In many ways we had a richer, more loving relationship than I had with my mother or brother. I became dependent on his advice and encouragement. The man who had been absent for so much of my life was now someone I relied upon. For better or for worse, he was family, and I was focusing on the "for better" part.

IV.

One day, my sister, Terry, showed up at my dorm. She was lugging a giant duffel bag and seemed almost hysterical. "Hope, you have to take this," she said. "I don't want it in my house."

The bag was full of my father's belongings, things he'd left at her house over the years. But now Terry was cutting my father out of her life and didn't want any trace of him in her house. He had invited a woman over when Terry wasn't home. So the next time he knocked on the door looking for a shower, Terry refused to let him in. At the time, my nephew was just a little boy, and Terry was concerned about protecting him. My father got upset and wrote her some threatening letters, saying that an "Italian vendetta" was on. After the second letter arrived, Terry called the police.

I was very angry. I thought she was overreacting, and I felt protective of him—his life was hard enough without his family turning on him. And now she had unloaded all of my father's crap on me. I was living in a tiny dorm room with roommates, and I didn't have any place to store his giant duffel.

But Terry was insistent. As she left, she warned me not to dare look in the bag.

I don't like being arbitrarily told what to do. Of course I looked through the bag as soon as she left. There were some sweet mementos: my brother's first home-run ball that he had given Dad the day he moved out of our house, a balsawood glider Marcus had painted for him, stones etched with portraits of my mom and Marcus, photos of me and Marcus, letters I had written him. But then there were also photo albums of naked women with disgusting letters that some of those women had written him. Many of them appeared to be prostitutes. It grossed me out, but I wasn't going to abandon him.

IV.

In December, I rejoined the national team. We played Mexico in a game in Texas, and this time I subbed in the second half for Siri. I let in two goals, including one memorably bad one—I tried to clear a ball and miskicked it. I was too far out of the goal to get back to make the save, and Mexico took a 2–1 lead. Fortunately, Cindy Parlow scored twice later in the game to get us the win, but after the game I was still feeling a little shaky.

But April hadn't given up on me. In January she named me to the traveling roster of a young team she was taking to China, for a two-game series with our longtime rivals. After my mishap against Mexico, I was determined to make a good impression. I was enjoying the trip. I felt that I got to know the veterans who were on the team, like Christie Pearce and Lorrie Fair. I was making some inroads and beginning to find a comfort level.

Early in the trip, April called me into her hotel room and told me to have a seat. I was very nervous. Was she going to tell me, again, that I wasn't ready to start? "Hope," she said. "I hear something is wrong with your father."

My stomach flipped and my heart started pounding. I felt faint. I stood up to head toward the door and then sat back down—not wanting to be rude to April or hurt my standing with her but desperate to get away and call my mom. Did she mean Glenn or my dad? Had there been an accident?

"Your father," April said, "has been accused of murder."

CHAPTER SEVEN

"I Should Have
Died a Long Time Ago . . ."

The day before I left for China, a grisly murder made headlines in Seattle. A forty-year-old real estate agent named Mike Emert was found dead in an upscale home for sale in Woodinville, an enclave northeast of the city. When the homeowner who had hired him returned, she found Emert's body face down in an upstairs bathtub with the water still running. He had been stabbed more than twenty times and, judging by the trail of blood leading up the stairs, had been dragged from the lower floor up into the bathroom.

By nightfall, police had identified my father as a "person of interest" and had taken him into custody for questioning. I didn't know it, but the night before our team left town, a detective knocked on Lesle's door and asked for my address. He told her my father was implicated in a murder case. Lesle was shocked—she had gotten to know my dad a little, and she couldn't believe the accusation, but her main concern was for me; she stalled the detective, telling him I was out of the country even though I wasn't leaving until the next morning. Police called my mother's home in Richland. They tracked down Marcus. They were on the hunt for any information they could find.

Of all the members of our family, I had had the most regular contact with my father, but I was six thousand miles away. Lesle and Amy were worried that either the police or the media would track me down in China, or that I would randomly find out—one of my teammates had a sister who was a Seattle cop. My coaches and family were eager to protect me as much as possible. Lesle called the team's sports psychologist, who was with us in China, and explained the situation.

"Don't tell Hope," Lesle told her. "She doesn't need to know about this until she gets home. We're trying to keep it quiet on campus. But she might find out somehow, and I want you to be aware."

Things didn't go exactly as planned. The psychologist told April, who just blurted out the bombshell: "Hope, your father has been accused of murder."

I gasped. Murder? I knew my father had a criminal past, and that trouble seemed to find him. I knew he presented himself as a tough guy. And I knew he had made strange threats in the past: the bomb scares, the vendetta against Terry. But I was certain the affectionate, caring man I had gotten to know was incapable of committing cold-blooded murder. I believed that with all my heart.

I was frantic. I called my mom and Marcus, tried to make sense of the whole thing. Was my father in custody? Had anyone seen him? Nobody knew where he was.

Back in my room, I huddled in front of a computer in my hotel in China, and read the lead of the story in the *Seattle Post-Intelligencer*:

He admits to a troubled past—to a life of street hustling and petty crime. And he acknowledges that he set up bogus meetings with female real estate agents as part of a shameful con game to meet women.

But he insists he's not a killer.

Nonetheless, authorities investigating the slaying of

Eastside Realtor Miko Emert are now focusing on Jeffrey John Solo—the mysterious man with a limp whom they consider a "person of interest" in the case.

Jeffrey John Solo. The man I knew as Gerry. His picture was on the paper's front page. The story said my father had come to the *Seattle Post-Intelligencer* building to tell his side of the story. Days earlier he had been taken into custody, had been given a polygraph test, had hair and blood samples taken, and then had been released. But he remained a "person of interest."

He matched the description of the suspect in a few key ways: he walked with a limp, carried a cane, had a thick New York accent, and admitted to hustling female real estate agents. He told the reporter that he would meet the agents in houses, get to talking, and then ask them out on dates. He said it was a con to get their money and confessed, "Like I said, I used women and did some bad things."

My father's criminal history was laid out for everyone to see: two years in Walla Walla State Penitentiary, several convictions in the Richland area—including for forgery and the bomb threats. My father told the newspaper things I'd never known: that he had been charged in a robbery conspiracy when he lived in Boston years earlier and had also been convicted of being in possession of stolen property in King County, Washington.

A quote from an unnamed source made my father sound like he was capable of anything, including murder. The reporter had called our home in Richland, and whoever answered said my dad was "the best con man I ever met." The person added, "He's lied to his kids for 12 years. It's a shame, because they deserve better than that."

Was that Glenn, answering the phone and spewing venom about my father? Was it someone else in my family? I was furious. But it was the final lines of the story that broke my heart. My father said he had only come forward to protect the reputation of his daughter.

"I don't care about myself or what happens to me. I should have died a long time ago," he said. "But my daughter, I don't want her to get hurt. That's why I'm telling my story. I didn't do this."

Alone in China, I stared at the computer screen and wept.

II.

We still had four days left on our trip, and I was getting another chance in goal. Because of Bri's ongoing weight and fitness issues and Siri's struggles in the Olympic gold medal game, I felt there was an opportunity for me to make an impression and start working toward the next World Cup, two years away. But it was hard to focus on soccer with all the drama swirling around me. Where was my father? Was he safe?

Yet I played well. As a young player, I had learned to shut out the many crises in my personal life whenever I stepped on the soccer field. That ability served me well in China. I got my chance against the Chinese national team in Hangzhou, where thirty thousand fans showed up to see us inaugurate a brand-new stadium that was built for the next World Cup, which China was scheduled to host. The crowd roared, and it seemed like they were right on top of us. They were still angry about the U.S. victory over China in the previous World Cup, and even though I wasn't Bri, they taunted me as if I had been the one who had saved the overtime penalty kick in 1999.

It was freezing when we walked onto the pitch. We took an early lead, but China tied us, 1–1, on a free kick that bent over our line and into the upper left corner of the goal. Overall, I had an excellent game. In the second half, I made a few diving saves. The ball got through our back line several times, but I didn't give up another goal. The game ended in a draw.

When we left China the next day, I didn't know what would

greet me at the airport when we landed. Would I be ambushed by reporters and photographers? The sensational story continued to make headlines—gruesome murders in well-to-do neighborhoods were not an everyday occurrence in Seattle. All the reports noted that Jeffrey John Solo had a nineteen-year-old daughter in Seattle. Though none identified me by name, it wouldn't take Sherlock Holmes to figure that the nineteen-year-old daughter from Richland with the same memorable last name, sometimes described as a "star athlete," was UW's goalkeeper.

Fortunately, Lesle had been doing damage control the entire time I'd been gone. She enlisted our sports information director to control the story on the UW end. She called our team together and warned that if anyone spoke to the media, they would be suspended. Lesle and Amy protected me. Their support during this family nightmare made me even more loyal to them and prouder that I had chosen UW.

Cheryl picked me up at the airport, and my fears of being ambushed went unrealized. There were no cameras or reporters. But my main concern wasn't bad publicity. It was my father.

"Let's go find your dad," Cheryl said.

The stories I had read said he'd been staying at a friend's apartment, but the friend had become upset by police harassment and had kicked him out. I went to his old spot in the woods off the freeway, but he wasn't there. I walked through parks in the rain, looking for him.

I finally went back to my apartment with Cheryl and cried for hours as she tried to console me.

After days of frantic worry, my father called. We decided to meet at REI, the large outdoor equipment store that was one of the few landmarks in downtown Seattle I was familiar with, because you could see it from the freeway.

When I saw him waiting for me outside the store, I ran into his arms. It was such a relief to see him, to see that he was all right. "Baby Hope, you know I didn't do this," he said.

"Of course I know that," I said.

He was cold and hungry. He told me the police had questioned him for hours, browbeating him in an attempt to get a confession. But he had stood his ground, telling them over and over, "Fuck off. I didn't do it." He said the harsh treatment might have broken him if he had been younger, that he could now understand how people confess to crimes they didn't commit. But as he liked to remind me, he was "a tough son of a bitch."

The police had distributed posters of him all around Kirkland, where the murdered man's stolen Escalade had been recovered. My father still sometimes hung out in downtown Kirkland after Terry had kicked him out of her house. But now he was blackballed, refused admittance into Starbucks or any of the fast-food restaurants where he often took shelter. Worst of all, the police had taken everything from him, he said, including his warm coat. And it was January. Fortunately, a detective who had taken a liking to him—and believed he was innocent—brought him a new coat. I took him to get some food. As he walked beside me, hobbling on two canes, I was painfully aware of his limp. It had gotten much worse. There was no way my dad could have dragged a man's body up a flight of stairs and lifted it into a bathtub.

I had never seen my father so upset. He felt he was being framed. He didn't understand why the police were hounding him. He had an alibi—he had been at a doctor's appointment at the VA Hospital the day the murder was committed. He had taken a lie detector test and was sure he had passed. But the police were still harassing him.

As my father told me of his ordeal, he broke down in tears. "You know, Baby Hope, I did a lot of bad things in my life," he said. "Maybe this is payback for all of that."

He had gone to the *Seattle Post-Intelligencer* out of fear that I would be linked to the news story and that my reputation would be harmed. He agreed to an exclusive interview in exchange for withholding my name.

"I just want to make sure you're protected," he told me.

My father had damaged a lot of people in his life, and hadn't cared about hurting the people who loved him. But now at sixty-two—at least that's how old the newspaper reports said he was—he seemed determined to protect at least one relationship. Ours.

III.

That spring April named me to the national team squad that traveled to Europe and then on to the Algarve Cup in Portugal. She was taking a very young team: all the national team veterans were getting ready for the inaugural season of the WUSA, the professional league they had founded. So our traveling roster was full of college players, including a few I had never heard of. Our average age was nineteen. Despite the hodgepodge of talent, it was fun to be with players of my own generation—and not excluded by the veterans. But it felt a little too comfortable.

It was the worst U.S. performance ever in the prestigious Portuguese tournament. We lost three games, including the two I started, to teams that had brought their full senior rosters. In a 3–0 loss to Canada, their veteran star, Charmaine Hooper, chipped a ball over me in the first half. And a new Canadian player named Christine Sinclair scored off a corner kick: it was the first battle of many between us. Sweden beat us, 2–0, in my second start.

While I was traveling, I heard that my father had been cleared in the Emert murder case. Sort of. A story in the *Seattle Post-Intelligencer* made it clear the police still had doubts about him. A King's County Sheriff's Office spokesperson, John Urquhart, was quoted as saying: "We don't believe that he was part and parcel to the homicide. We're still trying to figure out what, if any, connections to the crime Mr. Solo may have."

Urquhart also said that authorities had not ruled out the possibility that Emert's killer may have set Solo up to look like the killer or that he was somehow involved in another way.

My father had taken and passed two polygraph tests, and his alibi was solid: a physician at the VA Hospital confirmed that he had seen my father that day.

"He has a very strong alibi for the day before the murder, which we fully believe," Urquhart said.
      But Solo says he and his family suffered greatly as a result of the investigation.

My dad told the paper that the investigators were threatening when they talked to my mom and Marcus, and had even used me as leverage to try to get him to confess to the slaying. Again, my father said he went public only to protect me.

When I returned to Seattle, I could tell my father was frustrated. He didn't feel his name was fully cleared. He was still being harassed by police, banned by shopkeepers. The taint of the murder accusation lingered, and would for years. Marcus and I stood by him. Marcus had been traumatized by the murder investigation. The FBI had gone to Richland and talked to my mother, who had been storing my dad's old duffel bag from Terry's house in the secondhand store she now ran. Of course my mother had looked through it and seen the disgusting pictures of prostitutes. Marcus had taken the bag out of the store and destroyed the photos, but my mom told the FBI about the albums, so the FBI grilled Marcus. It was clear they thought that my father could be a suspect in the infamous Green River killings. Several prostitutes had been murdered over the years and at the time the killings were still unsolved. Just the mention of the Green River murders terrorized the Northwest at the time—and now someone was trying to link my father to that horror.

I knew that others in my family doubted whether my father was truly innocent. Their long-simmering animosity toward him was fueled by the lingering questions left by the police. My sister's husband told a detective about a time that my father had stolen some knives from him. Any past slight or misdeed was hauled out and used against him.

For a long time, I would hear other family members speculate about my father's role in the murder. Those doubts infuriated me. I knew he was innocent.

Meanwhile, the Emert murder remained unsolved. There wasn't any real closure for his widow and daughter. Or for my father.

IV.

The VA Hospital did more than just provide an alibi for my father. It threw him a lifeline.

He liked hanging out at the VA Hospital, shooting the breeze with other veterans. Through an outpatient program, homeless vets could get secondhand clothes, a cup of coffee, a sandwich. The first floor of the hospital was a gathering place that offered a little more dignity than a homeless shelter. A Vietnam veteran named Mark Sakura started the program on a volunteer basis. He knew my dad as Johnny and became quite friendly with him. My dad liked to talk, and Mark liked to listen. Mark really wanted his program to be useful to the homeless population. He picked my father's brain for information. What did the vets really need? Coats? Backpacks? Sleeping bags? Personal care items like toothpaste?

Shortly after Dad and Mark became friends, my father was implicated in Emert's murder. My dad was afraid it would ruin their friendship, but Mark believed in him, sensed a good heart beneath the rough exterior. "If you tell me you didn't do it, then nothing else matters," Mark told him.

Mark spent a lot of time with my dad, who liked to joke that they were like the mismatched cartoon characters Mutt and Jeff. My father was a loud, large, heavyset Italian American. Mark was a soft-spoken, small Japanese American. He would take my father to Burger King and get the two-for-one deals. When my father insisted he wasn't hungry, Mark would shrug and say, "You might as well eat it. I can't eat two." Just like me, he learned to help my dad in subtle ways, without hurting his pride.

Mark was an incredible resource. He understood how the system worked and how to help homeless people get on their feet. He helped my father sign up for Social Security benefits and disability. He helped him get full veteran benefits—tracking down his service record and clarifying at least one thing about my father's mysterious past: that he had, indeed, served in the navy. My father badly needed surgery for his knees, and Mark assisted in arranging the operation at the VA Hospital. While my father was recovering, Mark did something even more profound. He helped secure low-income housing at Hilltop House, an affordable complex for the elderly in downtown Seattle. In a quirk of bureaucracy, my father couldn't qualify for the housing if he was homeless. He needed to prove he had been living somewhere besides the street. So Mark filled out the paperwork and said that my dad had lived with him.

"A little white lie ain't hurting nobody," Mark told me.

Mark's mother-in-law had recently moved into an assisted-living facility, so he had all her furniture in storage. He gave it to my father to furnish his new studio apartment. He took him shopping for groceries, filling the refrigerator and cupboards in the small kitchen. He helped my father move in. My father had a roof. He had food.

After years on the street, he had a place to call home.

CHAPTER EIGHT

An Arm Like Frankenstein

After a slow start, I was getting the hang of college life. I dated a lot of guys, and I enjoyed the party scene around campus, so when the All-American Club—sports bar by day, trendy night-club after dark—opened near UW, I wanted to get in. Still several months away from my twenty-first birthday, I stood in front of an intimidating bouncer and presented the Washington driver's license I'd borrowed from a friend who looked vaguely like me.

The bouncer shined his flashlight in my face and then back down on the license. He shook his head. "Nope," he said.

That couldn't be the final verdict. They had already let Cheryl in, and she looked ten years old in her fake ID. I pleaded with the bouncer, who called over the club manager, a handsome dark-haired guy with a friendly smile. He looked at my ID and rolled his eyes. "I'm going to give you one chance," he said. "Tell me the truth. Is this you?"

For some reason I couldn't lie to him. "No," I said. "But can I have my ID back? It usually works." The manager started to turn away, but our friend Mark—a UW soccer player who possessed a legitimate ID—stepped in. "Dude," he said, pointing to me. "Don't you know who this is?"

"I have no idea who she is," the manager said. "And I don't really care."

"Come on, let her in," Mark said. "I won't let her drink. Trust me, she's cool."

The manager sighed. "Just this once," he warned and looked me in the eyes. "Remember—no drinking. I'm watching you. And," he added, pulling the ID back from me, "I'm keeping this."

When I thanked him, he warned me not to make a habit of it, but the next weekend, I was back in line behind the ropes, catching his eye. He smiled, rolled his eyes, and let me in again.

And that's how I met Adrian. A grown-up by my standards and seemingly worldly, he was twenty-five years old and managing nightclubs; he had played soccer in community college, and didn't care one way or the other about my soccer career. He made it clear that he'd rather watch water boil than women's soccer. I took that as a challenge.

Adrian liked to do the same stuff I did: shoot hoops or go snowboarding or just hang out. He was easy to be with, and pretty soon I was spending most of my free time with him. I still dated other guys, and he dated plenty of women, but when we were together, it felt special. And I needed a friend. There was a widening gap in my life as Cheryl and I grew apart. Malia had graduated, and every time I came back from a stint with the national team, I felt pushed farther out of Cheryl's circle. I was living a dual existence with my college and national teams, pulled between two sets of women who often seemed less like friends than work colleagues. I wasn't good at doing the things that kept friendships smooth—returning phone calls quickly or staying in touch while I traveled. But Adrian wasn't bothered and we could pick back up where we had left off, without a lot of drama.

He made me comfortable. He didn't pass judgment—not on my family or my background or my father. He had his own rocky past and complicated family matters. He'd grown up in West Seattle, also from a broken home. Though his parents eventually reconciled, his father had been physical with his mother when Adrian was young, which made him protective of the women in his life. For a time, he and his mother were homeless, moving from vacant room to vacant room in the hotel where his mother worked as a maid. As a kid, he had taken a swing at his vice principal, and had been in and out of reform schools. But he was resilient.

When my father met Adrian, they had an immediate connection, a recognition of mutual street smarts. My dad tested him, tried to get Adrian to do him favors like cash his check or give him a ride somewhere. Adrian called him on his bullshit, and a respect developed. They talked sports and joked around.

For a long, long time Adrian and I insisted—to outsiders and to each other—that we were just friends. We were strongly attracted to each other, but we were in denial about it, both so wrapped up with our own lives and busy schedules. We were afraid to commit, pushing each other away every time we got too close, establishing a pattern that would last for years.

II.

In 2001, before my junior year of college, I was named to the preseason list of candidates for the Hermann Trophy, the award given to the nation's outstanding collegiate soccer player. Just making the list was an honor—goalkeepers were rarely considered for the award. Lesle made sure that everyone—on our team, at UW, and on the outside—knew that the nomination was a testament to how important I was to the Huskies.

The season before, UW had won its first-ever Pac-10 conference championship. Eight of our games had been decided by one goal, and five of those were shutouts. That team had been special, a blue collar group. We had great senior leadership in Malia Arrant, Theresa Wagner, and Tami Bennett. I looked up to those upperclassmen and followed their lead. I may have stopped a lot of shots, but it was a collaborative effort. We finished the season ranked number three in the nation. UW soccer was on the map, and I had helped put it there. That was a great feeling.

Also on the Hermann Trophy list was my good friend Aly Wagner and a relatively unknown player named Abby Wambach from the University of Florida. Abby was a year older than me but hadn't yet been in the national-team pool. She was a raw, powerful player whose first significant national-team play was in the Nordic Cup in 2001 with our under-twenty-one team. Our coach, Jerry Smith, Brandi Chastain's husband, picked her. I didn't know much about Abby before training camp for the Nordic Cup, where we were roommates. She was rough around the edges but had great athleticism. At the Nordic Cup, she made an instant impact, scoring three goals but also drawing two yellow cards, which forced her to sit out our championship victory over Sweden. That was Abby in a nutshell: great ability combined with a power and force rarely seen in women's soccer. She sometimes ran right through opponents and intimidated them with her strength.

That September, Abby and I were among April's call-ups for the Nike U.S. Women's Cup training camp. The team was a blend of veterans, who had just finished their inaugural WUSA season, and young players. Five of us were interrupting our college seasons to play for the national team: a sign that the national team was serious about targeting the next generation of players and giving us meaningful playing time. I felt a bond with those other collegiate players who were being pulled out of school to play for the national team. Unlike my UW teammates, they lived the same dual life I did and understood the aspects of college life that we surrendered—the football games and parties and the ability to make weekend plans. Like me, they were packing up textbooks along with their cleats, saying good-bye to boyfriends and best friends, again and again. For us, soccer wasn't just a fun pastime. It was also our job.

I'd been in camp a few weeks when I tore my right groin in training. I flew home immediately to start my rehabilitation. I'd already missed two UW games and wanted to be ready to play for the Huskies for the rest of my junior year. Doctors told me the injury would keep me out for three weeks, but I didn't miss a game. It was the first significant injury I had suffered during college, the first time I had a Toradol shot to combat the pain. But I didn't want to miss any more UW games. I taped up the injury and played out the rest of the season, even though I was unable to kick with my right foot. The good news was that I found out I had a pretty decent left foot.

Despite my limited mobility, I had another good season. I made sixty-eight saves and helped the Huskies to a 12–4–1 record, second place in our conference. We were a good team, with a talented freshman class and more top recruits in the pipeline. One of our new players was Tina Frimpong, who had been a Washington high school sensation, one year behind me. Though Lesle had recruited Tina hard, she committed to Santa Clara. When she became pregnant at eighteen, Santa Clara was no longer an option, and she opted for UW, closer to her hometown of Vancouver, Washington. She missed the 2000 season and her daughter MacKenzie was born in March 2001; six months later, Tina was playing for us. MacKenzie's dad, Brad Ellertson, transferred to UW from Washington State, and they were working hard to be a family. I had so much respect for the way Tina was juggling her life to keep playing soccer despite the difficulties. We weren't particularly close then; I never could have predicted that a decade later she would be one of the most important people in my life.

Our team lost in the second round of the NCAA tournament that year, bounced yet again by Christine Sinclair and Portland. I didn't win the Hermann Trophy, but I got a consolation prize: I was named the Pac-10 player of the year, the first Washington player to receive the award and the first-ever goalkeeper.

III.

In February of my junior year, the U-21 national team was in Chihuahua, Mexico, playing against Mexico's senior team. Their star, Maribel Dominguez, took a free kick with ten minutes to play in a scoreless game. She sailed the ball toward the far post, and as I dove to block it, I hit the post and felt myself get caught on something. As the ball went into the net, my body lurched in a circle, still attached to the pole, and I thudded to the ground.

My teammates were shouting, "Get up, Hope! Get up!" They were running into the goal to get the ball—eager to tie the game—while I lay motionless, unable to move. Something was terribly wrong. I looked down to make sure my arm was still there because I couldn't feel it—was it still dangling from the post? The arm was there and I didn't see anything wrong. There wasn't any blood. There was no tear in the jersey. When I lifted up my jersey sleeve I gasped. A hole gaped in my forearm; the muscle and tendons were hanging out. I could see the yellow of the fat, the white of my bone, the maroon rippled texture of the muscle. My forearm had gotten caught on a hook on the inside of the goalpost and had been ripped wide open. I panicked, fearing that the insides of my arm were going to fall out. I took my filthy goalkeeper glove and covered the hole and sprinted off the field, with my defender, Natalie Spilger, running along beside me, screaming. On the sideline, my goalkeeper coach took one look at my arm and had to sit down. I turned paper white and went into shock.

Our team doctor went with me to a nearby hospital, where she made sure everything was disinfected and safe, then stitched up the jagged gash. It was hideous—my arm looked like a Frankenstein body part, connected to the rest of me by giant stitches.

That night in my hotel room, I couldn't sleep. My forearm was throbbing with pain, the sutures oozing. I couldn't feel my fingers and remembered the medical staff's concern about nerve damage. Would I ever be able to use my arm again? I started to panic. It was hard to breathe. What if my career was over? What would I do with my life? Could a rusty hook on a Mexican goalpost end all that? If I couldn't play, who was I?

I needed to escape the weight I felt on my chest, so I slid out of bed, down to the floor, as I had when I was a little girl saying my prayers for Grandma Alice. And down there on the cool tile floor in Mexico, I felt a sense of calm come over me. My inner confidence, the flame that I could always turn up on the soccer field, flared inside me. There was more to me than just being a soccer player. I had made myself into a great player. I could make myself into something else if I needed to. I had other talents. Even without soccer, I could make my way in the world.

I breathed in the earthy smell of the clay tile. "Hope," I said loud enough to wake up my roommate, "you're going to be OK."

IV.

My dad's new home at Hilltop was conveniently located near downtown Seattle, so I started to use it as my crash pad. In 2002, during my last full year at UW, I juggled international trips to Portugal for the Algarve Cup and to Iceland for another Nordic Cup championship. My arm healed and, aside from a nasty purple scar, was as good as new. I crammed through my classes to make sure I would graduate on time. And I earned money by coaching youth goalkeepers. Sleep was at a premium, so whenever I could, I went to see my dad. He'd make me some instant ramen noodles or fried rice and let me nap.

Free from the worry of whether he had enough to eat or where he was sleeping, my father was becoming the devoted father Marcus and I had always longed for. He now wanted to make sure *we* had enough to eat. Mark took him shopping and taught him how to pick good produce. My dad learned how to stretch what money he had—for example, by making sure a box of Satsuma oranges had some oranges he had "borrowed" from another box. He wrote letters and called to tell us how much he loved us. Marcus had season tickets to the Seattle Seahawks, and when he went to games, Dad would babysit Marcus's golden retriever, Henry. He loved that dog—they would go to a park, and Henry would try to chase the squirrels, pulling my dad on the leash. "Just ignore them, Henry," my dad would plead, talking to the dog the way he once talked to squirrels he lived with in the woods.

My father delighted in my accomplishments.

May 10, 2002

Well, Baby Hope, you threw out the first pitch at the Seattle Mariners and Boston Red Sox game, on this Friday night, a packed house.

You got your sign from the catcher, Ben Davis, and you shook him off. You wanted to throw your fastball, catcher laughed, you laughed, the crowd was going wild as you shook him off.

Now you are ready and you wind up and throw your fastball, it bounces up to the plate. Crowd goes ooooh and you put both hands up to wave to the crowd. They love you, Baby Hope.

So many memories and joy you have given your family. Thanks, you are the greatest. Love you,

Dad

V.

Lesle tried to schedule spring games in players' hometowns when possible. That was exciting when a team member was from California or Hawaii. But nobody wanted to go to Richland, except Cheryl and me. In March of my junior year, I got to go home. It was windy and cold, and tumbleweeds blew across the street. Our teammates laughed—many were from pretty suburbs in California or Colorado, and they couldn't get over how desolate and unsophisticated Richland was. Hanford had been declared one of the most toxic sites in America, which didn't make it more appealing. Whatever. I might be living in hip Seattle and running around the globe to play soccer, but that Columbia riverbank dust is in my soul.

My whole family came to the game, including my mother. And

I was so proud to see her. After several attempts, my mom stopped drinking on Halloween of 2000. She had tried quitting on her own, then in an outpatient rehab, but nothing lasted. But when she started attending Alcoholics Anonymous meetings, she stopped cold turkey. She was adjusting to her new life: she and Glenn had lost a lot of their hard-partying river friends. We stopped attending traditional annual events, like a big New Year's party. My grandparents made sure not to drink when Mom was around—and they loved their evening martini. Glenn stopped social drinking. Everyone supported her, and I started to see a real change in her. She seemed so much happier.

"Mom," I said, giving her a hug when we came to Richland. "I am so proud of you."

I had to laugh when Mr. Potter, the Richland athletic director—the same guy who had kicked me off the basketball team—came up to greet me with an embrace. I stiffened. "Don't act like you were a part of this, Mr. Potter," I said. I wasn't going to be a phony just to let him feel important.

VI.

Lesle believed our team would become stronger by being tested in tough nonconference games. We usually played powerhouses like Portland and Santa Clara. In my senior year, though, she outdid herself: she scheduled us in the Carolina Classic tournament in September, playing Duke and North Carolina. Those were two of the top teams in the country, but we were making our mark nationally: ranked number eleven to start the season. We lost both Carolina Classic games; I missed them both because I was with the national team for a game against Scotland in Columbus, Ohio. I got the start, and was replaced by Bri in the second half. Abby didn't start but came off the bench to score a hat trick (three goals in one game)—probably the moment she became indispensable to the national team.

I didn't know it, but that was the last game I would play for the national team for the next two and a half years. April was still encouraging and supportive, but Bri had regained her form and, having learned the hard way, was determined not to let go of the starting spot again.

I wanted to make the most of my senior year at UW. Our team had partied too much the year before, and the seniors decided to have a "dry" season. I didn't think it was a good idea—I didn't feel like policing the younger players, and I knew the rule would definitely get broken. Hell, we broke it ourselves—with senior-only parties in which we were sworn to secrecy about drinking. Not surprisingly, the younger players broke the rule too. The new players were struggling to balance the partying side of college with the hard work of soccer. I felt they were out of control, lacking focus and commitment. Still, the "dry" rule that everyone was ignoring became too big a distraction—too much energy and time went into trying to figure out how to handle violations.

It wasn't where our attention needed to be. On the field, our team was struggling. Our ambitious schedule hurt us: we lost eight games, seven to ranked opponents. We had a lot of talent, but everyone seemed to be pointing fingers rather than scoring goals. I was a captain, but I felt ineffective. I had one foot in the national-team camp and couldn't give the UW issues my complete attention. And I was frustrated by what I saw. In one team meeting, a freshman started to argue with Lesle about a formation she was implementing. I stood up. "This isn't fucking high school," I shouted. "Why don't you listen to someone who knows about the game?"

I stormed out. It wasn't an appropriate reaction for a senior captain, but I resented having a know-it-all freshman take over the meeting. When I had been a younger player, I looked up to our juniors and seniors. But now our team seemed irreparably broken. When we lost to UCLA in our final home weekend, I was disappointed. My senior season hadn't gone as I had hoped. No happy ending.

Lesle gave me a hug after the game. "I'm glad you have Adrian," she said. "I know you need someone to lean on away from the team."

When selections were made for the NCAA postseason tournament, UW was left out. The selection committee didn't consider our strength of schedule. They just saw all the losses. Portland, led by Christine Sinclair, won the national championship. I ended my career at UW with every school goalkeeper record, including my eighteen shutouts, 325 saves, and a goals-against average of 1.02. But statistics never mattered to me. The important thing was that—finally—I had learned to become a goalkeeper.

Not long after I first put on the purple UW jersey—choosing number 18 so that I could keep my options with a number a field player would wear—my goalkeeper coach, Amy, handed me a note that said, "A goalkeeper cannot win a game. A goalkeeper saves it." I made those words my computer screen-saver.

In high school, I had been the forward who won games. It was a huge mental adjustment to learn that my job was to save games. To be patient in goal. To anticipate what was needed. Amy taught me the nuances of being a goalkeeper. Before, I would stand in goal, the ball would come toward me, and I'd use my athletic ability to make the save. But thanks to Amy's tutelage and my time with the national team, I was becoming a much better tactical goalkeeper. I learned how to read my opponents' runs toward goal, how to position my defenders, how to see the angles. I learned when to come off my line and when to stay back, how to start a counterattack, how to anticipate and predict what was happening in front of me.

Amy—all five foot four of her—had to know the game to compete as a goalkeeper on the national team. She taught me that side and how to incorporate it with my athleticism. The intellectual side also made goalkeeping so much more interesting. It wasn't just ninety minutes of waiting for my defense to make a mistake. It was ninety minutes of tactics and strategy. The personality traits that had been shaped by my childhood—resilience and toughness—were assets at the position.

It had taken eight years, but I was finally a real goalkeeper.

VII.

In February of my senior year, Adrian and I flew to Atlanta for the WUSA draft. The professional league was starting its third season, and I was among the top players in the country, invited to attend the draft in person. I had already chosen an agent, Richard Motzkin, who represented high-profile players on the men's side, such as Landon Donovan and Alexi Lalas. And I had a deal in the works with Nike.

I knew I would have to leave my West Coast comfort zone to play in the WUSA. As expected, my friend Aly Wagner, who played at Santa Clara, was the first pick, going to San Diego. I knew the next three teams choosing were all on the East Coast. Christie Welsh went to New York with the second pick. The buzz in the draft room was that Boston—with a new coach Pia Sundhage—would select me with the third pick. But the Breakers took another player from Santa Clara, Devvyn Hawkins. My name was called on the fourth pick—I was going to play for the Philadelphia Charge. Philadelphia, Boston—it was all the same to me. I would have to move to the other side of the country. Away from my family, and away from Adrian.

I was now a professional soccer player. The fact that there was a professional league for women seemed like a natural development in a world where the 1999 World Cup had sold out NFL stadiums, where fans crushed against fences to see Mia Hamm, where girls like me had been rewarded all our lives for working hard and playing well. It seemed like a natural step—but for me it was still a scary one. "Oh my god, Adrian, I have to move to Philadelphia," I said. "I'm really going to miss you."

"Do you want me to come with you?" he said.

I thought he was kidding. "Would you really?" We were just friends, right? Really good friends.

He said, "When you love someone as much as I love you, it's not even a question of whether I'll come."

My breath caught in my chest. It was the first time he had said he loved me.

VIII.

I went back to Seattle and finished my classes, and then I was done with school. I went into the athletic building to say good-bye to Lesle and Amy and felt a wave of emotion. Going to UW was the best decision I ever made. If I had followed my original vow and gone as far away from home as possible, I might have never gotten to know my father, never improved my relationship with my mother, never learned as much about goalkeeping, never had coaches who would be role models and lifelong friends.

It was only fitting that I missed one more thing at UW because of soccer: my graduation ceremony. While my classmates donned robes and mortarboards, I was riding the bench for the Philadelphia Charge.

CHAPTER NINE

Made in the WUSA

The ball caromed off the crossbar, and Abby Wambach pounced on it, sending a rocket into the corner of the net. She was on fire; it was her third goal against us. But I couldn't do anything but watch, because I wasn't in the game. I was sitting on the bench while the Washington Freedom, a team that starred Abby and Mia Hamm, manhandled my Philadelphia Charge team.

Professional soccer wasn't turning out to be what I expected. The launch of the Women's United Soccer Association in 2001—the first professional soccer league for women—seemed to me like a natural evolution, not a revolution. Women's sports were growing stronger and more important every year. Why shouldn't we have our own league? When I was drafted by the WUSA, I thought I was joining the big time. I'd been in college and wasn't paying much attention to the league's growing pains or the dire forecasts. When Philadelphia drafted me, I felt I had arrived—a professional athlete, in the same category as Shaq or A-Rod. But by early May, I was learning the hard truth—women's professional soccer wasn't anything like the NBA or Major League Baseball. I had joined a league fighting desperately to stay alive. Corporate sponsorships weren't panning out, crowds were nowhere near as big as projected, and television ratings were abysmal. The league was in a downward economic spiral; I had barely unpacked before I was asked to take a pay cut, dropping my salary from $35,000 to $30,000.

I didn't understand the big-picture economics of the WUSA, but I could see we were running a bare-bones operation. We played our games at Villanova Stadium, training on a field of ancient and unforgiving Astroturf, and my back started to pay the price. This wasn't anything close to my beautiful training facility back at UW. Worse, we didn't have a goalkeeper coach. I went from working with a high-level coach, to basically training on my own. And it didn't take long to figure out that decisions by the coaches were often made for political reasons. Philadelphia was my first lesson that talent doesn't always win out. My coach, Mark Krikorian, had come to the WUSA from the University of Hartford. He coached the Charge to the semifinals in both of his first two seasons and was named Coach of the Year in 2002. He favored a goalkeeper named Melissa Moore, who was twenty-eight and had little experience at the national-team level. It seemed Mark felt he had found a diamond in the rough, and his feeling was vindicated when Moore won WUSA Goalkeeper of the Year honors in 2002. Melissa had played for Amy at New Mexico years earlier. She was a strong team leader, but I felt she wasn't a top-level goalkeeper. I was an up-and-coming goalkeeper, and he drafted me as an investment in the future, but it didn't seem to me that he wanted to play me.

AND SO I sat on the bench. I felt alone and homesick for the first time. After a lot of discussion, Adrian didn't come with me. He had too many business projects in Seattle, and we were both worried about the commitment that would have come with his moving to Philadelphia just to be with me.

Cheryl didn't come along either. And neither did Lesle and Amy. Everyone and everything was new. The East Coast was foreign to me—I missed the green of Seattle, and I had to learn how to cook. I called my mom and asked her to walk me through her lasagna recipe. Later, I called her to help me change a flat tire. Philadelphia was freezing until it abruptly became unbearably muggy. But the most unsettling thing was that since the Philadelphia Charge didn't have a goalkeeping coach, Melissa effectively took on the role. During practices, the coaches would send us off to the side to work together. We called Amy to ask for some basic drills—we were so used to being told what to do. Mark wanted Melissa to tutor me. How, I wondered, would anyone know if I beat her out? It didn't seem to me that I could compete for the job. I just wanted a fair shot.

So I sat and watched as our season disintegrated. We lost our first four games before I finally got a start on May 17 against New York. I had a shutout going until injury time of the second half, but we won 2–1, our first victory of the season. It didn't matter. I went back to the bench and watched Melissa struggle. Later on, in film sessions with Mark, I watched the scoring all over again and listened to both Mark and Melissa make excuses, talking about our team's poor marking or the opposition's uncanny ability.

No matter how bad the goal—and some of them were shocking—Mark never seemed to place the blame on Melissa. Nothing in college or national-team training had prepared me for the lack of accountability. I sat quietly for weeks, frustrated. I liked Mark, and I felt that we had a decent team—French star Marinette Pichon was among the league leaders in goals scored. I believed that all we needed was a stop here and there.

Finally, as the season dragged on, I decided to offer my opinion during one of our film sessions. "You were out of position," I said to Melissa, then turned to Mark. "Maybe we should get a goalkeeper coach to break down the film."

Mark didn't like that. He called Amy. "What's the deal with this kid?" he said.

"What do you mean? She's awesome. She's a hard worker. She wants to prove herself."

"Is she coachable?" Mark said. "She seems awfully immature."

Maybe I was. Mark was known as a coach you didn't confront.

I was getting worried about my career. I felt Mark's refusal to play me was hurting my chances for the national team, and the Women's World Cup was coming up in September—the first World Cup since the epic 1999 tournament—and it was back on U.S. soil. Every player in the national-team pool was training hard with the World Cup in mind. China had originally been slated to host the event, but the SARS epidemic of early 2003 caused a panic about travel to Asia. In May, FIFA decided to move the World Cup to the United States with just four months notice. The rationale was that the United States soccer federation could handle last-minute planning and that the tournament might bolster the struggling WUSA. China was awarded the rights to the 2007 World Cup.

Portland, which would serve as one of the host cities, was just three hours south of my home. For three years, I had been in and out of the national-team pool, and I felt I had a chance to make the roster this time. But I needed to play. In every Charge match, I saw national-team players starting for the opposition. Bri was starting for Atlanta. Siri was starting for the Washington Freedom and would ultimately lead them to the league championship. That was what the WUSA was supposed to be about: developing players with high-level regular competition. But I was stuck watching someone else's mistakes on video.

I heard that April actually lobbied Mark to get me some playing time, but he stuck with Melissa as the hot, muggy Philadelphia summer dragged on. I was miserable. Finally, after a 3–1 loss on July 26 to Carolina, the Charge was officially eliminated from playoff contention. We had been at the bottom of the league all season and had gone 0–5 in July. With nothing to lose, Mark decided to play me. It was, however, too late for my World Cup chances: April had to name her roster in less than a month.

I started the final three games of the season. Against Atlanta, I earned my first professional shutout in a 3–0 win. Against

Washington, I shut out the eventual champions, helping to hold Abby and Mia scoreless. In the season finale, at Carolina we tied 1–1, though we might have won if we had converted a late-game penalty kick. I finished the season with three wins and a tie and a little more confidence.

We got back to Philadelphia from Carolina and had a team exit meeting at the Villanova field. I drove my Chevy Blazer—already packed with all my belongings—to the meeting, and as soon as I was cleared to leave, I hit the road, heading west. I didn't even stay for the team party. Maybe I was being a lousy teammate, but I was incredibly homesick. I missed Adrian. I drove nonstop—pulling over only to power-nap in rest areas—back to Seattle where Adrian waited for me.

It had been a rough rookie season. I vowed to myself that my second season in the WUSA would be better.

II.

Sofia looked at me and laughed. "Your jeans, they're too . . ."— she made a big gesture with her hands—"I don't know the English word. Wide?"

We were having coffee on a cobblestoned street in Haga, the three-hundred-year-old neighborhood of Göteborg, Sweden. I was wearing jeans that were too wide from the knee down—not skinny jeans like the kind everyone in Europe was wearing. I had on white tennis shoes, which also made Sofia laugh. I might as well have stamped AMERICAN on my forehead.

"Come on, Hope," Sofia said, standing up. "We're going to go shopping."

We went down the street and walked into a stylish boutique. An hour later, I had skinny jeans, a ropey woolen scarf, and a pair of ankle boots. Thanks to Sofia, I looked a little more Euro. Which was a good thing, because I was now living in Europe. I was still a professional soccer player, but I was playing in Sweden.

Thirty-seven days after I played my last game for the Philadelphia Charge, the WUSA folded. Though I'd known the league was struggling, I was shocked. I got the call at the apartment in West Seattle I was sharing with Adrian. I plunked down hard on the couch, listening to a conference call announcing the death of the league just six days before the World Cup games were to begin. The players in the national-team pool were all distraught, particularly the '99ers who had helped found the league. We were all cast adrift. The WUSA had made a lot of mistakes along the way. Probably the biggest was assuming that the passion and power of the '99 World Cup could sustain an eight-team league. But Mia Hamm couldn't be on every team. The San Diego Spirit versus the San Jose CyberRays wasn't exactly a must-see event, especially when most members of the target audience—teenage soccer girls—had their own games to attend. The WUSA blew through its five-year budget in the first year, trying to create the illusion of big-time professional sports, with offices in New York, expensive travel, gratuitous perks, and too many league executives.

As I sat on my couch in Seattle I contemplated my future. How was I going to support myself? I was twenty-three and had been told for years that I had potential, potential, potential. But did the national team even have a spot for me? I was sick of hearing about my potential. I felt I was going backward. It was 2003, and I wasn't any further along than I had been in 2000. I hadn't played in a national-team game for over a year. What was I going to do?

I wasn't the only one worrying. The vibe for the '03 World Cup was nothing like it was in '99. The crowds were smaller and less enthusiastic—the roar in '99 had turned into a whisper. Because the games were in September and October, they competed with college football and the NFL, so no one paid attention. The stench of the failed WUSA seemed to cling to everything.

On October 5, the United States lost 3–0 to Germany in a semifinal game in Portland. There wouldn't be any repeat championship. I sat in the stands with Adrian, watching my teammates openly weep on the field. My good friend Cat Reddick fell to the ground and lay there sobbing until a veteran came over and pulled her to her feet. It was a depressing end to a sad summer for women's soccer.

While I figured out what to do with my life, I kept coaching kids. My friend Malia had become the coaching director of one of the biggest clubs in Seattle and she hired me as a goalkeeper coach and connected me with parents looking for private training. Thanks to Malia, I coached all around the Seattle area that winter—boys, girls, young and younger. I found the work fulfilling and felt that I connected with the kids, but I hated driving back and forth across Seattle and being in the cold and wet all day. Coaching in the Seattle winter is tough duty. I wasn't prepared to call that my career.

I spent a lot of time with my father during those months, curling up on his couch to nap between coaching gigs. I felt I could tell him anything—what I was thinking, how I was feeling. We talked about sports, about the future. Our relationship blossomed without the stress of the streets. But you could never take the streets out of my dad. One day we drove through a lousy neighborhood and stopped at a red light, where a bunch of tough guys, obviously up to no good, were hanging out on a corner. All of a sudden, my dad flashed a switchblade at them through the window, a warning not to mess with us.

"Dad," I yelled, and started laughing. He was forever the tough son of a bitch.

Adrian and I enjoyed living in West Seattle, near Alki Beach. We played beach volleyball and prowled our neighborhood cafés. As always, our time together was special, but we kept it casual. I was just staying at his apartment: no serious commitment. That's what we said, but we liked living together.

Around the holidays, my agent called. A First Division Swedish team, Kopparbergs/Göteborg, in southern Sweden, had offered me a contract. Why not, I thought? It sounded like an adventure, a chance to make more money than I could in the United States, and a way to prove to April and Phil that I was determined to get better. I needed game action, and I would get it in Sweden.

In February I flew to Göteborg and then headed directly to the Canary Islands for training camp, where I met my new teammates. I was the only American on the team. Playing in Sweden changed my life. Unencumbered by college obligations or family demands or the chase for the national-team carrot, I rediscovered my love for the game. I wasn't trying to please anyone or move up a ladder or prove anything to April. I relaxed and had fun.

Early on, I lived out in the country in a guesthouse on the team owner's estate with two players from Brazil, Daniela and Juliana. But my friends on the team insisted that I come stay in town, so I got an apartment in Göteborg, a beautiful city that was easy to navigate. I was making more money than I had made in Philadelphia, and I didn't have any expenses. The team covered my apartment, my food, my phone, my Internet, my car, and my gas. So I gave my teammates rides everywhere—none of the Swedes on the team drove cars because gas was so expensive and they weren't reimbursed. I was having fun.

Even better, I could tell I was improving on the field. The pace of the game was faster than in the WUSA; I had to make quicker decisions and take charge. Our team was playing well, and I was considered one of the top goalkeepers in a pretty good league.

I loved walking the cobblestoned streets of Haga, the old district, or wandering along the canal. I drank cider with my new friends and learned to toast by saying "Skål." Lotta Schelin and her older sister, Camilla, became my close friends, inviting me to their family home nearby and including me in their elaborate Easter dinner, where I learned to eat pickled herring. My closest friend was midfielder Sofia Palmqvist, who was a deep thinker. We were both in our twenties and trying to figure out life. We went kayaking together outside of town, talking about our lives and dreams. We played *Dance Dance Revolution* in my apartment and went to clubs in Göteborg. I also spent a lot of time alone, reading books like Dan Millman's *Way of the Peaceful Warrior*, about an athlete on a spiritual journey. I started a journal. I began to read the Bible. I wanted to find my center, to expand my heart and mind.

Now that I was far from my family, I appreciated their support and love even more. I called my dad and sent him postcards, and I called my mother almost every day. She had visited me in Philadelphia where—sharing a bed in my tiny studio apartment—she had opened up for the first time about her history with my father, telling me how they met and all the pain he put her through. I felt I knew her better now and I wanted to stay connected to her. Living on my own gave me perspective on the struggles she went through to make sure we had a home.

I had to move five thousand miles away to fully appreciate that.

III.

In late May 2004, I left my Swedish team and flew back to the United States for the Olympic residency camp in Southern California. April was finalizing her roster for the Athens Olympics, and—except for a few games with the Charge—she hadn't seen me play since September 2002. I had few expectations about making the Athens roster. I was just happy with my progress in Sweden, and I wasn't nervous about impressing the national team coaches. Everyone could tell that something about me had changed. On the field, I felt looser and more confident. I had an excellent two weeks of training and then returned to Sweden.

When the Athens roster was named in late June, the two goalkeepers on the team were Bri and Kristin Luckenbill. Luckenbill was a Dartmouth graduate who had started for three years for the Carolina WUSA team but hadn't played on the national level. Her emergence left me little hope of being named an alternate—I assumed that the final slot on the team would go to an experienced goalkeeper like Siri. But in early July—a few games before my Swedish team went on an extended break for the Olympics—goalkeeper coach Phil Wheddon called me. "Hope, we want you to be our alternate," Phil said. "We can see how much you've grown in Sweden. Because you've been playing competitive games we think you'd be better prepared than the goalkeepers who have only been able to train."

My first reaction was to reflect on the journey, all the hard work and sacrifices I had made along with my family. My second was to worry about my bank account. My mother was coming to visit me in Sweden, and I had planned a big trip to Italy with Adrian. Those non-refundable airline tickets put a damper on my excitement. But then April sent me an e-mail letting me know I didn't have to fly back to California for the final weeks of preparation—I could stay in Sweden, finish out the first half of my season, do my traveling, and then meet the team in Greece.

I immediately shot off an e-mail to Lesle and Amy.

> *I'm writing to tell you guys that I'm going to Greece as the third goalkeeper. Although I want to be the first! :) I feel very rewarded, and I feel a step closer to my dreams. It's a great feeling and I couldn't wait to tell you since you two have been through it all with me, right there by my side. It's taken several years, but slowly, it's all coming together, and I want to thank you for all your support and for truly believing in me. Washington, and all it had to offer, really set me straight!!! You guys are the best, and forever in my heart and mind! I love you. Hope.*

A few days later my mother arrived in Sweden on her first trip overseas. We were excited to be having an adventure together—it felt like a new chapter in our relationship. We drove my maroon Volvo north to Stockholm, over to Norway, up into the beautiful fjords. Like the locals—all of us weary of the long, dark winter—I was eager to take advantage of the beautiful Scandinavian summer, the long days and mild weather and outdoor lifestyle. We basked in the sun on the rocks outside Stockholm. We camped and swam in icy lakes. It reminded me of when I had been a little girl, camping on the beach in Happy Camp, Oregon. One night a little red fox came near our campfire, and my mother coaxed him closer with food. We nicknamed him Foxxy and viewed him as a good-luck symbol of our renewed connection.

I saw a different side of my mother in Scandinavia. She had been sober for a couple of years now and was clearheaded, strong, adventurous, funny, and fun—I saw a glimpse of the girl she must have been in the late 1970s, when she met my father. On a whim, we went into a store in Stockholm and both got our noses pierced. I had never thought of my mom as a girlfriend, someone fun to hang out with, but now we laughed and confided in each other. I had a new friend.

After my mother left, Adrian arrived, and we flew to Italy. I'd heard too much about it all my life to think it could live up to its reputation, but it was wonderful. We walked from town to town on Cinque Terre. We rented a boat and explored caves along the Italian Riviera. We ate pasta and drank red wine out of jugs and danced in the public squares of tiny villages. I sent my dad postcards from his ancestral land. I tried to find Solo family connections but didn't have much luck. Oh well. I told myself that "Solo" might not even be my dad's real name.

In early August, I had to meet the national team on Crete for training, while Adrian went off to travel in Turkey. I was always with the team on the field, but because I was an alternate, I was completely segregated the rest of the time. I couldn't even get into the team meals. Once again, I felt like an outsider. When the competition started and the team played in other parts of Greece, I went to Athens to wait and see if my services would be needed. I couldn't stay in the athlete's village, so I got housing through the U.S. Olympic Committee at a local university. There was a suite with two bedrooms. I shared a room with Pia Sundhage, who was scouting for our team; Paul Ellis, the head scout, was in the other room. We couldn't find any hotel rooms, so our massage therapist lent Adrian his credential so that he could stay on our couch.

I trained in the morning. Sometimes we played two on two, with Adrian, Paul, and Pia. But after that, I was free to do as I pleased. Nike helped me get tickets to Olympic events. We ate dinner late like the Athens locals, drinking wine in rooftop restaurants on warm nights, the Parthenon glowing in the distance.

I wasn't getting paid much more than a per diem. I had no perks as an Olympic athlete. I was isolated from my team. But in Athens I fell in love with the Olympics. As a fan, I saw the Olympic spirit, the pride of the Greeks, the enthusiasm in the stands, the enormity of the event. The Olympics were different from other sporting events; their meaning hadn't been damaged by all the modern commercialism and hype. Maybe being in Greece, the birthplace of the Games, helped me understand that there was something profound about this colossal gathering of the world's countries. I was determined to be a full participant the next time around.

My teammates rode a wave of emotion into the final. The gold-medal game against Brazil was the last competition for the core of the '99 team. Mia Hamm, Julie Foudy, and Joy Fawcett had announced that they would retire after the Games. No one was sure what the future held for Brandi Chastain or Kristine Lilly or Bri. They didn't say they were retiring, but an era was definitely ending.

For much of the gold-medal game, there was a sense that the world of soccer was undergoing a changing of the guard. Brazil—led by its skilled forward Marta—completely outplayed our team. I sat in the stands with Adrian, watching nervously. Brazil had scoring chance after scoring chance, hitting the post twice with potential game winners late in regulation. After ninety minutes, the game was tied 1–1. But in the twenty-second minute of overtime, Abby headed a corner kick in for the winning goal. Our team was able to kill the clock and finally celebrate.

I went to the after-party, which lasted through the sweltering Athens night and well into the sweltering Athens dawn. The '99ers clung together, weeping and laughing and telling tales in a code only they knew. I hung out on a back deck with my friends Cat

With (*clockwise from bottom left*) Marcus, Dad, David, Terry, and Mom. My mother worked hard to make us all feel like a family.

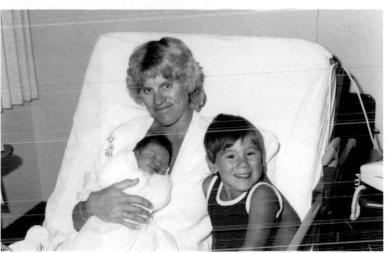

July 30, 1981, the day I was born, with my mom and Marcus.

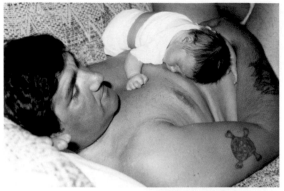

My father
cradling his
Baby Hope.

I idolized
my dad, who
I knew as
Gerry—one
of many
names he
went by.

I learned
to walk
by pulling
myself up on
Charlotte.

My dad and I forged an early connection through sports—
he was my very first soccer coach, in Richland, Washington.

I was always a forward—and prolific goal scorer—
on my youth and school teams.

Grandpa Pete was my father figure, standing by when I won Richland Homecoming Queen.

A rare family portrait at my high school graduation:
Dad, Terry, me, Mom, and Marcus.

With Mom, Glenn, and Marcus in the kitchen on Hoxie.

Cheryl (*left*) and I weren't angels—we definitely liked to party.
Here we are in college with our friends Megan and Van.

Training with legend Briana Scurry in 2007 kept me focused: I needed to have my job on lockdown. (*Julie Jacobson/ Associated Press*)

Despite my string of three 2007 World Cup shutouts, I was relegated to the bench against Brazil in the semifinal. I watched in horror as our team imploded. (*Mark Ralston/AFP/Getty Images*)

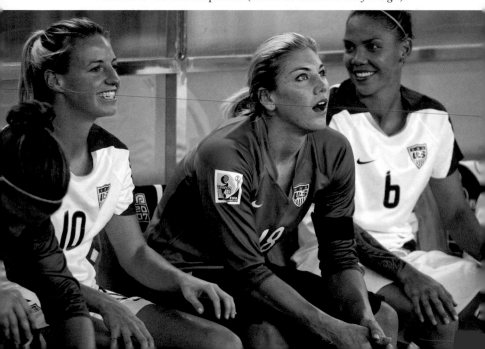

After I spoke up following Greg Ryan's decision to bench me,
the team treated me like a pariah and decided I couldn't suit up for the
"celebration tour." (*Kyle Ericson/Associated Press*)

With Carli Lloyd, my best friend on the national team
and the one teammate who publicly supported me in 2007.

I've known Tina Ellertson since we were teammates at the University of Washington, but it was in St. Louis that we became friends for life.

My manager and partner in crime Whitney helped shepherd me through the post–World Cup craziness: here we are at the FIFA Ballon D'Or in Zurich, where I celebrated my Golden Glove Award as best goalkeeper in the World Cup.

Reddick and Aly Wagner. As the sun rose over Piraeus harbor, I knew a new era was beginning for U.S. soccer. One that would include me.

IV.

I returned to Sweden for the end of our season, and all my new-found maturity and good feelings collapsed in a whirlwind of personal drama. After our romantic summer together, Adrian was acting distant and strange, and I heard he was spending a lot of time with some girl back in Seattle. A male soccer friend from home came to visit me in Sweden while he tried out with a Swedish team. Wounded by Adrian, I had a moment of weakness; my friend and I had a drunken fling. I was instantly remorseful. Sobbing on the phone, I confessed to Adrian.

"Thanks for telling me," he said. He sounded mature, but the distance between us grew.

That autumn the U.S. team went on a nine-game victory tour, celebrating the gold medal and bidding farewell to the '99ers. I wasn't invited to participate because I had been an alternate—a decision made by the veterans. Instead, I returned to Seattle after my Swedish season ended. Once there, I quickly figured out that I couldn't live with Adrian anymore. He would go out all the time and not tell me where he had been. He was still trying to punish me for what I'd done in Sweden.

One day, I'd had enough. I loaded up my car with all my belongings and moved out, crashing with my former teammate, Malia. Then I shared an apartment with Cheryl's brother Ben. I was depressed. My heart was broken. I didn't have anywhere to live. My beloved Seattle felt like a trap. I needed to leave.

Fortunately, my agent called with another contract offer: this time in Lyon, playing for Olympique Lyonnais, an established team offering great money and good benefits. In late December, I boarded a plane for France.

Several weeks later, as I was adjusting to life in Lyon, I got word from across the Atlantic of a huge national team shakeup. April had resigned as head coach.

One morning, my phone rang. "Hi, Hope," said the voice on the other end. "This is Greg Ryan."

CHAPTER TEN

Baa, Baa, Black Sheep

If I had made a list of all the people I thought might coach the national team, Greg Ryan would probably have been dead last. Greg had been April's unremarkable assistant coach, a terrier-faced man with a perpetually surprised expression. He mostly faded into the background, rarely talking and never taking charge at practice. If he had any leadership skills or technical savvy, I never saw it. I figured he got the job simply because he was a friend of April's.

But now, in February 2005, he was on the other end of the phone, telling me he was the interim national-team coach. And that I was on his roster for the upcoming Algarve Cup in Portugal. I felt bad for April. She had always been my supporter—all the way back to when I was first in the Olympic Development Program as a kid in Richland. She gave me my first break on the national team and was always straightforward and honest about what I needed to do to improve. Her departure was officially portrayed as a resignation, but there were reports that she had been forced out by the veteran players. I'd heard their grumblings—I believed they had been lobbying to get rid of her for years, unhappy with her soccer tactics, her communication skills, and her leadership style. I think the veterans felt they knew what was best for the team, and when they failed to win the 2000 Olympics and the 2003 World Cup, the players probably tried to use that as leverage against April. There were published reports that Brandi Chastain asked U.S. Soccer president Robert Contiguglia to fire April eight months before the Athens Olympics, but he refused.

Even winning the gold medal in Athens didn't save April's job. After Brazil had thoroughly outplayed us, it was reported that the veterans—even those who were retiring—sent a letter to April expressing their displeasure and asking her to resign. It seemed to me that now U.S. Soccer was no longer supportive of her, since the World Cup and Olympic cycle was over and a new four-year cycle was about to start. Rather than serve out the final ten months of her contract, April quit. The reported power struggle seemed to be indicative of the control the veteran players felt they had over the team. But they didn't control who would replace her. And now Greg Ryan was the head coach.

I wasn't the only person in Lyon getting a phone call from Greg. That winter, Lyon was a popular destination for Americans— Danielle Slaton, Aly Wagner, Lorrie Fair, and Christie Welsh had all signed to play with Olympique Lyonnais, an up-and-coming team run by the strong French men's club of the same name. We all lived together in residential housing and took weekend trips to Paris and the Alps to go skiing. I didn't like being with so many Americans. It made France seem less special than Sweden had been. Instead of meeting new people and rising to new challenges, I felt I was in an extension of U.S. training camp, with all the same issues, jealousies, and gossip reaching across the Atlantic to the base of the French Alps. I was also distraught over my breakup with Adrian.

In early March, Aly, Lorrie, Christie, and I flew to Lisbon for the Algarve Cup, joining a national team with a decidedly different look. Mia, Julie, and Joy had retired. Brandi wasn't on the roster. Bri was taking time off. Christie (Pearce) Rampone—now married, though she was always Pearcie to us—was pregnant. Only Kristine Lilly and Kate Markgraf remained from the '99ers, though Abby Wambach was so tight with them you would have thought she had stripped off her own jersey along with them in the Rose Bowl in July 1999.

Greg worked to win us over. April never seemed to have much fun, never had a drink, and was always super-serious. Greg was trying to be the exact opposite. He wore sandals and played his guitar for us. He told jokes. He had drinks in the hotel bar. He seemed to be trying hard to cultivate an image as a fun-loving, laid-back dude who would be an awesome guy to have around. During one of our first team dinners in Portugal, Greg cruised into the room with his guitar. "Hey, who's got a request?" he said, strumming the strings.

Awkward. We all just wanted to finish our meal and go Skype with our boyfriends. We didn't really want to sing "He's Got the Whole World in His Hands" with Greg. This wasn't summer camp. Some of my teammates rolled their eyes. Others applauded, seeing a way to get close to the new coach. I watched, fascinated but horrified.

Still, Portugal was fun that March. We didn't have a lot of expectations—we were starting a new four-year cycle and a new era. I didn't play the first game—our new goalkeeper coach, Bill Irwin, had worked with Nicole Barnhardt when she was a youth player and gave her the start, her first ever in international competition. We won 1–0. I got the next game, against Finland on March 11, 2005, my first national-team appearance since September 8, 2002, against Scotland in Columbus, Ohio, when I was a senior in college. That seemed like a long time ago. I knew that, thanks to two years as a professional player, I was a much better goalkeeper now.

Finland was surprisingly tough for us, but I didn't give up a goal, making four saves. Two days later, I started against Denmark, recording another clean sheet and helping our team to the tournament final against Germany. We won that game 1–0. Our defense was solid in front of me, but I made a few memorable saves, and reports termed it a "coming-out" party for me.

It was definitely a coming-out party for Greg as well, though U.S. Soccer officials said they were conducting a search for a full-time head coach. I heard rumors about some of the candidates:

some had worked in the WUSA, including Pia Sundhage, who had coached in Boston. Others were successful college coaches, such as Jerry Smith, who had built a powerhouse at Santa Clara. Pearcie, back home and pregnant, was supposed to be interviewing some of the candidates and passing information along to the rest of us. It seemed that the veterans favored Pia, who had been a great player. Of all the candidates, the one who seemed the least qualified was Greg Ryan. Before coming to the national team, he had coached at Colorado College, never earning an NCAA berth there before becoming April's vanilla assistant. The consensus on the team was that we needed a fresh start, and Greg was a leftover from the past. But it seemed to me that Greg was a pawn in a power struggle. The players were in negotiations for a new contract. According to re-ports, U.S. Soccer officials—many of whom were portrayed as not having cared at all about women's soccer until the 1999 team forced them to—wanted to gain more control over the women's team. The big personalities from the past had built the team from nothing and consequently felt entitled to ownership of that. U.S. Soccer wanted a coach who would do its bidding, including clearing out the entitled veterans. That probably meant Jerry Smith, who was married to Brandi Chastain, wasn't ever going to get a legitimate shot at the job. Greg didn't seem to have the players' backing, but by hiring him, the federation could send a clear message about who was boss.

We had unwittingly helped his cause. The four shutouts in Portu-gal were viewed as evidence that Ryan was the right man for the job and that the U.S. team hadn't missed a beat despite the changeover.

Three weeks after we won the Algarve Cup, when I was back in Lyon, Ryan was named the permanent head coach. "Oh well," I thought with a shrug.

II.

The needle pierced the middle of my back. "Ah!" I inhaled sharply. But I'd felt worse pain.

"Oui?" grunted the tattoo artist. "C'est bon?"

I was in a tattoo parlor in a funky neighborhood of Lyon. My French teammate Claire was with me—her friend had helped design the tattoo I was getting on my back:

Persecuted but not forsaken
Cast down but not destroyed

Here in a tattoo parlor off a French alley, I was trying to inject inspiration into my skin. Second Corinthians was a favorite of Grandma Alice's and the passage resonated with me. Claire's friend had sketched out a cool-looking inscription—a shadowy, edgy font for the tattoo artist to replicate. I was in an edgy period of my life.

After the Algarve Cup, Grandma Alice and Grandpa Pete came to visit me in Lyon. My adventurous grandparents flew to Portugal to support me in my starts for the national team, and now they wanted to see my new life in France. They rode the team bus to games with us and stayed in the residential housing I shared with the other Americans. We made meals in the kitchen and stayed up late playing cribbage. Grandma and Grandpa explored Lyon, even walking up the steep hill to the basilica that towers over the city. They found spiritual meaning and education in their travel.

When they left, I did my own exploring, including in tattoo parlors. I was in a post-Adrian mania. I got to know Claire's non-soccer-playing French friends. We drank red wine and ate Nutella crêpes and regularly ran off to Marseilles or Paris. I dated a lot of men. One French girl flirted with me for months, asking, "How do you know you don't like kissing girls if you've never tried it?"

"Trust me," I said. "I know I like men."

One night I got drunk and let her kiss me. I'd had gay teammates throughout my career—I thought maybe I should see their side of things. So we made out. Interesting but not life-changing. I was straight.

The soccer in France was frustrating. In Sweden, most of my

teammates spoke some English, but it was difficult communicating with my French back line. I tried to learn the right French words, but in the pressure of a game I would resort to English. If I said "away," they thought I was saying "J'ai"—I have it. So my defense thought I was calling for the ball. At times it felt as though I was trapped in a Monty Python skit.

III.

I came home that summer with nowhere to live. Even though we dated other people, Adrian and I continued to see each other—our friendship was too deep to abandon completely—but it was awkward, even painful. We just couldn't stay away from each other. Our families and friends didn't understand the nature of our relationship; some, like Cheryl, thought Adrian was a jerk. But other friends loved him. We were confusing everyone, including ourselves. Meanwhile, I was back on Malia's couch.

I had made enough money from my first three professional contracts that I felt I should buy an investment property. But I didn't have enough for a down payment. Adrian lent me the money. I wanted to draw up a contract and make monthly payments to him.

"Forget it," he said. "Pay me back when you sell it."

I didn't know when that would ever be, but I bought a tiny house in Kirkland, not far from where my sister, Terry, lived. It appealed to me because it was like a little cabin in the woods. It reminded me of how my father had lived for so many years, though he hadn't had walls around him. I intended to rent it out. Instead, I ended up living there for years—and Adrian kept refusing to let me pay him back.

In 2005, the U.S. team continued its transition. One of Greg's first acts as head coach was to tell Brandi Chastain that her services were no longer needed. Brandi hadn't retired after Athens, and she wanted the chance to try out and see if she could make the team. Greg refused to give it to her, causing an uproar in the press—the heroine of the 1999 World Cup had been fired!—and sending a clear message that this was a new era. I doubted Brandi was still good enough to play, but I felt she deserved the chance to try out. Briana Scurry hadn't officially retired, but the word around the team was that she was thinking about it. I took that with a grain of salt. Bri often needed time off after big tournaments, and I assumed she'd be back. But meanwhile, the starting job was mine.

We had a revolving door of goalkeeper coaches. Greg brought in several different coaches whose main experience had been on youth teams. They were telling us things like, "Make your hands in a W shape to catch the ball." I felt embarrassed: here we were playing at the highest level, and the coaches were instructing us as if we were in high school. Finally Ian Feuer came in—an accomplished English goalkeeper and coach. I loved working with Ian, but I didn't expect him to be around for long: he had a family and he could make a lot more money working somewhere else.

Even though the majority of the players in the pool had arrived post-1999, there was still a veteran cabal that controlled things. The key movers and shakers of the past were gone, so players like Kate Markgraf and Abby—who acted like a veteran—stepped into the void, taking over decision-making responsibilities for the team. There was definitely a divide on the team between "veterans" and "new players."

Truthfully, I didn't do much to try to win over the veteran group. The longer I was on the national team, the more I realized that my personality was different from many of my teammates. I wasn't outgoing and bubbly; I struggled socially in big groups. I didn't want to go to movies or to dinner in huge throngs that involved endless planning and negotiations and waiting around. I found it exhausting to be with twenty other women all the time—at training, on the bus, at every meal. I had a difficult time being social twenty-four hours a day. Other girls easily shared their innermost thoughts about boyfriends and family and personal issues, while I liked to keep my private business private. I felt the same as I had in high school: unwilling and unable to play the "social girl" game. But I knew that when I said "No thanks" to an invitation and closed my hotel room door so I could read or talk to my dad on the phone and recharge my energy supply, people thought I was being unfriendly.

"People just don't feel like they know you, Hope," Aly once told me. I knew that was true. It had been the same in high school and college. My lack of comfort in group situations made me feel as if I was dysfunctional, missing one of my X chromosomes.

Around this time, I read a magazine article about introverts. The article was like reading a master's thesis on my personality. Did I enjoy spending time alone or with just one or two friends? Check. While some people drew energy from others, thriving in big groups, was I exhausted and drained by too much social contact? Check. The article noted that, for introverts, trust was a major issue causing discomfort in groups and that those trust issues usually dated back to childhood. According to the article, introverts found it hard to feel comfortable and secure in large groups. While the loudest were usually viewed as leaders—Abby came quickly to mind—introverts could also lead. I was often called outspoken, because I was honest to the point of making others uncomfortable, but I wasn't loud or assertive. I had to find a way to lead in my own way. Now I had a name for why I felt as I did, why I preferred to be by myself. I was an introvert. I didn't know that made me a black sheep.

IV.

In 2006 Bri returned. She had decided to make one more run, though she would be thirty-six by the time the China World Cup began. I wasn't surprised to see her. Bri had always been nice to me when I was younger and wasn't a threat at all. But now the relationship had changed. There was more tension between us.

"It's your job to lose," Greg told me.

It was strange having a legend behind me, though it wasn't a bad thing: with Briana Scurry in the wings, I couldn't have an off game.

The pressure was on. But it was clear that Bri was going to have to do something extraordinary to win the job. I was far ahead of her in fitness, and the position had evolved in recent years: the kicking game was more important; footwork was emphasized more.

Without a professional league to keep us sharp, U.S. Soccer decided that residency camp was the best way to prepare for the World Cup. In 2006, we started a six-month live-in camp, which meant three weeks at a time in Southern California, training at the Home Depot Center, and one week at home. During those weeks when I got home, I tried to pack in everything: a trip to Richland to see my family, visits with my dad, local appearances, a coffee with Lesle and Amy. Adrian and I still had our weird connection. I was exhausted.

At camp, I rented an apartment by the ocean in Hermosa Beach with Christie Welsh. We lived in the same apartment complex Greg lived in. The night before camp began, Adrian and I were out at a nearby restaurant, and Greg and his new girlfriend were sitting in the bar. I was going to pretend I hadn't seen them, but Adrian said we should go over and say hello. I halfheartedly agreed. Greg was my boss now.

"Let me buy you a drink," Greg said.

"No, no, that's OK," I said, backing toward the door.

"Really, Hope, I insist," he said.

So Adrian and I sat at the bar and had drinks with Greg and his date. It seemed very odd to see him hanging out in a bar, especially since one of my teammates, Marci Miller, told me she wanted to play for Greg because he had strong Christian values. Marci had even followed Greg when he changed jobs—from the University of Wisconsin to Southern Methodist. Yet that summer in residency camp, Greg didn't seem to be that guy. I often saw him out with his girlfriend and in the apartment complex hot tub. He seemed to be playing the part of a stereotypical cool Californian.

I wasn't one to judge, though. I was partying myself, heavily at times. Sometimes I would drive to Vegas with a friend, party all night, and come back to training without having slept. And I dated dozens of men, often several at the same time. I started to wonder if I was like my father, if I was never going to be able to commit to one person.

My raging social life didn't hurt me on the field. I was always among the top players in fitness tests. Our new goalkeeping coach, Mark Dougherty, emphasized fitness, so I excelled with him. At one point, I had a streak of 1,054 minutes without giving up a goal from the run of play, an impressive stretch that ended with a goal by France in the 2006 Algarve Cup. I started every game at the Four Nations Cup in China and was named Goalkeeper of the Tournament. That year, I started eighteen of twenty-two national-team games. There wasn't any doubt about who was America's new goalkeeper.

Despite that, I still didn't feel that I had the full respect of the veterans. I sensed that the veterans didn't like the fact that Bri had been reduced to the role of backup. Every time Bri made a save, even in practice, they cheered like crazy for her. "Fuck yeah, Bri," Abby would scream when Bri made a routine save. Maybe it was because they'd seen Bri make a comeback before. Or maybe they had a more personal stake in her success—if Bri was being phased out, didn't that make them all expendable?

Everyone in the soccer world had expected a drop-off for our team after most of the stars of '99 departed, yet we still dominated. Under Greg, we hadn't lost a game (we lost the 2006 Algarve Cup final on penalty kicks to Germany, but it still counted as a tie). Though we didn't have the big names, we were still a team that could make America proud.

Residency camp was a revolving door. New players came and went as Greg constantly evaluated new talent. My old UW teammate Tina Frimpong became a regular in the pool. Another was Carli Lloyd, a blunt-spoken girl from New Jersey who—I later found out—thought I was incredibly intimidating.

In spite of his success, I saw signs of insecurity beginning to show in Greg as the year progressed. Instead of the laid-back guy he had tried to be early on, I saw him get upset about the smallest things: if the balls weren't pumped up right, if the goal was moved. I saw him arguing with his staff—the equipment managers and trainers. He didn't seem confident in his own decision-making capabilities.

One day he asked me to have coffee. As we sat at a local Starbucks, Greg peppered me with questions about our goalkeeping coach. Was I happy with Mark Dougherty? He said he wanted my opinion because I was the number one goalkeeper.

I liked Mark, but I had some reservations. My fitness was solid, but I believed my technique needed improvement. I felt awkward. "I have incredible respect for Mark," I said. "I think we have a great relationship."

Greg kept prodding, saying I needed to be honest.

I finally conceded that Phil Wheddon was one of the best goalkeeper coaches I had worked with. Phil had coached the men's team through the 2006 World Cup in Germany that summer but was now available. I was betraying Mark, but I needed to be honest.

The day after our meeting, Greg fired Mark. I heard later through the grapevine that Greg told Mark that I had come to him saying I wanted Phil back. If true, that was the craziest thing I'd ever heard: the head coach was putting such an important decision on me, a twenty-five-year-old goalkeeper. Mark never spoke to me again—and I don't blame him. But I was happy to be reunited with Phil. He had helped mold me in my early years with the national team and had supported me every step of the way, from my adventures in Europe to my role as alternate in Athens. He knew what I was capable of achieving.

I stuck close to Phil at training and tried to keep away from Greg and his mood swings. The World Cup was less than a year away, and I needed to make sure I had the goalkeeping job on lockdown.

I had a legend behind me, which kept me on edge.

IV.

Go!

I sprinted 800 meters, staying near the front with Aly. A minute rest.

Go!

Another 800.

Go!

And another . . .

I was the only goalkeeper doing all the 800s. In fact, I was one of the few players doing them—most viewed 800s as punishment for players who needed extra fitness work. But I wanted to do them. I hated that goalkeepers were often last in fitness. I wanted to be one of the fittest players on our team.

We did cone drills—sprint, turn, back—to five yards, ten yards, up to twenty-five yards out. Turn, stop, start, again. It was great work for strengthening our legs, ten sets. Up and down. Up and down. I dove for ball after ball, landing on my shoulder, ten, twenty, fifty, a hundred times.

V.

New Year's Day, 2007. The Women's World Cup was in September, and I was the team's starting goalkeeper. This was going to be my year. We won the Four Nations tournament in January in China, which felt like a World Cup preview, and we won the Algarve Cup again in March. I was already the second-most-capped goalkeeper in U.S. history.

In early April, we started another training camp in Southern California, one that would count us down to our departure for China. Because we would be traveling so much for our "send-off tour," there was no need to rent an apartment. I stayed at the Residence Inn in Torrance.

On Sunday morning, April 22, hours before the sun rose in

California, the World Cup draw took place in Wuhan, China. We were placed in the most difficult group of the four, along with Sweden, Nigeria, and North Korea. The inclusion of North Korea seemed to upset Greg. He had just seen them play China in a pre-draw match, and their talent was undeniable. The draw appeared to be a political move to keep the North Koreans away from host China. That benefited China but hurt us: we would open against one of the best yet least transparent teams in women's soccer. North Korea was hard to scout. The only time we had ever played North Korea was in the previous two World Cups.

But that Sunday morning, the politics of the World Cup draw was the last thing on my mind. I was alone in my room at the Residence Inn when my phone rang. "Hope," my mother said. "I have some terrible news about Liz."

My dear friend from high school, Liz Duncan, had been out for her usual Saturday run near her apartment in Seattle. She stopped on the median of a busy street, waiting for the light to change. A sixteen-year-old girl in a Pontiac Grand Am lost control of the car, jumped the curb, and hit Liz. She died at the scene.

I was distraught. Liz and I had been basketball and soccer teammates; we played hard and laughed hard. During college, we were friendly rivals: Liz played soccer for Washington State, and I loved seeing her on the field, trying to score against me. When we were both home from college, she would push me to go on training runs with her, mile after mile in the cold along the Columbia River. She had been a track star at Richland High, and she helped me get in the best shape of my life.

That morning Liz had been doing what she loved best: she ran every single day. I could envision her in a mesh running cap and black running tights, her ponytail swinging behind her. She had just registered for the Chicago Marathon. Her motto was "Life's short. Run long." She was days away from her twenty-seventh birthday.

I had never had anyone close to me die. I wasn't sure what to do. My mother stayed on the phone until I calmed down. Then I called Phil and asked if we could meet for coffee. I started to cross the street toward Starbucks, but I froze in the middle of the crosswalk—there were so many cars going in so many directions, lights blinking, loud noises. I rushed back to where I had started. A car had killed Liz on a street like this. How could life be so easily snuffed out? I broke down in tears.

"Phil, I think I need to go home," I said.

I felt tentative, unsure. Could I leave while we were preparing for a World Cup? Was it OK to attend the funeral of one of my best friends? Would my spot be in danger? Would I be letting down my team? "Hope, if you need to go, go," Phil said.

I did. Some things are more important than soccer. I spent a week in Richland. I wept over Liz's casket at the viewing. I mourned at her funeral. I spent time with her grieving mother. I came back to the team feeling fragile and cracked, as though one hard hit would break me open.

CHAPTER ELEVEN

"Only a Daughter Cries Like That"

Another hotel room. Another city. Another phone ringing.

I rolled out of bed and saw that I had missed a call. I had to stop and think for a moment. What day was it? What city was I in? Why was I here?

Friday, June 15. Cleveland. Tomorrow we had a game against China, the first in our "send-off" series leading to the World Cup. Our pregame meeting was in a few hours. I had been back training with the team for more than a month. After I returned from Liz's funeral, I was reserved, with a singular focus on my training. I wanted to draw inspiration from my strong athletic friend and honor her memory with my effort. I stopped drinking any alcohol, even on off days. I was all business.

Things were getting weird around the team. Greg was back from scouting North Korea and seemed uptight and angry. All anyone was talking about at team meals or on the bus was "What's wrong with Greg?" We still hadn't lost a game, but the World Cup was bearing down on us, and the pressure was clearly getting to him. Our sports psychologist came in to work on team-building. We had to do relay races balancing an egg on a spoon, passing the egg to a teammate without dropping it. A lot of people dropped the eggs.

"Did you feel like you let down your teammates when you dropped the egg?" she asked with a straight face.

I sat in the back and cringed. The exercise seemed absurd. I'd just lost one of my best friends, and we were talking about eggs. I wasn't sure how passing eggs around on spoons was going to help us win soccer games in China.

I was going to be late for breakfast. I picked up my phone and saw I had a message. I had missed a call from a 206 area code. That wasn't a good sign. Who would be calling me at five a.m. Seattle time?

"Hello, Miss Hope Solo?" a businesslike female voice said on the message. "Could you please call us back regarding Jeffrey John Solo?"

Oh God. What had happened? Had someone falsely accused my father again? I had talked to him just a few hours earlier, on Thursday evening, as I was walking back to our hotel from Game Four of the NBA Finals. My dad—who liked old-school athletes—was a huge Tim Duncan fan, so he was rooting for San Antonio; I was rooting for LeBron James and the Cavaliers. Dad was thrilled that I had a chance to go to the game and had bought him a championship hat, and he ribbed me after the Spurs completed the sweep of LeBron's team. I told him that he would have to wear this hat instead of keeping it wrapped in plastic like the others that I bought for him. He was his usual self—happy and joking and delighted to talk to me.

Full of dread, I hit redial. The same abrupt voice answered the phone.

"Hi," I said tentatively. "I'm calling about my dad? Jeffrey John Solo?"

"Oh, yes," She sounded like she was asking for my takeout order. "What kind of arrangement do you want to make for the body?"

My knees buckled and I slipped to the bed. "What's going on? What are you talking about?"

"I'm sorry," she said. "I thought you'd been informed. Your father passed away and you're listed as next of kin."

She kept talking but I couldn't hear her anymore.

"Oh my God, oh my God, oh my God . . ."

My roommate Cat came out of the bathroom and sat next to me. She figured out what must have happened through my moans. "Hope, you have to get home," she said. "Can you call your family? Do that, and I'll be right back." She went downstairs to tell my team.

I kept telling myself this wasn't real. My dad was supposed to be coming on a trip with me in just a few days. On June 23, our team would play Brazil in New York, and Marcus and my father would be there. We would take Dad on a trip to visit his boyhood haunts and maybe finally get some answers about his past. Best of all, my dad would be there in person to see me play with the national team for the first time. Every time I thought about our upcoming trip, I smiled. Dad couldn't have made this journey years earlier: his knees were too bad, his life too chaotic. But now he was stable, happy, and healthy. Mentally prepared to revisit the past.

Oh my God, oh my God.

Shaking, I dialed Marcus's number. I knew he was staying at Mom's.

"Wha . . . hello?" Marcus said. I had woken him from a sound sleep.

"Marcus," I said, trying to keep my voice calm. "Dad didn't make it through the night."

My strange wording confused him. It was too hard for me to say that our father had died. When Marcus finally understood what I was trying to tell him, he didn't respond with words, but a guttural animal-like wail. In the background, I heard my mother rush into his room and try to comfort him. She took the phone and I told her what I knew. But I didn't have any answers for them. I didn't feel equipped to deal with this. I felt like what I was. A little girl who had just lost her daddy.

Cat and Aly came back into my room. I couldn't stop crying or shaking. I was unsure what to do. What happens next?

I lay curled in a ball while things happened around me in a blur.

Someone booked me a flight home. Cat and Aly began to gather my things. My teammates came into the room, one by one, to check on me. Some were unsure how to act and stood awkwardly near the door, simply staring. They had never seen me so vulnerable and broken: I usually presented such a strong front. Marci Miller—older than many of my teammates—seemed to understand what was needed. She sat next to me on the bed and rubbed my leg, murmuring calming words. I latched onto her touch and voice and turned toward her for help. "I don't know what to do," I whimpered. "I can't do this."

I looked up and saw Bri sitting across from me, looking directly into my eyes. "You can do this Hope," she said. "Be strong."

When I didn't respond, she said again, "You can do this."

Bri had lost her father on Father's Day of 2004, just weeks before the Athens Olympics. She stared intently at me, as though passing her strength and experience through the air between us. I kept my eyes on her. "You can, Hope," Bri said. "You can do this." Then she got up and walked out of the room, like a woman on a mission.

Greg came in and stood awkwardly in the middle of the scene. I was in shock. Aly was on the phone. Cat was packing my bag. Marci was rubbing my leg. Other girls huddled on the bed or leaned against a wall. Greg walked over and patted me on the shoulder. "Take care, kiddo," he said. And then he walked out.

Aly and Cat arranged for a taxi to the airport. As we were leaving my room, Bri returned. She slipped a letter into my hand. "You can do this Hope," she said, again. "You're strong."

II.

At the airport, Aly and Cat checked me in, helped me get into the security line and hugged me good-bye. And then I was alone, sitting in a chair at my gate. For years, I had always called my dad before I flew, a ritual to ward off my fear of flying. I couldn't call him now. I was alone with my terrors, old and new.

Memories of my dad rushed at me. Dad holding me up to the basketball hoop in the driveway of the smiley-face house. Dad weeping as he proclaimed his innocence to me in front of REI. Dad reaching out to hug me near a damp Seattle soccer field. Showing me his tent in the woods. Pointing out the sights of Seattle from the top of the Space Needle. Sitting high in the stands in his purple University of Washington sweatshirt. Laughing as he tried to figure out a computer keyboard.

There was so much I still didn't know about him. So much more laughter to share. I put my head on my knees and sobbed.

After a few moments, I realized someone was standing near me. I looked up and saw an unfamiliar man with a kind expression, who said, "It's your father, isn't it?"

I nodded, wiping my eyes with my sleeve.

"Only a daughter cries like that for her father."

On the plane I pulled my hood over my head and opened Bri's letter.

She wrote from the heart, describing exactly how I felt. She knew because she had felt the same way—with her heart and soul ripped apart. "It will take time," she wrote, "and, to be honest, it will never go away completely." She encouraged me to hold on to my dad's spirit to help me get through these dark days, to carry him inside me and let myself cry when I needed to.

"You can do this, yes you can," she wrote. "Do it for both of you."

She closed by letting me know that she was there for me.

I flew west. I remembered that Sunday would be Father's Day.

III.

My father had been sleeping on the couch in the apartment of his friend, Beverly, who also lived at Hilltop. He hadn't felt right, and she had checked on him early in the morning. "I'm fine," he told her and went back to sleep. An hour later, he was dead; the cause of death was coronary artery disease.

Everyone in his life knew about his upcoming trip to New York. He bragged that he would see Baby Hope play at Giants Stadium, on the same field where Eli Manning played. He couldn't wait to travel with his two youngest children and show us his childhood landmarks. To take us on a carriage ride through Central Park and visit Yankee Stadium, where as a kid he had seen Mickey Mantle play. "I'm going to take them back to where it all started for me," he told his friend Mark.

He was happy. He couldn't wait for our trip. He had bought a suit for the journey and was already all packed, weeks in advance. The pain and craziness of his life had ceased. He was content, surrounding himself with family and good vibes.

One of the last things my father and I had done was paint my house, just a few weeks earlier. My little cabin in the woods was a dark brown, and I wanted to freshen it up. I picked out a cream color and a plum color for the trim. And then we had a painting party: me, Adrian, my dad, and my mother. I remember him working so hard to paint my shutters, though he was using primer that didn't cover well and he got frustrated as it slipped off and left streaks. He joked that we had given him an impossible job. He and Adrian painted the carport, each working on a different side, competing to see who could do a better job. My dad sat in a rocking chair with a long-handled roller, slapping paint on the wall and joking that two city boys like he and Adrian weren't used to such hard labor and needed a pay raise; meanwhile, my mother and I were doing all the hard work. But we were laughing all the time. The music was blasting. The weather was great. My dad's chatter never stopped.

Terry called that day. She was thinking about stopping by. "Dad's here," I told her. For almost seven years I'd done my best to keep them apart. She never came by.

That night we all went out to dinner: my mom, my dad, Adrian's parents, Adrian, and I. Like a normal family.

When I landed at Sea-Tac Airport, Adrian was waiting. He had been the second person I called. He loved my father, and even when things were difficult between us, he had been my dad's favorite. "Don't be upset about Adrian," Dad would tell me. "You two are in love. You just have to work it out."

In recent months, I realized my dad was right. I fell into Adrian's arms sobbing, and he wrapped me up. Then we drove to my little half-painted house in Kirkland, where my mother and Marcus were already waiting. I was drained, hollow, but I knew there was so much to do in just a few days. I needed to honor my father as best I could.

One blessing was knowing my father's wishes: he had told both me and Marcus he wanted to be cremated and have his ashes spread over the Snoqualmie Pass. I hated driving in bad weather, so in the winter, when I had to navigate the pass on my way to or from Richland, I would stay on the phone with my father until I felt safe. "When I die, scatter my ashes there so I can still look out for both of you," he had told us.

On Father's Day, I had a barbecue at my house to celebrate my father's life. Lesle and Amy came; so did Cheryl and Malia and Dad's friend Mark. It was the first time I had ever met my father's dear friend in person. Beverly came with her son. We had boards of photos of my dad set up. Adrian and Malia cooked for everybody.

During the gathering, Greg called. I already knew our team had beaten China in Cleveland. My teammates wore black armbands in honor of my father, and there was a moment of silence for him before the game. Bri had put my father's initials on her goalkeeper gloves and recorded a shutout. I was touched by their actions.

"I'm just checking in with you," Greg said. He told me to let him know when I was ready to come back and play with the team.

IV.

The next day, Marcus and I went to look at caskets. I was irritated by the incredible cost of ornate boxes, with leather padding and brass adornments that would just be burned up. The man who had been happy in a tent in the woods would have scoffed at the excess. Marcus and I found black humor in the absurdity of my father in a lavish casket. We decided not to get anything. We were going to dress my father in his beloved University of Washington sweats and a Native American Pride T-shirt he liked to wear, and cover him with a UW blanket—he didn't need any fancy trappings.

While we were there, my phone rang. It was Greg again. He must have gotten impatient waiting for me to call back. He wanted to know when I would be back. I stepped into the hall to talk. I told Greg what I had known all along, ever since I had left the hotel in Cleveland. I needed to play in the game in New York. It was the moment my father had been looking forward to, and even if he wasn't there, I wanted to fulfill the promise of our trip. I wanted to honor him by playing.

"Greg, I want to play against Brazil," I said. "I'll be there. I'll play."

He hesitated, then launched into minutiae about the travel and practice schedule. He thought I would miss too much training, but I knew the calendar. There was an off day and a travel day. I knew I would miss only one practice session. "I'll be there," I said. "I'll play. My dad would want me to."

Despite telling me he would honor my wishes, Greg told me that he thought I would be a distraction to the team. That he didn't think I would be emotionally ready.

What the fuck did he know about emotions? I thought. He was a man who had patted my shoulder and called me "kiddo" moments after I learned my father had died. One day he told me to let him know what I wanted to do; the next day he was telling me how I felt. Was I supposed to apologize because my father had died? Was I being punished? I couldn't believe it. I thought back to 2002, when I had roomed with Brandi Chastain when her mother, Lark, died of an aneurism. Brandi played the next day, and her teammates rallied behind her and picked her up. Eight months later, when Bri's dad died, she came back and played in the next scheduled game.

Greg told me I could sit on the bench with the team. He had made up his mind. He wasn't going to let me play in New York against Brazil.

V.

The plans for the memorial weren't going well. I felt overwhelmed: the list of things I had to do was endless. Phone calls to be made, the obituary to be written, cremation plans to be finalized, finding someone to officiate the service. I was trying to get things done. Marcus and I were arguing. Thankfully, Cheryl flew into town as soon as she heard the news and helped us get organized—she could tell we were paralyzed by our pain.

The night before the memorial, we were at my house, sitting outside in the yard, going over the plans when Marcus and I got in a terrible fight. I yelled at him for not helping and for partying instead of working. He lashed out at me. "You're taking this over," he said, "like you fucking take over everything."

I slapped him in the face. Even as my hand made contact with his skin, I knew I had made a terrible mistake. I sprinted back into my house, Marcus chasing me and calling me hateful names. My mother was right behind him, screaming for us to stop as I dove under my dining table. *Marcus is going to kill me*, I thought, *right here in my own house.*

Jesus Christ! I thought. I was twenty-five years old, my father had just died, and my brother and I were acting like animals. And I was cowering under a piece of furniture. This was our family, this was our inheritance.

VI.

Marcus didn't kill me, and we put together a moving memorial service. Everyone helped, including Cheryl, who found photos, helped write the obituary, got the programs printed and hand-folded them. We held the service at Hilltop; my father had made a lot of friends, and there was an outpouring of love and respect.

From every person who spoke, we learned something remarkable about my father. When he had been homeless, he had dressed up as Santa every year at the Fred Hutchinson Cancer Research Center, bringing joy to young children who were suffering. In the 1990s, when he was still living on the streets, he donated $35,000 in video equipment to that pediatric ward (where my father got all that electronic equipment remained a mystery that I decided was better left unexplored). At Hilltop he'd taught half the residents—men and women—how to play poker, arranging big games for dimes and nickels. He had wooed the Japanese ladies who lived at Hilltop with exotic mushrooms that his friend Mark picked in the woods and brought to him by the bagful. Mark brought a small bonsai tree to the service in his honor. Marcus's new dog Blue—who had replaced my dad's old friend Henry—was there. My grandparents came and Grandma Alice assured us that my father had been a Christian and that we would see him again. That eased our pain a bit.

My oldest brother, David, didn't attend the service, which upset me. Thanks to Marcus, David and my father had reconnected in recent years. The three of them had gone out to dinner one night when David was in Seattle on business. David's birthday is June 12, and my father had called him to wish him a happy birthday just three days before he died. In David's eyes, they had found some closure and peace in their relationship, and that was enough for him. But I still felt that David should have come to the memorial, to support Marcus and me, and to pay his respects. It was his father, for God's sake, the only one he would ever have.

My sister, Terry, did attend. She had never seen my father after the day she called the police on him, seven years earlier.

I was bitter that my father had died with the murder of Mike Emert still looming over him. The police had continued to harass him for years, and the case remained unsolved, a frustrating and sad episode that was proof to him that the authorities couldn't be trusted. Dad had been at peace with a lot in his life when he died, but not with that lingering stain. He spent hours thinking about it, going over details with Marcus, hoping to try to figure out what really happened.

When it was my turn to speak at the memorial, I said my father often seemed stuck in his ways but that he actually took computer classes to learn how to send me e-mails when I was away. He spent hours figuring out how to log on to the computer and poking at the keys to come up with a two-line e-mail saying he missed me. Sometimes he would mistakenly erase his finished product and have to start all over. He always laughed at himself when he told me about his technological struggles. In almost every e-mail he would write the same thing:

> *Baby Hope, be safe, have fun, go with your vibes, smile and be happy. You are the best. Love, Pops.*

I told how he had recently opened a bank account after a lifetime of keeping his money under his mattress. I told the secret of his happiness that he had passed along to me. "He guarded each and every memory with his whole heart," I said. "He was fueled by the love he shared with his friends and family, the moments between them, and he relived those happy memories over and over, bringing a new and fresh smile to his face each time. He knew that life could always be worse, so it was important to find joy in the simple things in life. My dad always said to me: 'Baby Hope, memories are for you, and nobody can take them away.'"

I ended by saying that my father would always be at my side and in the goal.

After the service, Marcus gathered his belongings from Hilltop. I joined him before he shut the door and saw the objects my father had carried from place to place, through the rain and cold, for so many years. The home-run ball Marcus had given him. The etched rock. A signed dollar bill from David from 1977. His carefully maintained scrapbooks were filled with pictures and keepsakes from all four of us: ticket stubs to David's football games, pictures of Terry, a letter from young David telling him about the 1980 Lakers-Sonics playoff games that ended with a plaintive, "I miss you Dad, I really love you a lot Dad." There were clippings about Dominic Woody's minor league baseball career—my dad had coached him back in Richland. There were letters in childish blocky writing to him from Marcus and me. My dad kept everything, carrying it with him for years through the Seattle rain. He had catalogued it and written little notes with observations and messages of love for his children.

Another scrapbook was filled with newspaper clippings, photos, and computer printouts detailing my entire soccer career, from Richland High to UW to the WUSA and all of my time with the national team. Everything was arranged in chronological order and carefully annotated. There was a Christmas card from Sofia, to "Mr. Italy," as she called my dad. There was an e-mail from me scolding him about watching his diet. I turned to the last page of the scrapbook. At the top, in my father's blocky handwriting, he had written: HOPE: WORLD CUP, 2007.

The page was blank.

CHAPTER TWELVE

Shadows

The ashes sifted through my fingers and floated on the still water of the lake in Central Park. We had found a quiet leafy corner, protected from the honking horns and human crush of Manhattan. The pilgrimage had taken place after all. Marcus, my mom, and I had brought our father home.

In my father's papers, we had found his military discharge from the navy. We found two different Social Security numbers. We found bits and pieces of the puzzle, but we couldn't find any documentation or history covering twenty years of my father's life. Those missing years probably took place somewhere in this vast city. But any answers were lost, now just ashes on my fingertips.

Some street artists were working nearby. "Let's get a portrait made," I said. "A family portrait." And so we spent part of the muggy afternoon sitting in Central Park, as the artists sketched us and then drew my father in from a photo of him that we carried with us. It was a true family portrait: the four of us. The family team, just as my father had envisioned. I was the goalkeeper, Marcus and my dad were strikers, and my mom was a defender—she knew how to protect me.

We took the carriage ride in the park that we had promised my father. We went to the Bronx, three country misfits out of place in the big city, and tracked down a couple of my father's old addresses, both not far from Yankee Stadium. We walked around the outside of the old ballpark and imagined my dad as a young boy, trying to bum a ticket.

GREG REFUSED TO budge about my playing against Brazil. My teammates—even Bri, who would get the start instead of me—thought he was being unreasonable. I knew that, given the chance, I would play with strength and inspiration; I thought of how NFL quarterback Brett Favre had played just a day after his own father had died. I had faith that I could play well through my emotions and sadness. I always had before.

But Greg insisted that I was mentally unprepared, so I decided I would play the part he had assigned me. I would grieve, and sit in the stands with my mom and Marcus, who had made the trip to support me. On June 23, I watched my team play Brazil. My teammates wore black armbands for my dad. Bri again kept his initials on her goalie gloves. We quickly went up 2–0. Both goals were scored on free kicks, one by Kristine Lilly and another that Cat took and Abby headed in. Brazil was an immensely talented team. They had Marta, the reigning FIFA Player of the Year, but they didn't have strong support from their federation between major tournaments. In fact, the team hadn't really played together since the '04 Olympics, when they had outplayed us but lost in the gold-medal match. They looked disorganized and ineffective. Bri was barely threatened as our team rolled to victory.

II.

"Hope!" Greg barked. "What the fuck are you doing?"

We were in Connecticut, training for our next game. We would leave for China in less than eight weeks. And Greg was riding my ass every day. I felt I had become the target for all his frustrations

and fears. My grief was near the surface. On the bus on the way to
training, I sat by myself, staring out the window and listening to
music. Tears trickled down my cheeks. I didn't talk much to anyone;
I felt as though every time I opened my mouth I might cry. I would
pause and collect myself while the bus cleared and then get off. But
when I leaned over to lace up my cleats, the tears would start again.

But the tears dried up on the field. My eyes were clear while I
zeroed in on shots. I was so focused that the pain went away. Soccer
training was what it had been when I was young: a chance to block
out everything bad in my life for the few hours I was on the field.

After I rejoined the team, Greg never said anything to me about
my father. He never asked how I was doing. Instead his demeanor
toward me seemed hostile. It seemed clear to me that he doubted
whether I was emotionally ready for the World Cup; it felt like he
was trying to break me, provoking me relentlessly through our
training sessions. I tried to ignore him. I worked with Phil, my
goalkeeper coach. If Greg thought yelling at me was a good moti-
vational tactic, he clearly knew nothing about me. I'd just lost my
father. I didn't give a shit what Greg Ryan thought about me. But
his antipathy for me became so noticeable that my teammates com-
mented on it. "Why is Greg being such an asshole to you?" they
asked me.

I'm pretty sure I know why. My theory is that he was a rookie
coach heading into his first major tournament. I was a young
goalkeeper about to play in my first major tournament. He was
probably freaking out about whether I could handle the pressure and my grief. He was likely feeling the pressure that comes
with coaching the favored American team, doubting himself and
doubting me. Yelling at me every day in practice probably made
him feel better.

One day, we had another team-building exercise: we all taped
sheets of paper to our backs and then went from teammate to teammate writing what we like about that person. The comments were
anonymous. At the end of the exercise, we took off the paper and

saw the things our teammates said. My paper was filled with positive messages.

"You are such a force. We believe in you so much."

"Your communication on and off the field and all the great advice you've given me, plus how strong you are."

"Always striving for more and pushing this team to be its best."

"Hopers—you are always the one I can talk to. You are one of my best friends."

"You are courageous. I am confident with you behind me."

"You are strong and courageous and you have made me a better person."

"You have pushed me to be better. Just know your dad is always watching."

III.

I was back in goal for our next game against Norway, on July 14 in Connecticut. Marcus and I had each taken a small container of our father's ashes, and kept them with us all the time. Marcus took my dad fishing. I carried my dad with me into the locker room. After all, he had always joked that he was helping me out in goal while he watched my games on television. "I'm going to trip those forwards for you," he would say gleefully.

I needed him to be right beside me, tripping forwards. We shut out Norway, 1–0.

I missed talking to him. He was the one who could comfort me, who could put all the pressure in perspective and make me laugh. He understood sports and knew what to say. Unable to call him as the biggest tournament of my life approached, I started writing to him in a journal.

July 15, 2007
Here I am sitting aboard a flight coming back home to Seattle. Seattle doesn't feel like home without you there. No longer

do I have a place to go to just talk, laugh, cry, eat or nap. This year, Dad—my first World Cup—I dedicate to you. You're coming to China with me and you're going to help me tend that goal. It was good to get back on the field after taking three weeks off. We shut out Norway together didn't we? I've never felt so at ease in the net. I didn't have a care in the world. I want to make your legacy live on.

I want to possess your "I don't give a fuck" attitude. Greg's a worm, Dad! A heartless soulless illogical man. Politics, right Dad? Fuck him. Not a word to me my first week back, not one word. In fact, he didn't even give me a day to get my feet wet again before he felt the need to ride me. . . .

You are so right that any time I feel lonely I can pull a memory out and then lock it back up for the next time I need it. Nobody can take my memories away. You've taught me so well, Dad. You have prepared me for life. You have taught me how to fight, how to love deeply, how not to get bullied, how to reach out to others, how not to judge, how to enjoy life, how to be happy no matter where I walk. You have taught me to be me, and you are such a part of me. I will carry your spirit inside me no matter where I go.

I wish I told you how much I loved you Dad. I wish I called you more. I wish I brought you over more. I wish I didn't act so fucking busy or like it was ever a burden to take you any-where. I am truly sorry if I ever made you feel that way. There was never a moment I didn't enjoy with you, never, Dad. I was always so proud of the man you were. We all make mistakes, Dad, but your heart was truly pure. I love you, Dad.

IV.

On my twenty-sixth birthday, Adrian took me to dinner at the res-taurant on top of the Space Needle. We looked out over Seattle as the restaurant revolved—east to the Cascades and my past, west toward China and my immediate future. I looked down on the streets where my father had lived for so many years. Eighteen years earlier, he had brought Marcus and me to this same spot, in a gesture of love that crippled our relationship for years.

The only birthday present I opened that day was from my father. When he cleaned out his apartment, Marcus found carefully wrapped and labeled birthday and Christmas presents for both of us. My father had missed so many birthdays and holidays that he was determined to be a good father and make up for lost time. Inside the box was a gold bracelet with Swarovski crystals. For years he joked that he only bought me "sporty" gifts and wanted to make sure I knew that he thought I was a beautiful young lady. And here was a ladylike gift for me.

Everything that happened reminded me of my father. I wanted to tell him about Barry Bonds breaking the career home-run record and my upcoming ESPN interview about him with Julie Foudy. I wanted to share every experience with him.

Aug. 9, 2007

I miss you an incredible amount. It's like I'm on a mission now. I've never felt so focused before. I'm not sure what I'd do if the World Cup wasn't around the corner, giving me something and somewhere to focus my energy. Once in a while I wonder if you sacrificed for me, Dad. It seems so strange to think. We've talked and waited for this day for years—for me to finally be part of a World Cup. Now it's here, it's all happening, Dad, and it's just not fair not to be able to go through it together, to talk about it all, to laugh at the commercials. I can't find words to explain how strange it all is. Why now, Dad? Why, when I'm finally getting the reward for all the years of sacrifice, of being away, of never finding time to spend with loved ones, it's tainted. The one single person I want to share all the glory with, as opposed to the years of heartache, is gone. Dad, I don't understand, unless you wanted to give me a reason to fight, to focus, to not get rattled. God knows, Dad, that I realize the many senseless things in life, and getting nervous in a soccer match seems so petty and very, very senseless.

I love you, Daddy. I hate to tell you but Barry Bonds finally did it. I'm sorry, Dad, but Hank Aaron will always be a hero. He'll never be caught. Barry, sports are changing and my dad never liked the showboats. I love you, Dad! Who will I go to, to pick out my college basketball brackets? Tomorrow I'll tell your story, Dad. I will tell it loud and proud and people all around the world will know my dad. Thanks for leaving me a story to tell.

V.

I had worked all my life for this moment, to make my father and the rest of my family proud, to fulfill my destiny. I was ready. I was in the best shape of my life, and I was proving it every day in practice. I felt confident in directing the defense, barking out orders.

Our last game in the States was a 4–0 victory over Finland at the Home Depot Center. We still hadn't lost a game in regulation since Greg had taken over as coach. We'd played forty-six games under Greg, and I had started thirty-six of them. We were issued gold World Cup uniforms. The message was clear: nothing less than a gold medal was acceptable.

Despite our record and gold shorts, we were leaving for China with little fanfare. Nike's ad campaign for the World Cup was "The Greatest Team You've Never Heard Of," which was an accurate description. While the American public could still name Mia Hamm and Brandi Chastain, we were strangers. We were still in the shadow of the '99ers. We were determined to change that—we were going to make our own history. On August 27, we boarded a plane in Los Angeles headed for Shanghai. My heart was heavy but my resolve had never been stronger.

This was my moment. Nothing was going to get in the way.

CHAPTER THIRTEEN

"You Can't Go by a Gut Feeling"

You're fucking fine! You're fine!"

I could hear Kate Markgraf screaming at me. The wet ball had just slipped off my fingertips and over my head, into the net.

A goal. In the very first game of the World Cup. I threw up my hands and shouted in frustration. We were tied 1–1 with North Korea in the second period on a wet slippery field in Chengdu.

"OK, OK," I told myself. "Come on, Hope." I was more pissed than rattled. Our opening game wasn't going well. This was why Greg Ryan had been tense ever since scouting North Korea. Their team was aggressive and skilled and was outplaying us. I was challenged immediately, with a hard shot just twelve seconds into the game. North Korea dominated possession. We were left chasing the ball.

That morning I had written in my journal.

Dad,

Game day, not sure how I feel. A little queasy but been that way for days. Trying to take a nap, but my eyes are twitching and I feel my heart beating against the mattress. I miss you Dad. I need you Dad. Help me live the moment. Dad, I love you so much. Wearing your armband. Got you with me. Picture in locker, bracelet and necklace on, ashes in goal, me and my dad in goal together. Time to show the world what these Solos are made of.

I felt strong and alive and focused in my first major tournament. We played a scoreless first half; I had a breakaway save and came out to stop through balls, cutting off their relentless attack. Soon after halftime, Abby put us on the board, hammering a pass from Kristine Lilly that skipped off the North Korean goalkeeper's gloves and into the net. It was glaring evidence of what I already knew: the conditions were rough for goalkeepers. The field was soaked, the ball was heavy and the slippery new commemorative design on the ball's surface only made it harder to handle.

Minutes after giving us the lead, Abby collided with a North Korean player and fell to the ground, blood gushing from a gash in her head. She went off for stitches as play continued but Greg didn't replace her. We kept glancing to the sideline to see if a sub was coming on, but continued to play a man down. North Korea—already far too comfortable—was clearly energized by Greg's decision to let us play shorthanded until Abby could return and stepped up the pressure. The North Koreans passed the ball with ease in front of our goal, eventually sending a pass wide to Kil Son Hui at the top of the penalty box. She lashed the ball toward me. I thought I could catch it. Instead the hard shot slipped through my wet gloves and into the goal. That made it 1–1.

Abby had been out for three minutes, and we were tied and struggling. Yet Greg still continued to let us play shorthanded. The message he was sending was pretty clear: *Without Abby we're doomed. Our subs are no good.*

I gathered my composure but was still under tremendous pressure. The North Korean players played kickball with each other while our team struggled for possession. After Carli was called for a foul, North Korea sent a free kick wide of the goal and then passed the ball among six different players. A shot heading toward the right post was deflected by Shannon Boxx directly in front of me; I was moving right, then tracked left with the deflection. But Kim Yong Ae pounced on the ball and shot it over my outstretched right hand.

Another goal. We were down 2–1. We had never lost a game in group play in World Cup history. I could see the alarm in my teammates' eyes. Greg seemed paralyzed on the sideline, doing nothing to stop North Korea's momentum. Finally, after ten long minutes and two North Korean goals, Abby came sprinting out on the field with eleven stitches in her head. Back at full strength, we calmed down. In the sixty-ninth minute, Heather O'Reilly buried a shot in the upper right corner of the net. We were even, 2–2, but North Korea continued to push forward. In stoppage time, they thought they had the winner on a hard shot, but I fully extended to my right to push the ball out of danger. Just seconds later, another North Korean player took a long shot directly at goal that I dove at and smothered. I was keeping us alive. Finally the whistle blew. We finished with a draw and a critical point in the group standings.

I wasn't happy about the goals—particularly the first one that had slipped off my gloves—but I was still proud. I had made a fistful of spectacular saves that kept our team in the game. I learned a rough lesson about trying to catch a slippery ball, a mistake I wouldn't make again. We came away with a point on a day when no one—not me, our field players, our coach—was at their best. Coming up big in the final seconds of the game only bolstered my confidence.

After the whistle, Greg came up to me on the field. He had a huge grin on his face. "Thank you for those saves," he said, giving me a hug. Then he pointed to the sky. "Somebody's watching out over you from up there," he said.

I stiffened. It was the first time since I'd returned from my father's memorial service—almost three months earlier—that Greg had openly acknowledged my loss. In those final weeks of training in the United States, he had never reached out to me or asked me how

I was doing. But now that I had come up big in a World Cup game, he was going to use my dad as a motivating factor? That offended me. But I didn't say anything. I just let him hug me while I seethed.

II.

The ashes were in a small container the size of my thumb that I placed in my locker before every game. Though I normally wouldn't wear my goalkeeper gloves out to the field, I did in China. I placed a tiny bit of ash in my left glove in the locker room. Out on the field, I put my right hand over my heart for the national anthem and held my left glove carefully by my side. When I walked into the goal, I made the sign of the cross, kissed my closed fist, then opened my glove and let the ashes drop, saying a little prayer to myself. I had meant what I had said at his memorial: my dad would always be in goal with me.

After the North Korea game, we stayed in gray Chengdu—a city famous for its lack of sunshine—for another few days to play Sweden, the third-ranked team in the world.

Sept 14, 2007
Game Two—so nervous, Dad. Please be with me. Help me
know that I have nothing to prove after last game. Help me
to live in the moment. Right through the fingers, Dad, but I
played so well. I just want to play relaxed, play in the moment,
enjoy every minute. Let's have fun, Dad.

Our game against Sweden was a much better outing for our team, with none of the tension and dramatics of the North Korea game. Abby scored twice, the first goal coming on a penalty kick, and our defense played much better. I saw my old friend Lotta Schelin—the rising star of the Swedish team—but she couldn't beat me. I had my first World Cup victory and shutout. I whispered a word of thanks to my dad.

We left Chengdu and headed to Shanghai, getting into the city just days before Typhoon Wipha. We played Nigeria—with the chance to win our group—in a steady downpour. Lori Chalupny scored just fifty-three seconds into the match, and Nigeria was on its heels the rest of the day. Still, late in the game, I was forced to make some saves to preserve the victory, another shutout.

Despite our difficult draw, we had won our group and were now in the quarterfinals against England. The game was in Tianjin, in northern China, a long trek from Shanghai. All our family members made the journey. The night before the game, I went over to the family hotel. My big support group had arrived in time for the Nigeria game: my mother; Marcus and his fiancée, Debbie; Aunt Susie; Grandma Alice and Grandpa Pete; Adrian; and Cheryl's parents, Mary and Dick. At the games, they wore black armbands to honor my father. It was comforting for me to be with my family. They were the only ones who really knew how much I missed my father and how badly I was hurting. I was painfully aware of all the time I had missed with him, rushing from one place to another, moments I could never get back. I wasn't going to make that same mistake with the rest of my family. And we all had something to celebrate in China: Marcus and Debbie had just found out they were going to have a baby, conceived just weeks after my father's death.

The night before the quarterfinal, I played cribbage with my grandparents and Adrian. Marcus and I talked about my dad. My mom—always the avid photographer—showed us all the pictures she had taken. It was very low-key. I got back to my room and puttered around before going to bed. As usual, I was one of the last ones to bed, battling my recurring insomnia.

Sept. 22, 2007
Hey dad. Why is today so hard? I'm scared today. Marcus is scared. I'm glad we could be together even just for a little bit—he's very emotional. Wants us to go all the way for you. Be there beside me in that lonesome goal. We play together in

this quarterfinal match against England. But I play for you, for everything that you taught me. Family first, right Dad?

England's team hadn't had much success at the senior level—this was the first time we had faced them in a World Cup match—but they were touted as an up-and-coming team. I considered Kelly Smith, whom I'd played with in Philadelphia, one of the top players in the world. We had a tense, scoreless first half—but our defense was strong. And then, in a ten-minute span in the second half, we scored three quick goals to put the game out of reach.

After the game, our celebration was subdued, tempered by our ambitions. We were almost to our ultimate goal. We were in the World Cup semifinals, as far as the 2003 team had advanced, but we wanted more. Our shaky start against North Korea appeared to have been a fluke. We had shown some nerves and inexperience against a good team but had rallied from adversity. I still didn't think we were playing like the world's number-one-ranked team. It was too much boot ball without a lot of creativity in our attack. But we hadn't lost in regulation in fifty games. We would face Brazil, a team that had appeared disorganized and unprepared in New York just three months earlier. I had three consecutive World Cup shutouts. I was on top of my game. I was ready.

III.

On Tuesday night, two days before the semifinal, we were eating dinner at the team hotel in Hangzhou. One of my first national team starts had come in Hangzhou in January of 2001, when I had learned my father was accused of murder. That seemed so long ago. The thought of that false accusation made me ache for my father's needless suffering. I wished so much that he could watch the upcoming semifinal . . . and trip Brazil's incredible player Marta for me.

Phil, my goalkeeper coach, came up behind me as I was eating and tapped me on the shoulder. "Hope," he said, bending down to speak in my ear. "Greg wants to see you in his room when dinner is over."

I stared at him. The balloon of confidence inside of me collapsed. "Why?" I asked.

Phil just looked at me and then walked away.

I pushed away my food, suddenly afraid I might get sick. I knew what was about to happen. Maybe I'd been expecting it for two years.

As I left the dining room, I saw Greg walk in to eat. He would be there awhile, so I went up to my room and called Adrian. When I tried to speak, the tears came instead. "I don't know what's going on," I finally said.

"You're fine, Hope," Adrian said. "Keep it together. You have to talk to him."

While I listened to Adrian, I started to breathe deeply to calm myself down. Adrian was right; I didn't want to be a wreck when I spoke to Greg. I hung up and my phone rang immediately. It was Phil, asking where I was.

"I'll be right down," I said.

I took the elevator to Greg's floor. When I entered his room, he was sitting in a chair playing his guitar and singing to himself. "Hey, Hope, do you know this song?" He smiled and strummed.

Seriously? He was about to tell me the most devastating thing I'd experienced in my soccer career and he wanted to chat about Pink Floyd? I just looked at him. *Don't fuck with me, Greg*, I thought as I sat down on the adjacent couch. I'm sure my face gave away my thoughts. When he saw my expression, Greg became a tough guy, the same asshole who had yelled at me all summer.

"Why are you late? I told you to be here at seven."

I looked at Phil, who was sitting at the other end of the couch I was perched on. "Actually, I was told to come after dinner," I said.

I put my hands on my knees and looked down at them, taking a deep breath to steady myself. Greg, sitting to my left, leaned forward and stuck his finger in my face. "You fucking look at me when I'm talking to you," he snapped. "I'm tired of you disrespecting me. You show up late and now you don't even make eye contact with me."

I was shocked. I knew this was going to be bad, but the fury in his voice stunned me. *OK*, I thought to myself, *you want me to look at you, asshole?* I looked down again, gathered myself and slowly turned my head to stare at him, never breaking eye contact as he derailed my career.

I wasn't ready for a major tournament, Greg said. He'd suspected it all along. And he could tell that in the first game when the ball went off my hands. He should have benched me after that soft goal. Bri had a winning record against Brazil, Greg said. She matched up better with Brazil's style. She singlehandedly won the gold medal in the 2004 Olympics against Brazil. And she had just played Brazil in New York.

I watched his mouth move. I heard the words coming out of it. I could see how they'd be printed in the newspapers, replayed on ESPN, crafted into headlines and sound bites. *Briana Scurry, one of the heroes of the 1999 World Cup, wins back her spot in goal.*

I was numb. Greg was waiting for a response. I didn't want to give him the satisfaction of weeping or raging. I worked hard to channel my fury into clear, precise words. "Greg, I have to respect your decision because you're my coach," I said. "But I disagree with you. It doesn't matter what Bri did three years ago. She hasn't played a game for more than three months, she hasn't been your number one for three years, and I'm playing the best I've ever played. I will never agree with your decision. And if anyone asks me, I will tell them that this is the wrong decision."

Greg smiled. He was back to being the cool guy. "That's why I love you, Hope," he said. "I expect my athletes to want to be on the field. To be angry if they don't play. I've given you four World Cup games. I've gotten you this far."

"*I've* gotten myself this far," I snapped. "Plenty of people—well before you came along—have believed in me along the way."

Greg wasn't finished. He told me that Lil and Abby had lobbied for Bri to get the start. "I agree with the captains," he said. "It's a gut feeling."

There had been a meeting behind my back? A decision based on whom they liked better? I looked at Greg and shook my head with disgust. He was a weak leader. He was ditching responsibility. Greg didn't have the balls to stand up for his decisions. He was passing the buck to the players.

"You can't go by a gut feeling, Greg," I said. "I've been your starting goalkeeper for three years. And now, in the biggest game of the tournament, you're pulling me because your gut tells you to?"

Greg didn't seem to like my tone. I wasn't crying. I wasn't folding. I wasn't making it easy. Instead, I was fighting back with words and logic, keeping my emotions tacked down. So he tried to provoke me, just as he had on the field all summer. He criticized my training session, saying Bri had been much sharper.

He could make up whatever reasons he wanted, but he couldn't attack my work ethic. He had told all the starters to take it easy in practice after the England game. We'd had four draining games in eleven days in the muggy monsoons of China. We had been specifically told to rest our bodies. I wasn't the only one holding back. Bri, on the other hand, hadn't played in three months—of course she was going all out.

I LOOKED OVER at Phil. I didn't know what to say. Logic was out the window. Greg was all over the place, his reasons for benching me shifting every time he opened his mouth. There was clearly no use arguing. He was panicking. And I was paying the price.

We were both silent. I had nothing left to say so I stood up to leave. Greg leaned over and pushed me back down on the couch. Hard. "You fucking leave when I say you can leave," he said.

I was stunned that he had touched me. I wanted to lash back, to hit him harder than I had hit Marcus or punched the cheerleader at the carnival or anyone else in my life. For a split second I really thought I would—I felt my hand move forward. But I wasn't going to let him provoke me. I restrained myself and glanced over at Phil, glad to have a witness. "Are we done?" I said icily.

I went back to my room shaking with anger.

For our short stay in Hangzhou, I was rooming with another goalkeeper, Nicole Barnhart, which was awkward. Usually goalkeepers don't room with each other. I preferred not to share my space with someone competing for my spot. I didn't want to confide in Barnie but she was in the room when I called Marcus. All the feelings I'd held in for the past half an hour came tumbling out. I cried and railed against Greg. I didn't make any attempt to hide my emotions.

Marcus was hurt too, but he told me that he loved me and how proud he was of me. That gave me strength. There was still something I needed to do.

III.

I walked out of my room and down the hallway to find Kristine Lilly. Lil was playing in her fifth World Cup. She was the last of the veterans from the first World Cup in 1991. We had never been close, but I respected her ability. But I wasn't intimidated by her résumé. She needed to hear me out.

"Lil, I've been your starting goalkeeper for three years," I said. "How can you decide—in the semifinals of the World Cup—that you want another goalkeeper?"

Lil looked shocked by my question, as though she never expected Greg to reveal their private conversation. She certainly didn't seem prepared for a confrontation. She stammered and told me she didn't think it mattered who was in goal.

"Lil, you're our captain," I said. "It should matter to you who's in goal. You should have an opinion. But if you don't, if you don't think it even matters at all, how can you go and lobby for Bri?"

When I said that, I thought I saw a flutter of doubt cross her eyes. Had she made a mistake? "I'm your starting goalkeeper for a reason," I went on. "Because I beat out the others. You should want the best players on the field. It's so arrogant to say that it doesn't matter who's in goal." I wasn't yelling. I was calm. "I've lost every ounce of respect I've had for you," I said.

I walked away. I went farther down the hall to find Abby and I told her exactly what I had told Lil. I felt even more betrayed by Abby—she and I were in the same generation of players.

"How could you turn your back on me?" I said.

At least Abby had an answer. "Hope, I think Bri is the better goalkeeper."

That shut me up. I didn't think it was true, and I didn't think Abby knew much about goalkeeping. But at least she had an opinion. At least she owned up to her part in the matter. I had to respect that.

I went back to my room and lay on the bed and called my mother. "I'm not playing against Brazil, Mom," I said, crying.

"Liar," my mother said with a laugh.

I wasn't lying. I wasn't having a bad dream. I rolled over and wept.

V.

The next day, we practiced at the stadium. I was dying inside, but I held my head high. There wasn't a huge American media contingent in China—it was an expensive trip, and most outlets were saving their funds to cover the Beijing Olympics the following year. But the reporters who were there got word of the goalkeeping change, and the topic dominated post-practice interviews. Greg rationalized his decision to the press by saying that he liked Bri's form in training and her history against Brazil. When asked if my confidence was shaken, Greg said that wasn't his concern, that the team was there to win the World Cup.

Lil stuck to her theory that such a monumental change didn't much matter. "It's not a huge deal from our team's perspective," she told reporters.

THE ESPN REPORTERS tracked me down. "I'm not happy with it, not one bit," I said. "But it is the coach's decision and I have to deal with it. And I have to be there for my team. They're going to need me. They're going to need all twenty-one players."

Sept. 27, 2007
Best in the world, Dad? I'm not so sure the world will see that. Can you believe this—semifinal game and I'll be on the bench. I need you there with me too, Dad. He's a coward like we always thought. What's going to happen, Dad? Has my career ended with the game against England? Dad, it's tough. My fight has been crushed. Please help me and Marcus get through this, Dad. I still play for you. With all my love—Baby Hope

On Thursday, September 27, the news that I had lost my start-ing job was beginning to reverberate back home, on blogs and sports shows. ESPN's commentators—Julie Foudy and former U.S. coach Tony DiCicco—expressed amazement at Greg's decision. Why would someone make such a radical change when things were going so well? "It makes a negative impact when you want to only be focusing on positive things," Julie said. "I think it's the wrong decision."

DiCicco agreed. "If there isn't a goalkeeper controversy, why make one?"

"This is the type of decision that keeps you employed or quickly gets you unemployed," ESPN commentator Rob Stone offered.

Because of the time difference, our games were airing at dawn in the United States. Back in Seattle, where it was still dark, Lesle Gallimore turned on the television and read the crawl across the screen. "Hope Solo replaced in goal by Briana Scurry." She fumbled for her phone to call Amy. "Is Hope hurt? What's going on?"

I didn't carry any ashes with me onto the field in Hangzhou. My dad wouldn't be beside me on the bench. And then the game started.

The worst World Cup game in U.S. history. In the 4–0 loss to Brazil, my team played like a group that had been blindsided.

CHAPTER FOURTEEN

Stepping into Liquid

When the carnage had ended and Brazil had danced off, I made my way across the field.

Abby stopped me. "Hope, I was wrong," she told me.

I nodded, but I was on a mission to find my family, to thank them for supporting me. I crossed the field to them, and Marcus leaned over the railing toward me, the pain showing on his face. In his hands he held tight his container of my father's ashes.

"This was supposed to be for Dad," he said, his voice quivering on the edge of tears.

That broke me open. I wanted so much to be strong for my family, to honor our father. I ached to make them proud. And now there was only more hurt. But I did draw strength just being near my family. And from Adrian, who, at the end of game, had run around the stadium to the stands above the tunnel where Greg Ryan was exiting the field, to yell at him, telling him what an idiot he was. Adrian had my back and didn't care who heard him.

As the stadium emptied, I reached up to squeeze my family's hands and say thank you. Finally, a security guard came to get me. I was the last player left behind. I said my good-byes and walked to the tunnel that led to the locker room. Adrian was still in the stands there, waiting for me. "Be strong, Hope," he said. "Be confident. Be honest. Don't be afraid to tell that asshole what you think."

Reporters were waiting for us in the bowels of the stadium, pressed up against the metal barricades, eager to capture our words on this historic defeat. Our press officer, Aaron Heifetz, stuck close to my side as I walked past reporters and the ESPN cameras. I was almost to the bus when a woman I didn't recognize leaned over the rail and asked me a question.

Heifetz answered for me. "She didn't play," he barked. "You only want to talk to people who played the game."

I stopped walking. I wasn't allowed to speak for myself? "Heif, this is *my* decision," I said, and turned toward the woman with the microphone.

"It was the wrong decision," I said. "And I think anybody that knows anything about the game knows that. There's no doubt in my mind I would have made those saves. And the fact of the matter is, it's not 2004 anymore. It's not 2004. It's 2007, and I think you have to live in the present. And you can't live by big names. You can't live in the past. It doesn't matter what somebody did in an Olympic gold medal game three years ago. Now is what matters, and that's what I think."

I turned away and headed toward the bus. "Don't ever tell me what interviews I can do," I said to Heifetz.

He was furious. He told me he was probably going to lose his job. He went back and reprimanded the reporter for hounding me and shepherded Bri past reporters without stopping.

I walked to the back of the team bus and sat down near my close friends. The mood was grim, the conversation muted. Players were exhausted, angry, in shock. "I just did an interview," I said to Carli, Tina, and whoever was nearby.

"What did you say?"

"I said I believed I would have made those saves."

"Uh oh, Hope," someone said with a laugh.

"I'm sure it's fine," Carli said.

"I don't know if it is," I said and put my earbuds in.

It didn't feel like anything was fine. Our team had just suffered its worst World Cup loss in history, our first loss in almost three years. In ninety minutes, everything we had worked for had been erased.

The bus pulled out of the stadium and took us to our Hangzhou hotel. The plan was to eat and have a quick visit with our families before the long bus ride back to Shanghai. While we were in the lobby, talking in subdued voices, the Brazilian team and their supporters came in. They were at the same hotel, a boneheaded move on the part of the Chinese organizers. The Brazilians danced around the lobby, doing the samba, beating their drums, snaking through the small groups of American supporters. You could feel the tension rise—I wouldn't have been surprised if a fistfight broke out. Brazil was celebrating in that uniquely Brazilian way, but they were rubbing our faces in the loss.

Soon we got back on the bus to ride through the night to Shanghai, where we would play a third-place game in a few days. Some people slept. Others checked their phones, talking to family back in the States, where it was still morning.

Carli texted with her trainer, James, in New Jersey. She turned to me. "Hope, James says this is blowing up back home," she said. "It's all over the news."

"What is?"

"Your interview."

For the rest of the ride, I stared out the window, watching the lights rush past in the dark night, replaying my words in my head. I had said what I thought about Greg's decision—I assumed he had told the press his reasoning for starting Bri. I felt justified in stating my point of view.

Once we got to the Westin Shanghai, Carli and Marci Miller—whom I roomed with in Shanghai—huddled with me in front of the computer. We found the interview on ESPN and watched it. "It's not so bad, is it?" I asked them. "That was meant for Greg, not Bri."

Carli and Marci hesitantly agreed. No, it wasn't horrible.

"Well," I said, trying to laugh, "I guess it's only a matter of time before I get hell from the older players."

Right then, my phone rang. I looked at Carli and Marci. "I guarantee you this is them," I said as I picked up.

It was Lil. She said the veterans wanted to talk to me and asked if I would come to their room.

II.

I walked down the hall. By now it was after midnight. I pushed open the door of Lil's room and saw the veterans grimly waiting for me. Kate Markgraf stood by the door. Lil, Shannon Boxx, Christie Rampone, Abby, and Bri sat on the beds. I walked across to the other side of the room and leaned against the wall.

They had seen the interview. I was told that I had, in their opinion, broken a team code.

"Well, I'm a professional athlete—of course I believe I could make a difference on the field," I said. "Just like you guys do," I added. "We should all believe we can make a difference or else why are we professional athletes?"

Kate Markgraf turned on me. "I can't even fucking look at you," she said. "Who the fuck do you think you are? I can't even be in the same room with you."

She walked out and slammed the door behind her. *Wow*, I thought, *that seems overly dramatic.*

Now there were five. I stood and listened as each had her say. They told me that you don't throw a teammate under the bus, that I had broken the code, that I had betrayed the team. I was told that I had ruined everything this team was built on, and that I had torn down what Julie Foudy and Mia and Lil and all the players who paved the way for us had created.

"This isn't about Julie Foudy or anyone else from the past," I said. "This is about our team. I would never do anything to hurt

Bri. I have so much respect for Bri. But as a professional athlete, I'm confident that I would have made a difference in the game. I believe in myself enough to know that I would have made an impact. I think all of us believe in ourselves enough to think we can affect the outcome."

"Are you even going to apologize to Bri?" someone asked.

I turned toward Bri. I wanted her to know that I wasn't trying to hurt her, not after everything she had done for me when my father died. I felt backed against the wall.

Bri spoke first. She told me I had hurt her very much. She said she had tried to be there for me when my father died and was shocked that I would do this to her.

"I'm sorry Bri," I said. "I really am. I didn't mean to hurt you. My comments were directed at Greg, not at you."

I could tell how awkward I sounded. I wanted to have a private moment with Bri but I was in a room full of angry women who demanded that I perform a public act of contrition. Everything felt forced. Staged.

"I hope, we've heard your side of things," Christie Rampone said. "You've heard how we feel. So how are we going to move forward and make this better?"

I looked at Pearcie with gratitude. She was the only one trying to lead us through the mess, to cut through the harsh words and angry feelings. The group decided that the way to move forward was for me to apologize to the entire team. They told me there would be a team meeting in the morning.

I went back to my room for a few tortured hours. I couldn't sleep. I cried most of the night and tried to figure out what to do. All my life I've said exactly what I thought and stood up for myself. But now I was in a firestorm for doing just that. I felt terrible that I had hurt Bri. She had been so kind to me when my father died. I vowed to talk to her in the morning and try to make things right between us.

The next morning when I stepped into the room, I saw Bri

standing by the door and I paused. "Bri, do you have a second?" I said. "Please know I would never want to hurt you. I have so much respect for you."

She turned away from me. "Hope, I can't even look at you right now," she said.

OK, I thought. *This is going to take time. This is going to be on Bri's terms. I have to be patient.*

I walked into the room and felt twenty sets of eyes bore into me. I was on stage. I said the same thing I had said to the smaller group in Lil's room the night before. "I never meant to hurt Bri," I said. "My comments were directed at Greg and his reasoning. I said I would have made those saves because I truly have to believe I could have made a difference."

I didn't see any sign of support. I saw hostility and anger. Hatred, even. Hard words were flung at me.

"You don't sound sincere."

"Do you even care what you've done?"

"How can you turn your back on the team?"

"Do you know how horrible you looked on television, pouting on the bench?"

"You've been feeling sorry for yourself since Greg told you that you weren't starting. Some of us sit on the bench every game."

I looked at my few close friends, hoping for a sympathetic face, but all I saw were blank, cold stares. I looked at the faces of the younger players, like Aly and Cat and Leslie Osborne and Lori Chalupny and Tina Frimpong, my former UW teammate. I had become a pariah. Everyone was following Lil and Abby. No one would stand up for me. Only Carli seemed to have any sympathy in her expression.

"You haven't even apologized to Bri," someone said.

I had already apologized to Bri in Lil's room the night before. I had just spoken to her again outside the door. But I apologized to Bri again, in front of everyone. I had maintained my composure through most of the meeting, but as I spoke, my voice broke. "I'm sorry Bri," I said. "I never meant to hurt you. I'm sorry that I did."

I was asked to leave the room while my fate was decided.

III.

We had a pool workout at the hotel later that morning, to help rejuvenate our legs. I felt awkward, unsure of where to go. No one spoke to me. I didn't know what had been decided after I left the room.

When I got into the pool, my teammates stayed away from me, as though I had some disease that could be transmitted through the water. After the workout, I got out of the pool first. As soon as I did, my teammates gathered for a team cheer.

Oh, God, I thought. *I don't look like a team player.*

I jumped back into the water. And then it dawned on me that the only reason they had done the cheer was because I was out of the pool.

After the workout, Greg spoke to a small gathering of press in the hotel lobby. Almost all the questions were about me. "There are always opportunities for reconciliation," he said. "We'll work to try to get past this hurdle."

But my teammates had already decided that reconciliation wasn't the answer. After I had left the meeting, they had deemed my apology insincere. I needed to be punished. They would not allow me to play in the third-place game. I couldn't even go to the game. I couldn't eat meals with the team. I was suspended. They also decided that I needed to call Julie Foudy to apologize to her for tarnishing the legacy she helped build, which seemed absurd to me.

Later that day, Greg called me into his room. He was smiling and friendly as he told me I was suspended. He told me that he had done bad things in his career, how once he stormed off the field after getting subbed out in a game. He suggested that I could move on, but it would be hard because I had let down my teammates.

"Greg, what I said wasn't directed at my teammates," I said. "It was directed at your decision. I wasn't putting down Bri. I was putting down your decision-making process."

Greg, who had already told me several different reasons for his decision, decided to drop another one on me now. He said that I had broken team rules, that on the night before the quarterfinal, I had missed curfew and a team dinner. He implied that I was out partying and not taking care of my body.

"I was at the family hotel playing cards with my grandparents," I said. "I took a cab home. I wasn't the only player there. I haven't even had a fucking drink in five months."

Now, twenty-four hours after the game, he decided I had violated a team rule? I felt that he was throwing darts, hoping to land on a decent reason for benching me, playing a game with my career.

After the meeting our team general manager, Cheryl Bailey, walked me back to my room. Cheryl seemed sympathetic. She handed me tissues and walked me around the hotel. She was the only one giving me any answers. She didn't say anything directly against Greg or my teammates, but I felt that she thought what was happening was bizarre. She helped me move out of Marci's room and into my own room.

Later that night, I logged onto MySpace, went to my page, and posted a comment.

I have felt compelled to clear the air regarding many of my post-game comments on Thursday night. I am not proud or happy the way things have come out. In my eyes there is no justification to put down a teammate. That is not what I was doing.

Although I stand strong in everything I said, the true disheartening moment for me was realizing it could look as though I was taking a direct shot at my own teammate. I would never throw such a low blow. Never.

I only wanted to speak of my own abilities yet also recognize that the past is the past. Things were taken out of context or

analyzed differently from my true meaning of my own words.
For that I am sorry. I hope everybody will come to know I have a
deep respect for this team and for Bri.

My phone buzzed. It was a text from Carli. "How are you? I'm
thinking about you. Hang in there."

I felt the warmth of her embrace. I still had a friend in the world.

Adrian came over that night to have dinner with me. I wasn't allowed to eat with the team, but I wasn't hungry anyway. While we
sat in the lobby with our food, Lil walked past us without a glance,
as though we weren't even there, as though we were furniture.

"Wow," Adrian said. "What a bitch."

IV.

On Saturday, the day before the third-place game, I was left behind
at the hotel while the team went to training. Our massage therapist, Kara, stayed to babysit me. I'm not sure what they were afraid
would happen if I were left alone: That I would call the press? Riffle
through my teammates' belongings? Harm myself?

I really wanted to be alone, but Kara seemed to think it would
be calming to watch a surf movie. She tried to make me comfortable. She burned incense. We watched *Step into Liquid*. I felt I was
in prison.

Our general manager Cheryl met with me after training. She
had more bad news. She told me I couldn't fly home with the team
on Monday.

All I wanted was to get home as quickly as possible. Instead, I
would have to wait for more than half a day after everyone else left
China before I could get a flight home late Monday night.

That afternoon, there was a press conference at the team hotel.
"We did not have Hope attend practice today," Greg said. "She will
not be attending the game tomorrow. We have moved forward with

twenty players who have stood by each other, who have battled for each other, and when the hard times came—and the Brazil game was a hard time—they stood strong."

Lil spoke. "How we look at everything with our group is we do what's best for the team," she said. "And what is best for the team is the twenty of us right now. I think the circumstance that happened and her going public has affected the whole group. I think having her with us is still a distraction."

Yes, I was definitely a distraction—it seemed to me that I was a *welcome* distraction from having to face up to the disaster of the Brazil game. As long as the focus was on me, Greg wasn't held accountable. The horrible loss wasn't the headline.

Lil spoke on and on about the team, the team, the team, missing the irony in her words. If we were such a team, why weren't my teammates willing to pick me up? I made a mistake, and I apologized. Why couldn't they reach out a hand and say, "We're pissed at you. You fucked up. We think you're a terrible person. But you're still our teammate."

Only Carli had reached out to me. My other longtime friends were treating me as though I was dead.

At least I had my family. They came to visit me at the hotel where our team was celebrating Pearcie's daughter Rylie's second birthday. I was sitting with my family in the bar outside the restaurant and we could hear everyone singing "Happy Birthday." We weren't invited in, but Grandma Alice went in to get a piece of cake and wish Rylie a happy birthday. She wasn't going to let them dictate how she would act. She was going to practice what she preached and still be my sweet grandma.

At some point—I can't remember when—I called Julie Foudy, who was in China doing commentary on the games. I told Julie I was sorry. It seemed like a strange thing to do, another staged act. I would have liked a real conversation with Julie, but that didn't seem possible.

On the day of the final World Cup games, I went for breakfast at the family hotel. In the lobby, I ran into Sunil Gulati, president of U.S. Soccer. He asked me to come up to his room to chat.

My heart sank. Sunil was the head of the federation. Was I going to be kicked off the team? Was I in for another lecture?

No, Sunil was friendly. He introduced me to his wife, Marcela. He didn't scold me. He just wanted to check how I was doing.

I told him I was okay, but eager to get home.

"You know," Sunil said, "if this had happened on a men's team, I think it would be quite a different situation." He pretended to throw a punch, implying that's how men would deal with it. "If you need anything, let me know," he said with a friendly smile.

The head of U.S. Soccer wasn't ostracizing me. That was one small bit of good news.

During the matches, I was confined to my hotel. My mother and Adrian stayed with me. "If my daughter's not allowed to be there, I won't be there either," my mom said. But the rest of my supporters went. My grandma wore her big billboard pin that she could program to flash different names. It usually flashed HOPE No. 18, but now she made it read BRI No. 1. My family wanted to show their support for Bri, to make it clear that what I said wasn't directed at Bri.

Back at the hotel, Adrian and Mom and I watched the games on a tiny television, listening to the commentary in Chinese. My teammates easily beat Norway and then celebrated as though they had won the World Cup. Abby scored two goals and ran to the bench for team high-fives, which looked to me like a staged moment to prove that all twenty were a team. When Lilly came out in the eighty-ninth minute, there was a big show of giving Bri the captain's armband. It all seemed like an act for the cameras; it was the sentimental send-off party they'd been planning all along.

In the final, Germany shut down Marta and easily handled Brazil.

The next morning, my team packed up and left China while I sat in my room. My family left while I stayed alone in the hotel for hours, waiting for my late-night flight. The hotel staff came around to say good-bye and were very kind. When I left for the airport, it was the first time I had been out of either the team or family hotel since arriving in Shanghai, almost ninety-six hours earlier. I had been isolated and had no idea what anyone thought about what had happened.

When I got in line to check in, I saw that I was on a flight with many U.S. team supporters and friends and boyfriends. I wanted to hide from them. But I couldn't. "I can't believe what happened to you," one man said. "I don't know how Ryan could bench one of the best goalkeepers in the world."

I was surprised. "Thank you," I said.

"Hang in there, Hope," another stranger said. "It's such a shame."

"We're rooting for you," his wife said.

I boarded the plane, sank into my seat, and left China behind.

CHAPTER FIFTEEN

"Don't Let the Devil Steal Your Joy"

Hotter.
    Hotter.
Hotter.

The plumes of steam billowed up, softening the periphery of my vision. The water scalded my foot as I stepped into the tub, but I slipped under the surface, my body burning, and drifted away.

Too hot!

I woke up sweating. I climbed out of the tub, wrapped myself in a towel and curled on the floor in a fetal position, where I fell back asleep.

Too cold!

I was shivering. I turned on the hot water tap of the bathtub, as hot as I could make it. I stepped back into the tub and sunk down again into the steaming water. Everything ached. It hurt to stand. To lie in my bed. The only comfort came in the bathtub or on the tile floor. I went from one to the other and back again, alternating between temperature extremes, trying to purge the pain from my body.

I had been home for days, isolated in my little cabin in Kirkland. I barely ate. In the bathtub, I could see my hipbones jutting up beneath my skin. I ignored my ringing phone. I didn't want to turn on my computer. The one person I wanted to talk to was gone. My father was dead, and his absence—uncoupled now from the pressure of the World Cup—overwhelmed me. I was paralyzed in a black hole of loss: Dad, Liz, the World Cup, my dreams, three years of striving toward a single goal, a lifetime of sport. I couldn't contemplate what was next. I couldn't envision playing soccer again. I couldn't move any farther than the bathtub. The only sensation that registered was heat.

I lay in the hot water and thought about my grandmother and her deep abiding faith and her capacity for forgiveness. I remembered the words she had said to me over the years: snippets of scripture, Christian sayings, encouraging phrases. She often spoke of forgiveness. Of having compassion for one's enemies. Of self-belief and remaining steadfast in your convictions. She said anger and hate were poison to the soul: "Don't let the devil steal your joy."

I hadn't always paid much attention, but her words had apparently soaked into my pores.

I thought of my mother's ability to forgive, how she smuggled cookies and cocoa to my father and painted my house with him and celebrated his life with Marcus and me, putting aside all the pain and hurt he had caused her.

I thought of how far down my father had been and how resilient he had been, not only to survive on the streets but to finally find joy in his life. I thought of how much he had ached, how he had hobbled in the woods on two canes with a smile despite the crippling blows he'd taken. Always with a word of love for my siblings and me. He was a fighter.

I stood up and got out of the tub. As I turned to leave the bathroom I saw Second Corinthians 4:9 on my back in the mirror.

Persecuted but not forsaken. Cast down but not destroyed.

II.

My phone kept ringing. All day, every day. Finally I answered it. It was my agent, Rich. He wanted me to join a conference call with the U.S. Soccer bosses, Sunil Gulati and Dan Flynn. And Greg Ryan.

The team had a "celebration tour" beginning on October 13 in St. Louis—just days away. It was supposed to be a victory tour, but we hadn't won anything. Still, there were three games scheduled against Mexico in three different cities. "Rich, I don't want to get on the call. I don't want to go on this fucking tour," I said. "I don't have the strength or energy. I don't want to go through all of this again."

Rich calmly said that was fine. He said he'd support me, no matter what I decided. But he also told me I should get on the call and tell Sunil and Dan. This was about my career.

I was beginning to understand that what happened at the World Cup had been huge news on sports networks and talk radio, unheard of for women's soccer, especially during football season. I was learning that many thought Greg's crazy decision and the team's behavior were far worse than my outburst. The ostracizing of Hope Solo was discussed nationwide, on TV sports shows and late night comedy shows. It was apparent that damage control was needed.

The Monday before the tour was scheduled to start, I sat on my couch with the phone against my ear, on a conference call with Sunil and Dan and Greg. Greg talked about how important it was for me to show real contrition. He pointed out that Marion Jones had just—that day—given back her Olympic medals out of shame for doping. He suggested that I give back my tour money and my bronze medal if I wanted to show true remorse. He said that I wouldn't be on the national team without him, that he had given me my opportunity.

"Greg, I've been in this program since 1999," I said. "I've been the starting goalkeeper on every age-level team for this country. You are not the one who opened doors for me. I've been with the national team longer than you've been here, and I'll remain on it longer than you do. I don't owe my starting spot to you: I earned it."

I felt the fire reignite inside of me. I wasn't going to let Greg Ryan control my career.

I wanted to be on the tour. "I'm going to be part of the celebration," I added. "Contractually it's my right to be there."

Greg told me that the team didn't want me there.

"Well, it's not up to the team anymore," I said. "I'm going to be there. I'm going to put myself through hell by being there, but I need to start this process."

I looked at a picture of Grandma Alice and Grandpa Pete on my refrigerator. "Refuse to remain offended," Grandma had once told me, quoting Galatians. "We shall reap if we do not lose heart."

"The sooner we get started, the sooner we can start healing," I said. Greg paused. He said he needed to discuss how to handle me with the team and then got off. Sunil and Dan remained on the line. Dan praised me for expressing myself clearly and being respectful. He told me to hang in there.

But truly, I still felt like giving up. Quitting the sport to which I had devoted my life. I couldn't imagine putting on the U.S. uniform and feeling proud, training alongside those women.

The tour began in a few days. A sympathetic teammate called me. She had been on a conference call with the team and the players' lawyer. "Hope, they're trying to take your money away," she said. "The don't want to pay you for the tour."

Carli's trainer, James Galanis, called me. I didn't know him well, but I saw that he had shaped her into a fighter. I respected him. And I knew I needed help. So I listened. "Get in the car, Hope," he said. "Drive to the field."

It was that basic. I needed someone to tell me what to do, how to restart my life, bring me back.

I started to pack for St. Louis.

III.

I flew to St. Louis on Thursday, October 12, two days before the game with Mexico. I flew through Chicago, where I sat at my gate, waiting for my connecting flight, filled with dread.

"Are you Hope Solo?"

I looked up and saw a man with a neatly trimmed goatee looking down at me. I nodded. "I'm Jeff Cooper," he said. "I'm the owner of the St. Louis WPS team."

I knew that the Women's Professional Soccer league was scheduled to start in the spring of 2009, a few months after the Beijing Olympics. Jeff was excited and full of energy and big ideas. He was also sympathetic about my situation. "Stand up for yourself, Hope," he told me as we boarded our flight. "Let me know if I can do anything for you."

The "Celebration Tour" roster had already been released, and my name was on it. Rich assured me that he had spoken several times with Dan Flynn, and there was a clear understanding of what would happen. We were going to move forward, put the World Cup behind us, point toward the 2008 Olympics. Dan—who lived in St. Louis—had canceled a trip to Switzerland to watch the men's national team play in order to stick close to home and monitor what happened with me.

By the time I reached the team hotel, it was late on Thursday night. I touched base with our general manager, Cheryl Bailey. She told me there would be a team meeting in the morning and gave me some words of advice. "One smile at a time," she said. "One hello at a time. You put your hand out and even if no one takes it, you keep on trying."

I checked into my room. I was rooming with Tina, who had volunteered to stay with me. I couldn't help but remember that she had never spoken up for me in China. But I could tell she wanted to make things better between us. "Hope," she said. "Guess what? I'm pregnant."

Tina and Brad had gotten married about a year earlier. I was so proud of how they had made it through the challenges of being teen parents and now they were adding to their family. That was her gift to me, her olive branch—I was one of the first people that she shared her news with. I hugged her.

The next morning Tina and Cat insisted I pray with them. We clasped hands and said a prayer of forgiveness. It felt phony. I went downstairs to a conference room. The chairs were arranged in a circle and my teammates were already seated. There was an open chair next to Carli. I sat down. I was so nervous that I was shaking. I didn't want to see any of these women—all I could think of was the hell I had gone through in Shanghai. I wanted to be back in my bathtub. Carli reached over and patted me on the leg. Everyone saw her do it.

Greg spoke first. He said that he knew it took courage for me to be here.

Well, I thought, that's a good start. But the start was also the end of "good." No more sympathy. Greg recited a laundry list of my transgressions: he said the goal in North Korea was one of the worst mistakes he had ever seen in a World Cup, yet he had stood by me. He accused me of breaking team policies by staying out too late the night before the England game. "I don't know how you could do this to your team," he said. "It takes a certain type of person to be able to do what you did. Something serious must have happened to you in your childhood."

His words lashed at me. Damn right something happened when I was a kid, I thought. I learned how to fight for myself.

I stared at him. Where was the part where we talked a bout moving forward and winning the Olympics in 2008? I fought my instinct to flee the room.

Greg said we couldn't move forward until everyone had expressed their feelings. So then the onslaught began.

Lil, the captain, started. She accused me of throwing the team under the bus. The accusations rushed in.

"We don't think you should be here. We think you should go home."

"You're a bad friend."

Each person who spoke stood up, as though we were in some sort of twelve-step meeting. "You're a terrible teammate."

"You threw us all under the bus."

"You just kept using your dad's death for sympathy."

That last jab was from Cat, my good friend. That hurt more than anything anyone else said. So much for forgiveness.

When it looked like they were done, I started to speak. "I . . ."

"Are you even sorry? You've never once been sincere."

"I can't stand this," Carli said under her breath and left the room. I put my head down as I was accused of planning my statement to the press. While it was true that I had told the back of the bus group that I had no problem commenting on Greg's decision if asked, it sounded as though I had concocted an elaborate plan for speaking to the press.

My close friends on the team remained silent, but had cold looks in their eyes. Tina looked miserable but didn't say anything.

I started rocking back and forth in my chair as the players went around the circle. I fought back tears. Carli came back in the room and sat back down beside me. "Stay strong, Hope," she whispered to me, and patted my leg. "Stay strong."

One of Greg's assistant coaches, Brett Hall, who had coached with Greg for years, finally spoke up. "Look, we all make mistakes," he said. "You have to pick that person up and move on as a team. You can't continue to make it worse; you want to forgive and move on."

His words hung heavily in the air. Greg shot him an angry look.

Finally, the meeting was adjourned. The message was clear: my teammates wished I had never shown up, and now they wanted me to go home, to make them look and feel better. Somewhere in the past few weeks, it must have registered with them that the image of the U.S. women's team had taken an enormous hit. The once beloved team was being called Mean Girls, its tactics likened to sorority hazing. Now everyone was in damage control but no one wanted to take any responsibility—for the disaster in China or for their behavior. But if I took the fall and left, they could go on pretending to be best friends and great teammates who would all have two fillings for each other.

The meeting had gone on so long that the team was late for training. Apparently heaping abuse on me was more important than game preparation. I stayed behind at the hotel and took notes on what had happened, something James Galanis had suggested I do for self-preservation.

Greg told reporters that he had "excused" my absence that day, as though it had been my choice to skip the workout.

At three p.m. I met with our general manager Cheryl Bailey and Dan Flynn. Dan was not happy when he learned what had happened. He told me to stay strong and not go home. He gave me a pep talk, saying I was the future of the team and that I was going to prove everyone wrong and be the best goalkeeper in the game. He told me to stay patient.

I had been in the hotel all day. It felt like prison, just like that hotel in Shanghai. Cheryl said she was worried about my health—she thought I looked as though I'd lost weight since China. She was right—I had lost ten pounds and looked diminished. She insisted that we walk down to T.G.I. Friday's for dinner. I ordered French onion soup and raspberry lemonade; Cheryl urged me to also have ice cream for dessert. It felt good to be out of the hotel, walking on the street, getting smiles and eye-contact from friendly Midwesterners.

Back at the hotel, it was time for another meeting, this time with Lil and Cheryl. Lil insisted that I have a flight booked to go home if it came to that. "Is having Hope leave what's best for the image of the team?" Cheryl asked. "What can Hope do to help the team?"

Lil thought. Her solution? She suggested I carry the team equipment at practice.

I wanted to laugh but it wasn't funny. Did they want me to polish their boots too?

They decided I would sit on the bench in street clothes and that I wouldn't be on the field for the national anthem. By now it was late. I had a flight booked at 6.20 in the morning, but Cheryl told me not to take it. She said I needed to meet with Greg again in the morning before anything was decided.

I was on autopilot, dead inside, pushed from one meeting to the next.

On Saturday morning, I met with Greg. I had a sense he had been told by U.S. Soccer that he couldn't send me home. But he seemed determined to make me miserable, telling me that the team didn't want me on their bench.

"Well, I want to be here," I said. "I'm going to sit on the bench."

We had another team meeting, and the parameters of my punishment were laid out. I wasn't allowed to suit up. I wasn't allowed to be on the field for the national anthem. I wasn't allowed to eat with the team. I certainly wasn't allowed to interact with fans or sign autographs. One more condition: I had to offer a formal apology. This time, in writing.

Aaron Heifetz, our press officer, met with me—he had written a draft and wanted me to rubber-stamp his words. I was appalled by some of the language in the draft. Heifetz said that I wasn't suiting up, "because I need to earn the right to wear the national team uniform." He wrote, "What I did violates what this team is about and that is a reflection on me and me alone," and "My teammates have acted professionally and appropriately through this and they do not deserve what I have brought on this team."

"I'm not approving this," I said and pulled out my phone to call Rich. But it was Saturday morning in California and he was at his kids' soccer games. I called Lesle—who wrote her own version of an apology and e-mailed it to me. But there wasn't time, Heifetz insisted, for long edits. This had to be released before game time. He was furious when I took out my pen and started crossing out phrases. He seemed as angry as one of the players. I thought he might burst into tears.

I headed into another meeting with Greg and Cheryl to go over the logistics of my involvement. I didn't realize banishment required so much strategic planning. I was to sit in the front of the bus next to Cheryl. I was not allowed in the team locker room or the team huddle. During team warm-ups, I was to remain on the sideline, away from the team. I was not allowed into team meals. I was going to be moved out of Tina's room right away, back to isolation.

A few hours before the game in St. Louis, the official apology was released:

> I would like to apologize to my teammates, coaches and everyone else adversely affected by my comments at the Women's World Cup. This public apology comes later than it should have, but I hope that does not diminish the fact that I am truly sorry. I made a mistake and I take full responsibility for my actions. I let my teammates down and have lost their trust.
>
> I would like to especially apologize to Greg Ryan and Briana Scurry. There is no excuse for insulting a coach or a teammate. My focus now is solely on reconciliation with the team. I am here to support the team for these games, but after apologizing in person to all my teammates and the coaches, I have made the choice not to suit up for these games since I believe this is the first step in the healing process.
>
> As I work to regain the team's trust, I will not be making any more public comments at this time. The healing process has started, but I understand that I have a lot of work to do with my teammates and that is my focus moving forward.

It wasn't long before I got an e-mail from my Aunt Susie. "Did you really make that statement," she wrote, "or is someone putting words in your mouth?"

V.

While the team warmed up for its first game, I stood on the field awkwardly, unsure of what to do. Our general manager Cheryl talked to me. So did our assistant coach Brett. I was wearing jeans and tennis shoes, which seemed weird. I waited inside the tunnel while the anthems were played and the teams shook hands. After the pregame ceremony was finished, I walked back into the stadium, and cheers went up around me. Some fans shouted jeers at Greg Ryan. Signs were held aloft in the stands: FREE HOPE SOLO and HOPE APOLOGIZED, THE TEAM OSTRACIZED. I heard some people chanting my name. The plan to make me invisible had backfired.

As I sat on the bench, Carli was the only player who would sit near me. Another strategic move planned out in a meeting: Who is the one player who doesn't hate Hope? Though the public was being told that our team had reconciled and was moving forward, no one spoke a word in my direction. When my teammates came off the field, I reached out—as everyone on the bench does—to give high-fives. A few of my teammates touched my hand, but most avoided me.

This meaningless friendly match attracted an inordinate amount of attention. That night, the Rockies and the Diamondbacks played extra innings in a National League Championship Series. As the managers ran out of bench players, one of the announcers quipped, "Looks like the only person who hasn't played tonight is Hope Solo."

After the game, the team signed autographs, but I was hurried onto the bus, where I sat, as planned, in the front next to Cheryl. As my teammates filed on, they avoided looking at me. Except for Christie Rampone, who paused at my seat and said, "How you doing?"

"OK, Pearcie," I said, my eyes starting to well. Her tiny bit of kindness almost burst me open.

Back at the team hotel, everyone exited the bus and headed to the elevator. I walked onto an elevator that was already carrying several of my teammates. After I stepped through the doors, my teammates got off. "I'm not getting on with her," one player said loudly.

As the elevator doors closed, I burst out laughing. On my ride up to my room, a dam between pain and humor broke. This had become ludicrous.

The next morning, the absurdity continued. At the airport, I went through security by myself. I sat by myself on the flight to Portland. My adult teammates were acting as though I were radioactive, but I took Cheryl's advice to heart: one interaction at a time.

"Hi, Chups," I said, when Lori Chalupny walked by me at training.

"Hey, Tarp," I said as I passed Lindsay Tarpley.

I made eye contact. I smiled. And sometimes I got eye contact back. I started keeping score. *Eye contact! Yay, one victory for me!*

When we got to Portland, the Nike athletes were invited to go to the Niketown store for a shopping spree. They sent a Suburban for us. When I got in the car, other players got out, preferring to skip the trip than ride with me. But I wasn't missing a chance to interact with my friends at Nike. I was worried about my livelihood, but they were supportive. Stacey Chapman, one of the company's top marketing executives, hugged me when she saw me. She had been in China and witnessed how I had been treated, reporting back to Lesle how horrible the situation was. "Fake it 'til you make it," she said. "Keep smiling."

I also met with Joe Elsmore, the head of Nike's soccer marketing branch. He told me that he had pulled a planned advertising campaign that had emphasized the importance of team. Joe told me he couldn't approve such a campaign, in light of what was happening. So now I had another soccer power broker voicing support for me.

One night I went to dinner with goalkeeper coach Phil Wheddon, the first time we had talked since China. The disconnect with Phil was particularly painful because I had been so close to him. We drank a bottle of wine: it was the first time I had had any alcohol since April. He told me I was the best goalkeeper in the tournament. I probably would have won the award.

God, that hurt. One of my dreams was to be considered the "best goalkeeper in the world." I had worked so hard for that and it stung to know that it had been within my grasp. Phil seemed sympathetic. He was the only one who knew what had happened between me and Greg. I wanted to hear more words of support from Phil, but I could tell he was worried about his job. I understood—it was his livelihood. Greg was his boss and was acting increasingly nasty toward him. In St. Louis I overheard Greg demand that Phil get out of his sight, and sarcastically suggest that he "go hang out with your buddy Hope" at the end of the bench. Once beside me, Phil had motioned for our massage therapist to come and sit between us. Even my longtime coach was distancing himself from me.

In Portland, there was team business to take care of: the new league was preparing to launch soon, and all of the national team players would be allocated to different WPS clubs. Though it was more than a year away, we were supposed to turn in our top three preferences. There was a meeting with the team lawyer to go over everything.

I wasn't allowed into the meeting, so Abby came up to me. She told me she needed my top three picks. It was the first time she had talked to me outside of a team meeting since China. I had zero trust that they would honor my preferences, no confidence that the team lawyer—who I was convinced was beholden to the veterans—would keep my business private. "Abby, you're not allowing me into the meeting, but you expect me to turn in my picks to you?" I said. "I'll give them to my agent."

I e-mailed Rich my preferences: 1. St. Louis, 2. St. Louis, 3. St. Louis. My chance meeting on the airplane with Jeffrey Cooper had convinced me that I wanted to play for him. But I sure as hell wasn't telling my teammates—I was certain they would try to sabotage me.

Later that day, on the bus, I got a text. It was from Chups, who was sitting at the back of the bus. She had walked right past me. She told me she was worried about me and still considered us friends.

Wow, I thought. A breakthrough.

My mood improved dramatically in Portland. I was in my Northwest comfort zone. My family and friends came to the game. On the field, I juggled the ball and goofed around; after the game, I defied the rules prohibiting me from signing autographs and went into the stands and embraced fans who had offered their support. I went out with my grandparents and Malia and her brothers after the game, and then Malia and I stayed out drinking and talking. Malia stayed in my isolation room with me. It felt so good to have someone to laugh with and confide in. The next morning, I missed the team bus to the airport. I texted Cheryl Bailey and said I'd just meet them there.

"What are they going to do?" I laughed to Malia as she drove me to the airport. "Kick me off the team?"

By the time we got to Albuquerque, I was feeling better, but the team was cracking at the seams. Carli told me that Abby had cornered her and berated her for talking to me, telling her she had jeopardized her position on the team. Carli said Abby accused her of being like me—antisocial and always in her own room.

Carli went to Greg and asked what the hell that was all about. Greg assured her that Abby's views didn't come from him.

In Albuquerque I went for coffee with our assistant coach, Brett. Brett was a tough guy, a demanding coach, but he had a forgiving heart. He told me that I was in a shitty situation but I could learn from it. He said he thought hard times could mold greatness. "If you have to go through this, at least get something out of it," he said.

In the lobby of the hotel, Dan Flynn made a point of talking to me, as he had at other stops, to see how I was doing and buy me coffee. Everyone on the team could see that one of the main bosses of U.S. Soccer was behind me. By phone, Rich kept encouraging me to hold on and be patient. He was talking to Dan regularly. He seemed to think something dramatic was about to happen. On the final day of the tour, I heard that Greg and Phil had a bitter argument.

In the finale of the "celebration tour," we tied Mexico 1–1. Natasha replaced Abby in the second half, which meant that Abby was on the bench. She loudly picked apart Carli's play from her seat near me. It was uncomfortable—finally Aly leaned over and told

Abby to relax. After the game, I stood out on the field for a long time, watching my team sign autographs.

Aly came up to me on the field. "Hope, I miss my friend," she said.

I knew I'd talk to Aly at some point. But something had broken forever between us.

After the game, Greg asked me to meet him on the second floor of the hotel outside the conference rooms. He sat at one end of the long table. I sat down at the other. He slid something across the table toward me.

I caught it just before it dropped off the end of the table. It was my World Cup bronze medal, in a tiny Ziploc bag. This was my medal ceremony.

He formally shook my hand. Then Greg turned and went down the escalator, to where Sunil and Dan were waiting for him. I watched him descend.

It was over. The tour, the season, the year. This team would never be the same.

The next morning on the bus, everyone was hugging each other good-bye. Hugging everyone but me. I was alone, a player without a team. At the airport, I ate some breakfast. A group of my teammates sat at a table close by but didn't say a word to me, not even Tina. I knew she would soon be calling me, her bubbly and friendly self. But at that table, with Abby, she couldn't even acknowledge me. The journey that had started with such hope and promise three years earlier was ending in bitterness and loss.

I flew home. When I landed in Seattle and turned on my phone, I had a message from Cheryl Bailey. "Hope," she said, "I wanted you to know that Greg has been fired."

CHAPTER SIXTEEN

The New #1

Greg Ryan was gone, but that didn't mean my problems were over. Three years earlier, I hadn't thought a head coaching change was a big deal. I believed talent won out. I was much wiser now.

Would U.S. Soccer choose a coach beholden to the veterans? The search committee was Mia Hamm, Dan Flynn, and Sunil Gulati. I figured Mia would look for a coach who would support the veterans, one who would take the side of Lil and Abby. Could any candidate possibly have an open mind about me? I wasn't sure of anything these days. As I waited in my cabin in Seattle to find out who would be named coach, I read through the mail and e-mail that had piled up since the World Cup. I was noticing trends. Men seemed to be more understanding and forgiving of what happened in China than women were. Men seemed to think what I'd said was no big deal—that it was nothing worse than what male athletes routinely say. They also noted that if men don't like each other, they fight it out and then forget about it the next day.

In my mail, I found a small card with a Colorado postmark. It was from Greg Ryan. He wrote that to err is human and to forgive is divine. He added that we all make mistakes and need to forgive and that he hoped that would happen with me and my teammates.

It seemed to be an odd time to say I needed to receive forgiveness. I had to wonder if his words were a plea for himself.

My mailboxes also contained a dark, frightening chunk of mail. I was accused of racism, of having tried to take a job away from a hardworking African-American woman. I was called hateful names, and I received death threats. I had a stalker who wrote to me about my father, and called me a slut. I gave the worst letters and e-mails to the police. I didn't know how some of the mail had made it to my home address—if envelopes got to my house, that meant these crazy people could get there too. I was scared.

My step-dad Glenn took me to a friend of his in the Tri-Cities who was a self-defense expert. He gave me a self-defense course and helped me install a security system in my house. That year, my Christmas present from Glenn was a Sig Sauer 9 mm pistol—he took me out to the target range and taught me how to shoot it. Glenn wanted to give me the tools to protect myself. He was worried—a dad concerned about his daughter. We had come a long way together.

Marcus was also worried. He and my dad had never liked my living alone. Late one night, he startled me by knocking on my front door. I looked through my peephole and all I saw was Marcus, but when I opened the door, there on the doorstep was a wriggling, wagging, bundle of affection—a golden retriever puppy. Leo was the son of Marcus's dog Blue. I had desperately missed having a dog, but I didn't know how I would take care of one with all my travel. "We'll all help take care of him," Marcus said. "I don't want you to be here alone."

From that moment on, the first thing I did whenever I got back to Seattle was pick up my Leo from whoever was watching him for me.

II.

On November 13, our general manager, Cheryl Bailey, called me with the big news. The new coach of the national team was Pia Sundhage. Pia was a pioneer of the women's game. For two decades, she had played in Sweden, leading her country to World

Cups in 1991 and 1995. After coaching in Sweden, she came to the WUSA as an assistant in Philadelphia—I had heard a lot of good things about her, but by the time I was drafted by Philadelphia, she had become Boston's head coach. Both Lil and Kate Markgraf played for her with the Breakers, and Pia had been the veterans' first choice to take over after April was fired. Those were red flags for me, but I had gotten to know Pia in Athens, where we shared housing and trained and even went out and drank beer together. I liked her—I thought she was funny and interesting, and I was told she was a great coach.

Cheryl Bailey sent me the schedule of the upcoming training camp. She told me that Pia had been told in detail about the past two months of turmoil. Two weeks before Christmas, we gathered in Southern California for a four-day camp to meet Pia. Bri was there, so was Barnie. I didn't know where I fit in—or if I fit in anywhere. I had no desire to be there or see my teammates. I was still exhausted from everything that had happened in the past eight months.

I walked into the hotel and saw my teammates embracing each other, excited to be reunited, squealing and laughing. But they got quiet as I walked down the hall to my room. No one greeted or hugged me. I kept my head down and went to the equipment room to get my gear.

"Hey, Hope, how are you?" asked a friendly voice. I looked up. It was Jesse Bignami, our equipment manager. He gave me a big hug, my first real welcome. A second later, Abby walked into the room. "What's up, Biggs?" Abby said to Jesse.

I was still invisible.

We had our first team meeting. Pia talked a little bit about the schedule going forward, her plan and philosophy. Then she pulled out her guitar, explaining that English wasn't her native language and that she would sing us a song.

She started to strum her guitar and sing, "Come gather 'round, people / Wherever you roam . . ."

Our new coach was singing Bob Dylan's anthem of transition. We listened in amazement as she finished up with the main chorus: "For the times they are a-changin'."

I smiled. I love it.

When Pia finished, she asked us: "Do you want to win?"

"Yes!" came the loud response.

"Well, to win you need a goalkeeper," Pia said. "I don't expect you to forget. But I do expect you to forgive. The Olympics are right around the corner, so let's get to work."

Meeting adjourned.

III.

I felt like shit on the field. I knew I wasn't playing well, that my lack of comfort and confidence was showing every day in practice. Pia came up to me during every practice to check on me. "How you doing today?" she'd say.

"I'm OK, Pia," I'd tell her.

During the four-day camp, Pia met with many players and heard many sides to the story. She listened. She observed. She saw how isolated I was. Toward the end of camp, she sat down with me and asked questions. "I don't know what happened, and I don't know if I want to know what happened," she told me. "But in the end, we move on. I'm not making the choice for you. You have to make the choice whether you're on board."

I didn't have much to say. She could see for herself how I was struggling.

"I want you to trust me, Hope," she said. "Let's look forward instead of back. As long as you keep playing well, it makes my job easier." Pia said I needed to "keep" playing well, though we both knew I wasn't performing like a starting goalkeeper. But she was giving me an opening.

The team came back together in early January to prepare for the Four Nations Tournament in China. Word was out that Lil was pregnant with her first child and would miss the entire year, including the Beijing Olympics. That meant that one more of the '99ers was gone, at least for the immediate future. I was happy Lil was moving on with her life; a major hurdle had just been moved out of my path. I felt the shadow beginning to fade.

But even without Lil, the veterans were still trying to control our new coach. I found out through the grapevine that several veterans—even ones who were no longer on the team—had told Pia I wasn't ready to play, that I needed to learn how to sit on the bench and be a team player. But I was learning to trust my new coach. Pia seemed like someone who made her own decisions. She was looking at the big picture, thinking about who she would need in Beijing in August. She named me to the Four Nations roster, and in China I started two out of three games: Bri got the other game. Even though I didn't feel I had earned the starts, I played well enough. I kept to myself, sharing a room with Carli. I took my friend Stacey's advice: "Fake it 'til you make it." I smiled. I gave a few high-fives. I yelled, "Good job," from the bench to my team-mates. Faking anything went against my basic philosophy of life, but I could genuinely applaud a good play or appreciate a skillful move. I concentrated on moving forward.

Pia started bringing in new young players like Tobin Heath and Lauren Cheney. They didn't share our recent tortured history; they had fresh eyes and fresh attitudes. Pearcie had taken over the captain's armband from Lil. She was a confident, thoughtful leader; I remembered that in the hotel room in Shanghai, she had been the only veteran to try to move forward, and that on the celebration tour she had been the only veteran to stop and speak to me. She didn't just talk about leadership; she showed it.

A few weeks after we won the Four Nations, we headed to Portugal for the Algarve Cup. Bri was left off the roster—Barnie and I split the four games. We played well, and for the first time in almost a year, I felt relaxed and happy with my team. Maybe it was the mild Portuguese weather and the beautiful surroundings.

Maybe it was because the veterans' circle had shrunk in size and power. Everyone seemed to be in a good mood. After we won, we all—Pia included—went dancing.

The calendar between the World Cup and the Olympics was condensed and intense. We were a different team than we had been just a few months ago, with a different coach, who wanted to play a different style. There wasn't time to dwell on hurt feelings. The schedule was full: after Portugal we headed to Mexico to qualify for the Olympics, which we did with three wins and a tie.

While in Southern California for training camp, I was getting closer to Jesse, our equipment manager. I still stayed in touch with Adrian all the time, but he was busy with his own life. Jesse worked for U.S. Soccer and had had his own run-ins with Greg Ryan; he knew so much about the politics of my situation that I could turn to him for advice and support. He made me feel special and loved, something I needed at that low point. I still was feeling that my life was in flux. When I went home, I missed my father terribly. When I looked in the mirror, I felt I needed a change.

"I'm going to dye my hair brown," I told one of my Nike reps.

"We've already shot our Olympic campaigns," she said. "We want you to be recognizable. You're going to be one of the faces of the team."

So I stayed blond.

After our trip to Mexico, we had a handful of friendly games in the United States: two with Australia, in North Carolina and Alabama, and another with Canada in Washington, D.C. At those games, I took some abuse from Scurry fans. I heard boos behind the goal, and heckling.

"You're no Scurry."

"You'll never be as good as Bri. You suck, Solo."

"Get off the field."

I pretended that I didn't hear them.

As we edged closer to the Olympics, the press started to pay more attention to the team. How, reporters wondered, could this broken team heal? They started asking hard questions, ripping off the Band-Aid and seeing what was underneath. In Washington, D.C., Grant Wahl from *Sports Illustrated* sat down with both Bri and me separately and asked us to revisit the details of 2007.

"I guess *Sports Illustrated* is doing a story," I said to Bri later.

"Yeah," she said.

We decided we should talk. For eight months, I'd been dreading this conversation, but at a café near our hotel, Bri and I talked for more than two hours. There was no anger. I apologized again, and she said she forgave me. We spoke of our fathers. Bri told me she had always thought I was a good kid before the World Cup. "I still think you're a good kid," she said.

We hugged. The scar was always going to be there, on both our careers. But the wound seemed to have finally healed.

IV.

When the Olympic roster was named in June, Barnie and I were the goalkeepers. Bri was the alternate. It was the first time she wasn't on the roster for a world championship since the 1991 World Cup. An era had ended, and I felt it was time to mark the start of a new one. I had worn number 18 since college, when I still hoped to be a field player. But that was so long ago—I was a goalkeeper now, one of the best in the world. Goalkeepers traditionally wear number 1. Even though Bri had been a backup for most of the past three years, she had retained the number 1 jersey—she had that right as our most senior player. I knew that requesting the number 1 jersey now could be portrayed—once again—as me stabbing Bri in the back, but I felt strongly that the number 1 jersey should be worn by the starting goalkeeper. It was soccer tradition. And it represented a fresh start.

I told Aaron Heifetz and Cheryl Bailey that I wanted to make the change before the roster was sent to FIFA, and after a little hesitation, the change was made. My goalkeeper coach, Phil, approved—he told me that I had earned the number 1. A few teammates asked me what was up with changing my jersey, and I told them the truth: I wanted to wear the traditional goalkeeper number. The people it affected the most were my family members, because they all now had a collection of obsolete number 18 jerseys.

Secure in my place on the team, I started to make plans for my loved ones to come to the Olympics. Asking anyone to make two trips to China in the space of one year was a big request, and I had already received so much support for the World Cup that I wasn't sure what to expect. I was grateful for the support I was receiving—my mom was coming and my grandparents were committed. They were getting older, and international travel was becoming more difficult. Grandma said it might be the last time that she left "God's second paradise."

Marcus wasn't going to come, but he had the best reason of all to skip the Olympics. He and his fiancée, Debbie, had become parents of a baby boy in April. Johnny was named for my father—and he had been conceived soon after my father's death and was born a few days after my father's birthday and a day after my grandpa's birthday. His birth brought joy and a sense of renewal to all of us.

Our last game before the Olympics was against Brazil in San Diego. Brazil, as usual, had struggled between the major tournaments and had been the last team to qualify for the Olympics. It was a warm night in July and the stadium was packed with enthusiastic fans. In the first half, Abby and Andréia Rosa went into a hard tackle and Abby never got up. She was flat on the ground and lifted her head to signal to the bench for help. I had never seen Abby in that kind of pain—not even when she had her head split open against North Korea.

The game came to a stop. Pearcie ran over to Abby. The paramedics lifted Abby onto a stretcher and placed an Aircast on her leg. She was taken to the hospital while the game continued. We won the game 1–0, but everyone on the team was in shock.

We found out after the game that Abby had broken both her left tibia and fibula. That's exactly what Abby—completely lucid—had told Pearcie on the field.

Abby—our force, our scoring threat—was out of the Olympics. We were going to have to win without her. Abby and I still didn't have much of a relationship, but we had reached a kind of détente: we agreed to disagree about what had happened in China. We were both key to the team's success: the goal scorer and the goal stopper. I couldn't imagine our team without her.

Some of the players were staying the night in San Diego while the rest of us were heading back to Los Angeles. I wanted to go to the hospital to see Abby, to let her know how important I thought she was to the team, to tell her that I wished nothing but the best for her. But the bus back to Los Angeles was waiting, so I left Abby behind in the hospital, where she had surgery to place a titanium rod and screws in her leg. I sent her a text.

Hey Abby, thinking of you.

A few days later, we boarded the plane headed for Beijing. We hadn't lost a game since Pia took over—our last loss was the World Cup game against Brazil. I looked around at my teammates. There was no Lil, no Abby. Bri was only there as an alternate. Shannon Boxx, who had made it clear through comments to the press that she didn't want to revisit the past and just wanted to play soccer, was all business. Kate Markgraf, Pearcie, and I had formed a working relationship as the core of the defense. Aly and I dealt with each other, but our relationship was never going to be the same, and we both knew it. Cat wasn't there—she was injured. Tina had just had baby Mya. We were a completely different team. The times had indeed changed.

V.

God damn it, what was wrong with me? Why was I playing like this? I had never felt this nervous. The Olympics had started just five minutes ago, and I had already let in two goals. We had barely started our Olympic journey, and we were already facing elimination. If we were boxers, we might have been TKO'd.

We were playing our first game against Norway in Qinhuang-dao, a seaport east of Beijing. We had arrived before most of the rest of Team USA, landing in China two weeks before our first game, which gave us time to adjust to the heat and the "haze," as the Chinese euphemistically called the ever-present smog. But the long acclimation period didn't do anything to calm my nerves. I had never been more scared to play a soccer game.

I knew how many people wanted me to fail. Sure, there were others who supported me, but I was keenly aware of how many were rooting against me and how important it was to prove them wrong. By the morning of our first game, August 6—two days before Opening Ceremonies—the accumulated weight of the past eleven months had settled in the pit of my stomach.

When I took the field, I had too much adrenaline rushing through me. In the first two minutes, I made a terrible decision. Lori Chalupny was marking the Norwegian captain, and was in perfect position. But I charged off my line and tried to punch the ball out, but I clocked Chups in the head instead. The goal was left untended and a Norwegian player easily headed the ball into the empty net. Not only had I made an error, I had injured Chups—our best defender. She left the game with a concussion.

The mistake rattled me. But it wasn't what led to the next goal—there wasn't really much I could do when Markgraf made a bad pass right to a Norwegian forward who brought the ball down into the box and blasted a shot past me. Now we were down 2–0. And that's the way the game stayed. It was our first-ever loss in Olympic group play, the U.S. team's only Olympic loss other than that golden goal defeat to Norway in Sydney in 2000. I was furious with myself. I couldn't believe we had lost our very first game and that our entire Olympics were suddenly at risk, all because I had worried about what other people thought. *What the fuck am I doing?* I thought. *Why the fuck am I letting the critics get to me?*

It was the first time in my life that I had felt influenced by the opinions of others. I hadn't been able to shut out the distractions on the soccer field. I thought of my dad—how he had always ignored those who judged him with a "Fuck off" attitude.

Fuck everyone, I thought.

We stayed in Qinhuangdao while the extravagant opening ceremonies unspooled in the Bird's Nest in Beijing. We watched them on TV, but I couldn't fully enjoy the spectacle. The thrill of being at the Olympics had given way to the desperate business of trying to recover and win an Olympic medal. We were already being ripped to shreds in the press. *We could never win without Abby. The World Cup wounds couldn't heal. We weren't a unified team.* In the eyes of the American media, we were already eliminated, forever in the shadow of the '99 team.

But Pia stayed positive. She didn't let us get down about the Norway result, and when we played Japan on August 9, we came out determined and attacking. In the first half, Carli scored a goal, and I played much better. We won 1–0 and headed to Shenyang to play New Zealand. What seemed impossible a few days earlier— winning our group—was within our grasp, if we won our game big and Japan beat Norway. I knew I couldn't afford to let in a goal. We did our part, winning 4–0. At the end of the game we celebrated and then heard the score of the Japan game: the Japanese had beaten Norway 3–1.

Our celebration circle on the field was an especially joyous one. We had overcome a disastrous loss—just ten months after the bitterness that ripped our team apart, we were playing resilient, tough, unified soccer. It felt good. It felt like fate.

Before and after every game, I talked to Adrian on the phone. I was dating Jesse now, and Adrian was dating someone else, but I still needed him. Before the Olympics, I had pleaded with him to come to China. "Adrian, you're one of the most important people in my life. I can't imagine getting through these games without you. I bought a plane ticket for you. Please come."

But he didn't. Still, he got up early back in Seattle to watch every game on television—interrupting his life to support me. He answered my calls at any hour of the night, and he took care of Leo.

In the quarterfinals, we played Canada in Shanghai. Midway through the first half we were leading 1–0 when rain began to pour down and lightning flashed around the stadium. The match was delayed for an hour and a half because of lightning strikes. I called Adrian. He kept me focused and calm through the long break.

When the game resumed, my old nemesis, Christine Sinclair, blasted a shot past my extended body to tie the game. It took eleven minutes of overtime before Natasha Kai, who had come on to replace Heather O'Reilly when overtime began, scored on a diving header to put us in the semifinals, where we would meet Japan again.

VI.

Our manager handed me an envelope. "This is for you, Hope."

Inside was a letter from Abby. Back home in upstate New York, she was rehabilitating, watching us and reflecting on the team. She had thought about coming to China but decided she would be a distraction. Instead, she wrote each of her teammates a letter. Even me.

She told me that she understood that as a goalkeeper I needed to have a strong belief in myself. She said that in the past year she learned to accept people for who they are. She said that she had tried to turn me into a villain for being myself.

"That isn't honest. That isn't compassionate. That is controlling and manipulative. I am sorry I was like that," Abby wrote.

She said that my skill in goal frustrated her constantly in practice and that she appreciated my ability. She encouraged me to show
the world my softer side.

"You have a chance to show everyone who you really are," she
wrote. "I believe you'll show everyone you're a winner."

I folded up the letter. I was blown away by the thought and feeling Abby had put into it. She could have written a perfunctory, "Go
for the gold!" but she had truly thought about our relationship and
what was at stake. I was humbled and inspired. She had reached out
across the ravine that separated us and I knew I would grasp her
hand. We didn't have to be best friends, but we had to be teammates. We needed each other.

Finally, after our quarterfinal, we traveled to Beijing, where
the Olympic action was happening, and moved into the Olympic
Village. The semifinal and final were at Workers Stadium, an old
stadium removed from the Olympic Park, in a bustling part of Beijing. We had never lost to Japan, but we knew how dangerous the
Japanese were. Just as we took the field for warm-ups, the other
semifinal game was ending. In a major upset, Brazil had manhandled Germany, 4–1, ousting the tournament favorite and exacting
revenge for their World Cup loss.

When our semifinal began, Japan seemed intent on continuing
the day of upsets. Japan jumped out in front in the first half, scoring
on a corner kick. We tied the game late in the first half on an attack
that I started with a long goal kick. Just before the half we scored
again, and never relinquished the lead. The final was 4–2.

I had played fine for the first five games of the tournament, but
I hadn't been required to be a game-changer. In every major tournament, a team needs its goalkeeper to come up huge in at least
one game, and that hadn't happened yet. The game hadn't called my
name. But I would be ready when it did. We were in the gold-medal
game. And our opponent was Brazil.

VII.

In recent months, I had returned to my comfortable spot at the back of the bus, where I could zone out and listen to music. On the ride to Workers Stadium on August 21, I looked out the window and thought about my yearlong odyssey from a stadium in Hangzhou to a stadium in Beijing. I felt so strong, both mentally and physically prepared. I knew I had done everything to be ready for this moment. We pulled up to the stadium, and when I stood to get up off the bus, I looked over at Carli. Our eyes locked. We smiled a sort of half-smile that spoke everything that needed to be said. We were at once relaxed and confident. "Well," I said. "Here we go."

Carli nodded. "Here we go."

BRAZIL'S STARS, CRISTIANE and Marta, were determined from the start to pick up where they left off in the World Cup, firing shot after shot at me. I dove to smother shots, punched balls out, collided with players. The game was calling my name. In the seventy-second minute, Marta got behind two of our defenders and into the six-yard box. She shot at me from point blank range: as she came at me I read that she would hit the ball left to the far post, but she quickly changed and blasted the ball to my right. I had to react instantaneously, throwing up my arm to block the rocket shot, which felt like it would take off my arm. The force of the blow was so loud some observers thought the ball had struck the post. No, it had struck me, ricocheting out of danger. Marta thrust her hands up in frustration.

Regulation time ended in a 0–0 draw. We would play two fifteen-minute halves of overtime. Six minutes into overtime, Carli had a give-and-go with Amy Rodriguez and blasted a left-footed shot from the top of the box. It landed in the corner of the goal. We led 1–0.

"Hell yeah!" I said, at the far end of the field, but refrained from celebrating. I knew we still had twenty-four minutes to play and Brazil was relentless.

Marta beat our defense again and sailed a ball past me, just over the crossbar. Time seemed to have stopped, stretching out into the muggy Chinese night. Ball after ball was slotted through without anyone touching them. I pushed balls out with my fingertips, with one hand. We had been playing forever, an eternal battle, and still the whistle didn't come. As the seconds ticked down, Brazil earned corner after corner. Finally I saw the referee glance at her watch. It had to be time.

Renata Costa lofted another corner. Cristiane got her head on it. I made the save.

And then the whistle blew.

CHAPTER SEVENTEEN

Pretty Damn Sweet

I sprinted out of the goal toward Carli and threw my arms around her. I wasn't thinking about the irony, the two ostracized teammates with the winning goal and the shutout. I just wanted to hug my friend in celebration. A celebration I'd been awaiting my entire life. We had our gold medal.

We collapsed onto each other, my teammates and I, a jumble of cleats and tears and joy and sweat. Pia—our coach, who had believed in me—lifted me off the ground in a bear hug. Brazil's Cristiane sat on the field, distraught, wailing in despair. Their goalkeeper, Barbara, lay prone across the face of the goal, weeping. Marta walked in small circles, looking stunned and confused.

We had done it. *Just* us. This unrecognized group that had lost its star player in July. We had won a major championship. We had done it without Mia Hamm, without Brandi Chastain, without Julie Foudy, without Kristine Lilly. We had stepped out of the shadow.

There was someone else I needed to share the moment with, someone who was back home in Washington, cradling his infant son, Johnny. Only Marcus really knew how shattered and vulnerable I had been at the World Cup. Before this game, I felt sure I would need to talk to him, so I had wrapped my cell phone in a white towel and placed it with my water bottle next to the goal. Marcus's number was pre-dialed. I ran back to the goal from the celebration, retrieved my phone, and punched SEND.

"We did it! We did it!" I shouted into the phone over the noise. "We fucking did it!"

We did it. My teammates and I. Marcus and I.

"Hell yes!" he shouted back. "I'm so proud of you, Hope."

We were both laughing and crying, barely able to hear each other over the noise. "This is for dad," he said over and over.

When we were little kids, alone and scared in that Seattle police station, when we were fighting and clawing at each other in the house on Hoxie, who imagined there would be an Olympic gold medal to bind us?

In my white towel, I had also placed a giant plastic gold medal—a ridiculous made-in-China prop that my mom and I had found in a Beijing marketplace. I put it on and ran over to where my family sat. My mom laughed in delight at my silly medal. My grandpa had such an enormous smile. My teammates and I reached up to the stands for high-fives and hugs. Pearcie's daughter Rylie was passed down to her. American flags were handed down, and some of my teammates ran around the stadium wrapped in them. Everyone was celebrating.

Later on, I heard some say how selfish I had been because I had ignored my teammates in order to talk on my phone and prance around with a tacky fake medal. That I was still a "Solo act." I was far beyond caring who judged how I celebrated something I had worked for my entire life. Never again would I worry about what others thought.

When the podium was finally set up on the field for the medal ceremony, we put on our white jackets, specifically made for the gold medal ceremony. As we lined up to step up on the podium, Bri came up to me and nodded. "I told you that you could do it, Hope," she said. Had she really? It didn't matter. We hugged.

I bowed my head and felt the medal slip around my neck. I heard the anthem play, saw my Grandma with her red, white, and blue sweater and blinking HOPE No. 1 sign pinned above her heart, singing at the top of her lungs. My grandpa was beaming with pride. My mother looked at me with so much love and amazement. They all shared this medal with me.

I thought of that moment years ago at the Sea-Tac Airport and how proud my dad had been when I won the gold medal in the Pan-American Games: he stopped strangers to tell them about how great his daughter was. I imagined how much he would have loved to see the gold medal hanging from my neck right now.

When we went back into the locker room, I stared at my medal for a very long time. I couldn't find my gloves, which were covered with writing: my dad's initials, words of inspiration from my grandma. I went back out to the field to look for them, but they were gone, probably snagged by some photographer looking for a souvenir.

When I came through the mixed zone on the way to the bus, there was a mob of reporters waiting for me, pressed up against the metal barricades, shouting questions about redemption and Greg Ryan and vindication. I had just won an Olympic gold medal. I wasn't thinking about the past, not about failures or hurts and certainly not about Greg. This was my happiest moment. I was not going to let the devil steal my joy.

"How," someone asked, "does the moment feel?"

"It's unreal to me," I said. "It's like a storybook ending. It's something you see in Hollywood, a fairy tale, and yet it was playing out. And my life doesn't play out that way all the time, you know? There have been a lot of hardships. I was just hoping this one time it would really come through. But honestly, that was wishful thinking. I knew it was a long road, a long journey. And I knew it was too perfect an ending to actually happen. Nothing ever goes right with my family and my life, so this was too perfect."

II.

As I've said many times: I don't believe in happy endings. I'm not a bitter cynic, just a realist bracing for whatever life delivers next. People who believe in happily ever after, who hadn't been dealt hardships and heartbreaks, always seemed a little naïve to me. But I have to admit that those hours after winning the Olympics were pretty damn sweet. When I was interviewed by ESPN's Jeremy Schaap several hours after the game, I told him, "For the first time in my life, I can say that I'm genuinely joyful and happy."

After the game, we went to the U.S. Soccer House in Beijing and celebrated with friends and family. Dan Flynn told us how proud he was of us. Pia spoke about the incredible journey we'd been on. Every time Carli and I made eye contact, we laughed and laughed.

It was so late, but no one wanted our gold-medal night to end. I jumped in a cab with Pia and some others, and we headed to a bar. Most of my teammates were too exhausted to go out, but a few of us partied and danced through the night.

At one point, Pia came up to me and said, "Why don't the coaches get a gold medal too?"

I agreed that it didn't seem fair. "Here you go, Pia," I said, slipping my medal over her silver hair. "You wear mine tonight."

I wanted to share this victory with her. I wanted to share it with the world.

III.

A few days after I got home, Jesse and I rented a Winnebago and headed to the Gorge Amphitheater on the Columbia River—just a hundred miles away from Richland—for a three-day Dave Matthews concert that we dubbed our Gold Medal Celebration Tour. Sofia Palmqvist flew in to celebrate with me, and other friends came from Richland and Seattle. We decorated the RV in Olympic rings. We brought our mountain bikes and cruised around, partying too hard.

Some Olympians stick their gold medals in a safe deposit box as soon as they get home. Not me. Before we left for the games, I made a bet with my friends that if we won, I'd wear mine at the gorge with my swimsuit. That's what I did. I wore it while we played drinking games, and I wore it everywhere I went until the ribbon began to fray. I was proud of being an eastern Washington girl with a gold medal around my dusty neck.

Two weeks after I got home, the team started a victory tour, beginning with three games against Ireland. This time I wasn't dreading being reunited with my teammates. Our first stop was Philadelphia, where our players' attorney, John Langel, was based. One of our first priorities was a team meeting with John to decide how to split our victory-tour money and gold-medal bonus. We were paid during the year by the national team, but the pool of money that came with the victory tour was our real payday.

When we got to Langel's office, I was surprised when I heard the plans for allocating the money. Bri was scheduled to receive a huge share, far more than our other alternates would receive. When I had been an alternate in Athens, I hadn't received any of the celebration tour money. I had a feeling I was witnessing a World Cup–type scenario all over again: a decision had been made for sentimental reasons, as a personal sendoff, rather than based on agreed-upon rules.

I took a deep breath. Bri was in the room. I knew that if I spoke up, it was going to be viewed as Hope versus Bri all over again. But I felt strongly that it was time for some consistency in how we treated people and some honest discussion. There couldn't be two sets of rules: one for the old veterans and one for everyone else. As Pia had said with her song, times had changed. We proved it on the field in Beijing. Now it was time to prove it off the field.

"I'm wondering," I said, my voice quavering, "why we're paying Bri so much? And if we pay Bri that much, why aren't we paying the other alternates the same amount?"

The few remaining veterans spoke up. "Well," I was told, "they didn't travel. Bri traveled to China."

"Yeah, but they were still training back home in case someone got hurt," I said. "They were still fulfilling their obligation as alternates. It wasn't their choice not to travel. Why aren't all the alternates paid the same?"

I saw some people's eyes roll. Here we go, I could see them thinking.

"I also don't think—since we have to make the decision—that we should be discussing this in front of the alternates," I said.

I didn't want to be disrespectful, but I thought we needed to have a fair discussion. Bri was sent out of the room. "I just want to understand the reasoning," I said to our lawyer.

"This is the way we've always done it," I was told. "This is the precedent that was set in 2000 and 2004."

I was silent. I looked at him. I'm sure my teammates were thinking, *Well, that shut her up.* "Maybe you've forgotten," I said, "but I was your alternate in 2004, and I didn't get paid anything. So are we following a precedent that was set, or does every separate team decide what it wants to do with their bonus money?"

I was told that must have been a mistake—that I should have been paid.

"Whether it was a mistake or not, I didn't get paid," I said. "I traveled to Greece. I missed part of my season in Sweden."

All of a sudden there was discussion in the room. A few veterans were adamant that Bri should be treated differently, but other players started to ask questions. The right questions: they asked about precedents, about the rationale behind decisions, about what was fair. I was a bit shocked as I looked around the room—it was the first time I had ever seen the entire team participating in a decision-making process.

We took a silent vote. I didn't care how the voting went. I was just proud that our team was participating in the decision without feeling intimidated. We decided that all alternates would get paid the same, whether or not they had traveled. The majority prevailed against the position taken by the old guard. It wasn't about money or what happened to me in 2004. It was about taking ownership of the team. We had finally escaped the shadow.

IV.

The coach of the women's soccer team at Arizona State was a good friend of Jesse's. He asked if I would make an appearance at one of their games, bring my gold medal, and sign some autographs. No problem. I had a free day after the last tour game against Ireland.

One problem: ASU was playing Michigan. Where Greg Ryan was now coaching. I hadn't seen Greg since Albuquerque, when he had tossed me my bronze World Cup medal and then gone downstairs to be fired. While I signed autographs and took pictures with ASU fans—who all wanted to touch my medal—I kept wondering if I was going to run into Greg. After the game, I went out on the field to meet the ASU team, and I saw Greg on the sideline. It felt as though everyone from both teams was staring at us. I had the gold medal, I was back on the team, I had a new coach—I could afford to be gracious. I walked up to Greg—it would have been awkward to avoid him.

"Hi Greg," I said reaching out to shake his hand. "It looks like things are going well for you. You remember Jesse, right?"

It seemed like a dumb question. Jesse worked for U.S. Soccer and had told me of his own conflicts with Greg.

Jesse stuck out his hand. "Hi Greg," he said.

Greg just glared at us and rudely told Jesse to keep his hand.

Holy shit. That was way more hostile than I expected. Greg must have forgotten the note he sent me: To forgive is divine. I turned to walk away, and then changed my mind. I turned back. "You know, Greg, we're both adults, and I thought we could be mature enough to get over what happened a year ago," I said. "But I guess not."

I lifted my gold medal up into his line of vision and—as he had instructed me once—looked him dead in the eye. And then

I walked away. Greg was still stuck somewhere in 2007, bitter and small-minded. I had moved on.

V.

The thing about happy endings is, they don't last very long. In the early morning hours of October 31, my phone rang. It was Adrian. He needed me the way I had needed him sixteen months earlier. His dad, Bob Galaviz, had been over at his home the evening before. As it had been for my dad and me, Adrian and his father—after years of separation and turmoil—had built a strong and loving relationship. That night he gave Adrian an extra long, tight hug before he walked out to his car. Bob was driving south on Interstate 5 through Seattle when a car heading north jumped the grassy median and started plowing up the highway in the wrong direction. It hit one car, smashed into Bob's car, then hit two more vehicles before coming to a stop. The police later said the driver had blacked out at the wheel. He killed two people, the sixty-one-year-old wife of the driver in the first car that was struck and Adrian's father. Bob was fifty-five years old.

Adrian got the phone call from the police. He had to go to his mother's workplace and tell her what had happened. I was in Richmond, Virginia, where we were preparing to play South Korea as part of our victory tour, when Adrian called.

"Hope, I need you."

I had seen Adrian's father right after the Olympics. As soon as I got back from China, I found Adrian. It didn't matter that I was planning a Winnebago tour with Jesse—I needed to share everything about the Olympics with him. We were bopping around Seattle and stopped by for a visit with his father, who had been watching Leo.

Bob wanted to hear all about the Olympics. "You've got to bring me that gold medal—I want to see it," he said.

"I'll bring it next time," I promised.

"I miss you," he said giving me a long hug. "You have to come see me more often."

As we left the house that day, Adrian's father told his son something that was an echo of what my father had once told me. "Adrian, don't lose this one. You two have to figure it out."

But we hadn't figured it out. I was seeing Jesse, Adrian was seeing someone else. We were never ready to commit.

I told Pia I had to leave the tour. I told Jesse I had to go to Adrian. "You need to do what you need to do," Jesse said.

And what I needed to do was be with Adrian. I flew west for another funeral. I brought my gold medal, even though it was too late.

CHAPTER EIGHTEEN

Unprofessional Professionals

The air was icy. I shivered as I glanced over at Kristine Lilly. We were standing on a New York City sidewalk on the *Today* show to promote the launch of the WPS, our new professional league. Why the producers picked us to promote the league, I'm not quite sure. But there we were, the longtime legend and the newly minted gold medalist making nice, with no one but the two of us aware of the tension.

We took the same car service to the set and didn't speak a word to each other. Matt Lauer tried to put a soccer ball under Kristine's belly to illustrate how pregnant she had been a few months earlier. Meredith Vieira asked about the 2008 Olympic gold medal performance. "It's been quite a year," I said, thinking back to the hellfire I had walked through just twelve months before. "It's a perfect time to kickstart a new league."

That was an overly optimistic statement. It really wasn't a perfect time to start a new league. Or even a good time. The economy was bad and about to get a lot worse, but the WPS had already been postponed for the '07 World Cup and the '08 Olympics.

It was a strange launch, straight into the headwind of a recession. We had only seven teams, with the promise of an eighth. Some owners weren't fully committed—AEG, a major player in Major League Soccer, only agreed to run the L.A. Sol short-term and was looking to sell. Some of the proposed teams, such as the one in Dallas, never materialized. The league's goals were modest, and commissioner Tonya Antonucci didn't make big pronouncements. Still, every story written about the league was slathered in a thick coat of skepticism—the WUSA had failed even with players like Mia Hamm, the economy was terrible, and the league had a low-budget feel. When the uniforms were unveiled—during New York's Fashion Week, no less—the kits included a skirt-like wrap. The goalkeeper jerseys were hot pink, and the shorts were padded, the kind of gear parents might buy at the Sports Basement for their twelve-year-old daughter. The whole thing screamed girly marketing, as though Sepp Blatter—the FIFA president who once said women soccer players should wear tight shorts to get attention—was the mastermind.

"There's no way in hell I'm wearing that," I said when I saw the goalkeeper uniform.

That got me in trouble with league officials. I was dissing a product being pushed by Puma, the league's only major sponsor. No one wanted to do anything that would upset Puma, including standing up for what was right. But our owner, Jeff Cooper, stood by me. He bought real goalkeeper jerseys—Puma brand—and had them fitted and numbered for us. The league was furious with him, but he wanted the players to be happy and feel professional. "Go ahead and fine me," he said.

I loved playing for Jeff. He was the black sheep of the league because he said what he thought, because he argued, and because he stood up for his players. I felt incredibly loyal to him. I also became close friends with our general manager, Tim Owens, and his family, who made me feel at home in St. Louis. I liked our coach, Jorge Barcellos, who had coached Brazil at the Olympics. I had a terrific contract. I lived downtown—exactly where I was warned not to settle. It was gritty but interesting: I lived in a hip loft, met diverse types of people, and walked to St. Louis Cardinals baseball games. That year we had only four national-team games after the March Algarve Cup, so I had a lot of time to explore my new home.

We didn't have a dominant personality who overwhelmed the

team. Chups, Tina, and I were the national team players on our team. Jill Loyden was my backup. We had an eclectic mix. I became close friends with Kia McNeill. Brazil's Daniela—whom I'd played with in Sweden—was our best offensive player.

One of the best things was the growing friendship between Tina and me. I'd known her for years, first at UW and later with the national team. I was scarred by the fact that she had never stood up for me in China, but in St. Louis, we bonded. I got to know and love her daughters, Mackenzie and Mya—I became their aunt Hope. Tina and I started to work seriously on soccer together: she had embraced her switch to defense and wanted to be the best defender she could be. She asked me a lot of questions. We spent hours together on the field, working on defensive strategy.

That season we finally talked about what had happened at the 2007 World Cup. "When I think back on my life, I'll always remember that," she said. "Of you rocking back and forth and crying in that room and me thinking, *No one deserves this.* I just didn't know what to do, Hope. It was awful." We cried talking about it. Tina and I were a lot alike, both outsiders for different reasons.

"Hope, you're a strong person," Tina said. "You're a truth-teller. People aren't comfortable with that."

The WPS officials sure didn't seem comfortable with it. They seemed more concerned about pleasing Puma and twisting our schedule to get a TV contract than doing what was right on the field. I was happy in St. Louis, but I wasn't happy with WPS: they kept saying they were the best in the world, but I'd played overseas. I'd seen how other leagues operated. The officiating was terrible, the uniforms were lame, and the disparity in pay was enormous. I wasn't terribly optimistic about the future.

II.

The most important thing that happened to my soccer career in 2009 wasn't the launch of the WPS. It was the arrival of Paul

Rogers in my life. After the 2008 Olympics, Phil Wheddon left to become the women's head coach at Syracuse. Paul was hired as our new goalkeeper coach and came to Portugal with us that March. He had worked at Florida State for my old Philadelphia Charge coach, Mark Krikorian, and FSU made it to the NCAA Final Four two years in a row. A really great goalkeeper coach is a rarity: I knew because I'd had dozens of them by then. Paul was English, arrogant, confident, and demanding. I loved him. He immediately told me I sucked. He told Nicole Barnhart the same thing. *Who is this guy?* I thought, looking at Barnie.

And then Paul set about correcting our bad habits. We broke down film—not just game footage but practice film. We examined tiny technical details like our balance, our first steps, the weight distribution in our feet, how far out our elbows were. It was the kind of intricate examination I'd never been exposed to before.

Barnie and I could see all our faults, right there on film. It wasn't pleasant. *Wow!* I thought. *We really* do *suck.*

But then Paul set about building us back up. He worked at a different level than anyone who had ever coached me: he could spot little things, like balancing too much on my toes, or exactly at what spot in my dive my arms started to reach out. Barnie and I started to get better. I was thrilled. I had a gold medal, but I also had new goals. I knew there was so much more I could do, and I had finally found the coach who could take my work ethic and desire for instruction and push me harder than I had ever been pushed.

In that first tournament with Paul, I had three shutouts in the Algarve Cup, and was named the MVP. Later, when I was named U.S. Soccer female player of the year for 2009, I made sure that I thanked Paul "for helping me think about the position in a more sophisticated way, both technically and tactically."

When I got back from Portugal, I told Jeff that Paul was the best goalkeeper coach I'd ever worked with, and Jeff hired him right away. Jeff wanted what was best for his players—all the more reason to be loyal to him.

III.

That spring we finally spread my dad's ashes, close to the anniversary of his birthday. As a family, we hiked to waterfalls up near the Snoqualmie Pass that I always hated to drive alone. We all came: Marcus and Debbie, with Johnny in a backpack, Terry, Jeff, and their son Christian, Mom, and Adrian. We took turns carrying Johnny. We had Blue and Leo with us, and we hiked through the spring snow to a bridge over a swollen mountain stream.

In the months after my father died, we had learned more about him. Marcus had gone through his papers and requested his naval records. My father had been in the navy during the Lebanon crisis in 1958. A year later, he received an honorable discharge because he contracted tuberculosis; he was treated with chemotherapy, and received full disability. While he was on disability, he worked as a machine operator at the Department of Motor Vehicles in Dorchester, Massachusetts. There was proof that he had played semipro football in Massachusetts. When he was twenty-six, he requested a name change from Beyers to Solo. And then the trail stopped.

Why did he change his name? What was he doing in Massachusetts? Why was he so determined to keep his history a mystery? I was never going to know the answer.

We stopped at the wooden rail and poured the ashes—mixed with flower petals—down into the clear water of the Cascades runoff. We watched the petals float away to some unknown destination. "Thanks, Dad," I whispered. "You made me who I am."

IV.

My fears about the solvency of the new league were well-founded. Our season ended in the semifinals, with a loss to eventual champion Sky Blue, who beat the L.A. Sol—Marta's team. The Sol had the best regular-season record, but a few months later had shut down operations. AEG hadn't been able to find a buyer, and folded it up. All the Sol players entered a dispersal draft. Shannon

Boxx ended up on our team, as did Japan's Aya Miyama, who became a close friend of mine. Aya said she had heard a lot about me when she was with the Sol.

"Hope, you're not what I expected," Aya told me. "The players on the Sol described you in a way that doesn't match how you really are."

Just a few weeks into our second season, Jeff called a meeting. His business partners had defaulted on their contract to fund the team through the season, so Jeff told us he had no choice but to pull the plug. As of June 1, we were all free agents; my awesome three-year contract wasn't going to be honored. I immediately signed with the Atlanta Beat, as did Tina, Chups, Aya, and a few of our other players. But I only played one game with Atlanta before leaving the country to go to the men's World Cup in South Africa.

Kia and I traveled with Team Up, a program affiliated with the Right to Play organization, reaching out to young people in the slums of Soweto, using soccer as a bridge for HIV-prevention education. We went to villages, met kids, and played soccer with them. I loved laughing and joking with them as they tried to get a shot past me. I was overwhelmed by their excitement at receiving a simple T-shirt or one of the bracelets I'd brought to give away. I was inspired by these children who were so knowledgeable about the HIV virus and prevention and so determined to make a difference in their communities.

I had never been to a men's World Cup. Over the years, I had become friendly with Landon Donovan—we had the same agent— and I knew several of the other players, including goalkeeper Tim Howard. I attended all three of the U.S. games in group play, and also saw Spain, South Africa, Argentina, and the Netherlands play—seven games in seven days. The atmosphere was unbelievable—I enjoyed meeting the locals, blowing the *vuvuzelas* (plastic horns), experiencing the international excitement. I saw why the World Cup was often called the world's best sporting event, and I swore I'd never miss another.

But the games were only the second-best part of my trip. I've traveled the world playing soccer, but those moments with kids on the dirt fields in Soweto were among the most profound experiences I've ever had. I saw the full power of what a sport could do, how it could unite people and change the world. I asked the kids what they wanted to do when they grew up. Their dreams were very real and very specific. But one little girl said, "I don't have any dreams."

I hugged her. She broke my heart. By the end of our interaction, she told me that she did have a dream. "To teach everybody about safe sex," she said.

I was proud of her for dreaming to make a difference in the world. On that trip, I realized that I—too—could make a difference.

V.

When I got back to Atlanta, our team still hadn't won a game. I arrived in time to play in the All-Star game in Atlanta: I was on a team captained by Abby Wambach—she picked her roster, and Marta picked the other team. It was a fun day, but not much else about the league was fun as that second season wound down.

Our team was playing in Boston one night in August, and the people behind the net were being obnoxious. I was accustomed to being booed and heckled in visiting stadiums—there were always references to 2007 and Bri. I figured it was better for the women's game if it wasn't all ponytails and smiley faces. If people wanted to view me as a villain, I didn't care. I actually liked the edginess it brought to my game, the knowledge that they viewed me as a threat.

But that night, the members of a Breakers fan club called the Riptide went way too far. The heckling became incredibly racist: they shouted taunts about "eating sushi" to my Japanese teammate, Aya, and yelled slurs in fake Japanese accents. They said horrible things to Kia and to Eniola Aluko, who was born in

Nigeria. With only a couple of thousand people in attendance, the jeers echoed around the stadium and were impossible to ignore. It was ugly, and it made me sick. I was so pissed off that I left after the game without signing autographs. Later I went on Twitter and explained why I hadn't stuck around, that a few fans had ruined it for everyone:

> To all the Boston fans and especially the young children that I didn't sign autographs for I'm sorry. I will not stand for . . .

> an organization who can so blatantly disrespect the athletes that come to play. Perhaps the WPS or Boston themselves . . .

> can finally take a stance to the profanity, racism and crude remarks that are made by their so called 'fan club.'

> To the true fans, I hope to catch you at the next game. Thanks for your support and love for the game.

MY COMMENTS CREATED an uproar. The Boston fans posted hateful things on soccer blogs and to my Twitter account. The Boston team denied that anything racist had taken place. It started to feel like a cover-up. I was accused of lying and being a prima donna who couldn't handle heckling. But when a handful of Boston fans wrote letters to the team saying they had to walk out of the game with their children because the language and behavior was so inappropriate, an apology was sent to our team.

A week later our coach was fired and James Galanis was brought in as interim coach. The owner asked me for a recommendation, and the first person I thought of was James, whom I had met through Carli. He knew how to push me and when to back off. A few weeks later, we were playing the Washington Freedom. Both teams needed a win to get into the playoffs. It was the craziest officiating I'd ever seen: calls were changed for no reason and goals disallowed. We lost 1–0, a result completely gifted to Washington by the center ref, who appeared in awe of Abby. I thought she might ask Abby to autograph the red card she pulled out of her pocket to show one of our players. I couldn't stand it. The league was a joke. The officiating, rather than getting better, seemed to be getting worse.

THAT NIGHT I vented on Twitter, willing to accept the standard $250 fine for criticizing officials:

> It's official, the refs are straight bad. Its clear the league wanted DC in playoffs. I have truly never seen anything like this. It's sad. . . .

> We play with 10, DC with 12 . . . I am done playing in a league where the game is no longer in control of the players.

> Multiple choice question. Why did the refs call back our goal? Is it A) Free kick taken before the whistle B) Indirect not direct C) Offsides D) Foul

> Those are all the reasons we heard so I think E is the only one that makes sense.

> E) We just want Washington to win regardless.

Twitter gave me the ability to talk directly to fans. The WPS, which had encouraged players to tweet, didn't love Twitter so much anymore.

League officials slapped me with a one-game suspension, eight hours of community service, and a $2,500 fine. When Tony DiCicco had ripped the officiating a year earlier, he was fined $200. When high-profile players like Kate Markgraf and Pearcie said things about the refs, they were barely disciplined. The league was acting out of desperation. It was clearly falling apart: its commissioner had just been forced out, and several teams were on the brink of shutting down. But don't say anything's wrong! Just smile and keep on playing!

The season was over. I didn't know if there would be another one. But I had bigger concerns than whether the WPS was going to survive. My entire career was at risk.

V.

My right shoulder had been throbbing and aching for years, the result of more than a decade of abuse—hard landings on dives, bone-rattling contact with players and the turf. I was the Queen of Advil, but I refused to give in to the pain. After Portugal in 2009, I had an MRI because doctors suspected I had a torn ligament in my elbow. Turned out I did have an injured elbow, but the doctor was most concerned about my shoulder: he said it was disintegrating, that there was nothing holding it together.

"My shoulder is the least of my worries," I told him. "I've been living with that pain for years."

They told me surgery to repair my elbow would require twelve-months of recovery, so I decided not to have that operation because I wouldn't be ready for the World Cup. So I just plodded ahead. My shoulder got worse and worse as the year progressed, until it was screaming at me with every dive and every block.

Listen to me! My shoulder screamed. *I'm your livelihood. You had better take care of me.*

My closest teammates, Aya and Tina, were concerned. They saw how much pain I was in every day. They kept encouraging me to take care of it. One day, toward the end of that second WPS season, I gasped in pain and walked off the practice field. I couldn't take it anymore. I went home to Seattle and started to gather medical opinions. If I had listened to my body instead of trying to tough it out, I would have had surgery right after the 2008 Olympics. But now I faced a decision: surgery on my shoulder and elbow would mean that I would miss the 2011 World Cup. Surgery on just my shoulder still put me at risk of missing the World Cup. No surgery meant there was a chance that my shoulder would blow at any minute.

And the World Cup was just ten months away.

I talked to Pia. What would my status be if I had the surgery? I knew better than to assume that any starting position was written in stone. She assured me that when I was medically cleared, I'd return as the starter.

One night, I called Paul four different times, bouncing around like a moth trapped in a lamp. I was going to get the surgery and bust through my rehab. No I wasn't, I would just suffer through the pain. Yes, I don't think I can keep going without surgery. No—what if I don't come back? I didn't know what to do.

On September 21, I was on a conference call with the WPS. My appeal was denied. The ridiculous league was upholding my punishment. I listened from Birmingham, Alabama, where I was meeting with Dr. James Andrews, the world-renowned orthopedic surgeon.

First, he did a physical strength test. "You're fine, kiddo," he said.

I was surprised. Then he went to his computer and looked at the images. My muscles around my shoulder were so strong that Dr. Andrews was fooled into thinking the shoulder was functional. In truth, the muscles were the only things holding the joint together. "Can you be here at six a.m. tomorrow?" Dr. Andrews asked.

The decision was made for me. I was having surgery.

CHAPTER NINETEEN

Seattle's Finest

When I could finally open my eyes, I tried to take inventory. I was alone—in a hospital bed, my right shoulder bandaged and immobile, my head hazy from a potent dose of painkillers.

Dr. Andrews came in to see me. "The surgery took a very long time," he said. "It was extremely complicated." He had expected a ninety-minute operation; it took three and a half hours. It took so long that the anesthesia started to wear off in the middle of the operation and I needed another dose. Dr. Andrews told me he'd found extensive damage: a 360-degree tear of my labrum—the cuff of cartilage around the shoulder—the same injury that had almost ended the career of New Orleans Saints quarterback Drew Brees. My biceps tendon was detached from my shoulder, and the capsule—the ligaments that keep the joint in place—was severely torn. The articular cartilage on the bone was shot. Bone chunks were floating around.

Dr. Andrews repaired the labrum and used thirteen anchors—eleven took hold—to secure the shoulder. He micro-fractured the bone around the labrum in hopes of regenerating cartilage. He pulled up my biceps tendon from where it had curled down my arm and reattached it with another anchor.

I tried to absorb everything he was telling me through my drug-induced haze, but only one thing registered: my shoulder had been wrecked. And my return to soccer was in jeopardy.

Not long after Dr. Andrews left, the pain in my shoulder erupted, a sickening all-consuming kind of hurt. I needed more painkillers, but the IV pumping drugs directly into me wasn't working. The nurses finally got it fixed, and it flooded my body with pain medication and relief, but I had a terrible allergic reaction to the drugs, and itched all night. The nurses dosed me with Benadryl to help with that, and finally, at around seven a.m.—more than twenty-four hours after my surgery—I started to drift asleep.

"Hello?"

I snapped awake. Two young men were in my room ready to take me down to rehab.

"Already?"

Yes, already. I was trying to condense a twelve-to-eighteen month rehab into six months. I had to get back for the World Cup. I had to start rehab immediately.

I was miserable, but there was nothing I could do. These two strangers helped me get dressed—there was no time for modesty. I felt like hiding so I asked them to put my sunglasses on my face. They did, then put me in a wheelchair and wheeled me down to the rehab clinic—every bump and turn on the journey causing me to grimace in pain. I imagine I made a pretty picture: all drugged up with stringy hair and sunglasses in the Andrews "locker room," the place where some of the most famous athletes in U.S. sports history had worked through pain and injury: Michael Jordan, Drew Brees, Brett Favre. I tried to go to the bathroom by myself but couldn't manage to even pull my hair back. I was still throwing up, and the therapists had to send the receptionist to help me get on and off the toilet. My humiliation was complete.

That first morning, the therapist took my arm out of the sling and had me straighten my arm. That's all I had to do. I thought I was going to die. A Tampa Bay Rays pitcher who'd had shoulder surgery four months earlier was in the clinic working out; he looked at me with deep sympathy. "I don't miss those days," he said.

I never took off my sunglasses. I didn't want anyone to see the tears in my eyes.

II.

I stayed in Alabama for several weeks, miserable and in incredible pain. I felt helpless, having to ask for assistance to eat, to get dressed, to wash my hair. Jesse stayed with me in Birmingham, taking care of me, for which I was grateful. Through e-mail, my goalkeeper coach, Paul, monitored every step of my recovery. He asked me to send him a record of every exercise I did in therapy, even if it was just five curls with the elastic armband. He wanted to be kept abreast of the entire process, step by step, so that—true to his nature—he could make an intricately detailed, focused plan for when I returned to the team.

After a couple of weeks I left Alabama; I went to Atlanta to pack up my belongings. The national team was training there, getting ready to head to Mexico for World Cup qualifying, but I couldn't have inspired much confidence—I was a drugged-up mess.

I headed back to Seattle, where my mom stayed with me. She saw to my every need and ignored my nastiness—the drugs made me feel terrible, and my sense of helplessness was frustrating. I wasn't pleasant to be around, but my mom stayed, driving me an hour each way to my physical therapy in Gig Harbor.

I tracked the qualifying games online. The first three games were lopsided victories over Haiti, Guatemala, and Costa Rica. But on November 5, our team lost to Mexico 2–1. It was our first-ever loss to Mexico, and it put our backs against the wall: we had to beat Costa Rica in a third-place match in Cancún and then play a home-and-home with Italy for the right to play in the World Cup.

One more loss and we probably wouldn't be going to Germany. I was in shock, and I started to beat myself up, second-guessing my decision to have surgery. The team was tired from a grueling WPS schedule that didn't provide time off before qualifying. We hadn't been playing together, and part of our struggle was the new possession-oriented system that Pia had put in. And, of course I thought I could have made a difference. The team's struggles only added to my misery. I could barely move my arm two inches to the side. I couldn't raise it at all. It was hard to imagine playing in the World Cup in just a few months. That is, if our team made it to the World Cup.

On November 20, I woke up early to track the game in Italy. It was agonizing, almost as bad as the rehab session that awaited me later in the day. Our team couldn't score, and the game went into extra time. Finally in the ninety-fourth minute, our youngest team member, Alex Morgan—who had just finished her senior year at Cal—pushed a shot past the diving Italian goalkeeper for the 1–0 victory. We still had life. But it was torture, watching from afar, unable to do anything to help. I decided to meet my team in Illinois for the final do-or-die game against Italy. Everyone was a little shocked to see the shape I was in. I had lost weight, and my arm had completely atrophied from lack of exercise.

"You need to gain some muscle," Pia said.

"I'm trying," I said.

The game was tense. Italy dominated much of the run of play, but Amy Rodriguez's goal late in the first half stood up. Barnie played great, and we won 1–0. We were going to Germany next summer. But who would be the starting goalkeeper?

II.

Snap. Crackle. Pop. Moan.

My shoulder sounded like a bowl of cereal, as my therapists Bruce Shell and Dave Andrews helped me stretch through my pain to break up the scar tissue. They pushed me all winter. When I was in Los Angeles, the head trainer for the men's team, Ivan Pierra, was in charge of my rehab. I suffered, but I fought my ass off. "This is among the most serious shoulder injuries that I've ever seen, and I've been working in sports for twenty-eight years," Bruce told ESPN. "And I can't imagine too many worse injuries, from a traumatic standpoint."

Sometimes our sessions lasted six hours. Pain and suffering was my full-time job. I was taking painkillers every night to sleep. I was pushing myself as hard as I could. The team went to China in January, but I wasn't ready to travel with them—again I watched online. The results were mixed: we lost in our first game to Sweden. Though we won two other games, we didn't dominate in any of them.

In March, I was medically cleared to join the team, so I joined them in camp for the Algarve Cup. I could sense tension—a vibe that seemed very familiar. The World Cup was just three months away and Pia, like Greg four years earlier, seemed to be starting to stress out. She hadn't faced much pressure until now. When she took over before the '08 Olympics, she had inherited a damaged, dysfunctional team: getting to the gold medal game eight months later was a bonus. But she'd guided the top-ranked team in the world for three years now. The players were the ones she had chosen. The team was struggling, and it didn't help that her starting goalkeeper could barely move.

I was mentally ready to get back to work, but I was weak physically. I started simply, working on my footwork. Everything—things that had once been so easy for me—was difficult. I got frustrated and I started to lose confidence. I had been so impatient in rehab, where that mind-set worked for me, but on the field I had to learn to be patient. Paul wouldn't let me face a shot until we got to Portugal. There, he tossed balls to me. I was scared to react, so fearful of the pain. Every time I touched the ball, I was in agony. The first time I dove I thought my shoulder anchors would rip loose. *If I can't do this*, I thought, grimacing from a soft-tossed ball, *how the hell am I going to stop Abby's shots?*

I looked in Paul's eyes to see if I could spot doubt, but I didn't.

He never questioned me. Instead, he guided me in baby steps. Four shots to each side of my body one day, five shots the next. A little bit more confidence every day. He was protective and patient—creating drills in conjunction with my therapists that would increase both my range of motion and my healing. "You're going to have pain," Paul said, "so you're going to have to learn to manage it."

PAUL'S APPROACH WAS perfect. He pushed me just hard enough so that I was progressing without risking re-injury. He never panicked about my pain or my grimaces. He kept my confidence up and also kept Barnie sharp. He got me to the point where I felt so good that I was eager for more action, but he still wouldn't let me practice with the team. He didn't want to do anything that would be a setback—mentally or physically. He wanted to keep moving forward.

III.

"You're not starting." Paul looked at me as he delivered the news.

We were in London to play a friendly against England. At long last, I was medically cleared to play. We were six months past my surgery, eleven weeks away from the World Cup opener. I needed to start—I was running out of time. I'd been working toward game day, April 2—my dad's birthday—for months as my target goal. Pia had already announced her starting lineup at practice and I was in it. I was excited. Now Paul said I wasn't starting.

"We only have four games left before the World Cup," I said. "I need time to prepare."

"You'll get the second half," Paul said. When I protested, he asked, "Do you think you beat out Barnie?"

"Hell no, I haven't beat out Barnie," I said. "She's playing the best I've ever seen her. But you've said you want me to be your starting goalkeeper for the World Cup and I need to get games.

I need to make mistakes now so that I don't make them closer to the World Cup. Now you're only giving me three-and-a-half games to get ready for our most important tournament."

But Paul didn't think I was ready. It was the biggest argument he and I had ever had. I knew he didn't want to wreck my confidence, but I needed as many minutes as possible after sitting out for six months. I had been following a plan we had laid out back in September, and now the plan was changing. I felt I had done my part, and I trusted my coaches to uphold their end.

Paul told me to clean myself up and go meet with Pia. She took one look at my face and knew I was upset. "What are you feeling?" she said.

I told her that I needed every minute I could get and that she was taking a crucial forty-five minutes away from me.

"You don't think you can be ready in three-and-a-half games? You need these forty-five minutes to be ready for the World Cup?"

I could hear the doubt in her voice. Pia was losing faith in me.

"Pia, I'll be ready for the World Cup if you only give me two games. I'll do whatever it takes. But you know as well as I do that every minute counts."

"Get yourself ready to play in the second half then," she said, dismissing me.

She doubted me. And when people doubt me, I became more determined. *I'm going to prove to her that I'm ready*, I thought.

Paul and I were fine, despite our argument. He liked that I had voiced my opinion and often told me so: he said it was better than trying to guess what someone was thinking. I later apologized to him for saying I had lost trust in him: I never had. Not for a moment.

I entered the game in the second half, my first live action since my last game of the WPS season. We were down 2–1 when I came in. We hadn't played very well in the first half and Barnie had seen a ton of action. I didn't see much action at all, which was irritating. I needed to make some tough decisions, get challenged. Still, it felt great to get back on the field. Paul was pleased—nothing had happened to damage the most important part of my game, my confidence. But our team lost the game, our first loss ever to England and our first loss in a friendly since the team lost to Denmark during the 2004 Olympic victory tour, back in another era.

What—the media started to wonder—was wrong with the U.S. national team?

IV.

Pia snapped at me. "Shut the fuck up, Hope."

I was stunned. Pia, Paul, and I were having a meeting about the medical staff—I didn't feel that I was getting proper care for my shoulder, and I was lobbying for my therapists, Bruce and Dave, to be added to the staff. They had come to Portugal, and everyone on the team had raved about them. I was completely indebted to them and to Ivan, the men's team trainer. They had all worked as a team to get me ready for the World Cup, and it looked as though all our combined hard work was paying off. I was almost there. But without my team of therapists in camp, my progress had stalled. I had a list of issues about the team's training staff. We had people who could tape ankles and hand out Advil but they weren't qualified to guide an athlete back from major surgery in a compressed schedule. I was getting frustrated and running out of time.

"You have captains for a reason," Pia barked at me.

That pissed me off. Abby regularly expressed her opinion, and she wasn't a captain. Boxxy expressed her opinion, and she wasn't a captain. Pearcie—who *was* our captain—often asked for my opinion about the training staff, because she knew how closely I worked with them and how critical the staff was to our entire team's well-being. I told Pia that, but she didn't want to hear it. Six weeks before the World Cup and I was having a conflict with my coach. Was the shitstorm coming my way again?

The next morning, on my way down to breakfast, I was in the elevator when Pia stepped in. I didn't say anything, just looked down at my newspaper.

"How you doing?" she said.

"Fine, Pia," I said. "How are you?"

"I'm good."

And we were fine from then on out.

V.

The WPS was still going. Sort of. I had signed with a team called the MagicJack. The Washington Freedom franchise had been purchased by Dan Borislow, the inventor of the MagicJack phone technology, and he moved the team to his hometown of Boca Raton, renamed it for his company, and signed a bunch of national-team players.

The league officials and most of the fans hated him. What little tradition there was in the WPS included the Freedom, Mia Hamm's original team, which had been owned by John Hendricks, the Discovery Channel founder who had originally bankrolled the WUSA. But even Hendricks wanted out of the WPS, and in December 2010, Dan bought the team. WPS thought he was going to be their savior, but Dan did things his way.

The league hated the fact that Dan was using the team to promote his company and that he wouldn't abide by league rules. He didn't have a team website or media director. He didn't put up the sponsors' advertising and didn't share game film with the rest of the league. But I think the biggest reason the league hated him was because it needed him so desperately, and he knew it. Investors were dropping out, teams were folding, and the league was now down to just five teams. It was a slow death march.

But I liked Dan. Sure, he disrespected people and did some crazy things, but he called bullshit on just about everything the league did. He was a rich guy who bought the team because he liked soccer, had a daughter who played, and he was looking for unique ways to promote his business. He was innovative and different—our version of Dallas Mavericks owner Mark Cuban. And it wasn't as though the league had been successful and highly professional before he arrived.

I made my first start for the MagicJack on May 1. I'd told them I was ready in late April, but I wasn't—that way, that idiotic one-game suspension for my Twitter comments about the officiating was served while I was still rehabbing. I was happy to be playing in the WPS this time; it was good to get some more games under my belt, considering how few opportunities were left to play for the national team. A bunch of my national-team teammates, including Abby and Pearcie, were playing for the MagicJack.

But the experience was bizarre. The MagicJack coach quit after the team won its first three games, so our team was coached by Pearcie and Dan. It was strange but really not all that much of a departure from the screwball behavior that had marked the league's entire existence. And I was too focused on my shoulder and the World Cup to worry about anything that happened in the WPS. I was trying to prioritize everything in my life. I broke up with Jesse that spring. He wanted a commitment that I had never been able to give him. When I was back in Seattle rehabilitating, I was—of course—spending time with Adrian; we couldn't stay away from each other. I knew I wasn't being fair to Jesse but even though I was twenty-nine now, I was scared of settling down. My inability to commit made me wonder yet again if I was like my father—unable to have a grown-up, functioning relationship.

On May 14, I finally got my first national-team start in Columbus against Japan. Mentally I was ready, but my arm felt terrible. At least I was tested—I had a good tip-over save and some tough balls on set pieces. We beat Japan 2–0 that day and by the same score four days later in North Carolina.

VI.

As we counted down the days to the World Cup, I got a call from my dad's old friend Mark Sakura. "Hope, did you know the murder of Mike Emert has been solved?" he said. "Did you know your father was no longer a suspect?"

And then he proceeded to tell me a story straight out of CSI. In the fall of 2010, Mike Emert's widow, Mary Beth, was told there was a DNA match—they had found her husband's killer. But the killer was now dead. A retired Seattle cop named Gary Krueger had been involved in a home invasion in March, 2010. Krueger tried to force his way into the upscale home of an orthopedic surgeon; when the police were called, Krueger fled, stole a boat in Lake Washington, and capsized it. His body wasn't pulled out of the lake until September. At that time, his DNA was put into a database and came up as a solid match for DNA found at the Emert crime scene: skin under Emert's fingernails and blood in his stolen SUV.

I was stunned. We had never even been told there was any DNA at the scene that could have cleared my father. But that wasn't the end of the story. Krueger had been a rogue cop in the late 1970s. After he retired in 1980, he turned to criminal schemes and was a suspect in a couple of murders, including Emert's. Krueger was finally convicted for a series of bank robberies and went to prison, where his DNA should have been collected and entered into the database. But it wasn't collected until he was released on parole in 2007, and then it was never entered into the database. There was no explanation about the cause of the three-and-a-half-year delay. Marcus had made some phone calls. One of his sources in the police department told him that it was clear that my father had been framed. Krueger had intentionally dressed like him, adopted a New York accent and a limp, and arranged to meet Emert at a place where my dad hung out.

In addition, there was another cop, John Powers, who had been fired several years earlier for a number of offenses, including improperly using a department computer to get information on individuals and sharing his findings with people outside of the department. One of the individuals he gathered information on was my dad. Powers ran my father's criminal history, printed it out, and gave it to a pawnshop owner named Rob Chandler, who was Mike Emert's brother-in-law. That was how so many people involved in the case knew so many private things about my father—a fact that had always confused him. Despite our best efforts, we couldn't unravel the connections between Krueger and Powers—the rogue cops had worked for Seattle PD in different eras. But it was apparent that my father had somehow been the victim of corruption, and it seemed to me that the department was eager to sweep the connections under the rug because the crooked police officers were two of their own.

THE MORE WE learned, the angrier I became. My dad was officially cleared now that the murder was solved, but that should have happened years earlier, while he was alive. My father died with that accusation still haunting him. He had been the victim of the Seattle police. I guess he'd been right to never trust authorities to do the right thing. No one from the police department ever called to apologize or explain why they had harassed the wrong man for almost seven years.

One of the last times I saw my dad—when we painted my little cabin in the woods.

Marcus, Mom, and me outside Yankee Stadium on our pilgrimage to honor my dad. My dad's ashes are contained in Marcus's bracelet, and I am holding his cross.

The first thing I did after we won the gold medal
was call Marcus back home in Washington.

During the World Cup, my name launched almost as many marriage proposals as bad puns. (*Sideline Sports Photography, LLC - 2012*)

Grandma Alice and Grandpa Pete were my rocks: they traveled the world to cheer me on.

Making a save against Brazil in the 2011 World Cup—the game felt epic from the start. (*Sideline Sports Photography, LLC - 2012*)

The first person I found to celebrate the Brazil victory with was Abby— our problems from four years earlier were a distant memory. (*Marcio Jose Sanchez/Associated Press*)

I wouldn't have been able to make it through the World Cup without my medical staff; here I'm celebrating with Bruce Snell. (*Scott Heavey/Getty Images*)

During the penalty shootout against Brazil, I could see my UW coaches Amy Griffin (*right*) and Lesle Gallimore (*left*) mouthing words of encouragement. They had supported me since high school, and now I was having a private moment with them in front of millions of people worldwide.

Adrian and I could never stay apart for long.

We share the same sense of adventure and fun—
here we are on vacation in Thailand.

Back home in Washington with my dog, Leo, and my nephew, Johnny, who was named for my dad.

I was out of my comfort zone on *Dancing with the Stars*— my contentious relationship with my partner, Maksim Chmerkovskiy, didn't help. (*Disney/ABC Television Group/ Getty*)

I'm not afraid of taking risks. (*Luis Sanchis*)

CHAPTER TWENTY

It Just Takes One

The granite Alps sliced the cobalt sky behind us, a stark symbol of the heights our team was trying to reach. We were on a practice field near our hotel in Leogang, Austria. For ten days, we stayed at a high-end spa, getting acclimated to the time change and focusing on the weeks ahead. We hiked and practiced yoga and took gondola rides to the snowy tops of the mountains. Pia played guitar in meetings and seemed more relaxed now that we were isolated. We felt strong. We played a closed-door game against Norway and lost, but I wasn't bothered by that—I thought it was probably a good thing to get some mistakes out of the way.

I tried not to think about the 2007 World Cup. That experience taught me how unpredictable life is. The lesson was to enjoy every moment and opportunity. I vowed to lock in every memory so that I could have it for the rest of my life—the way my father had taught me. I also reflected on how far the team had come in four years, how much we enjoyed each other's company, and how well we functioned as a unit. There wasn't the segregation between young players and veterans or the cliques that had existed in 2007. No one expected us all to be best friends. It wasn't perceived as an affront to team camaraderie if I took my book and went off to read, or if I shut the door to my room. If a young player raised her hand

and asked a question, no one viewed it as an impertinent challenge to authority. No one was worried about the small stuff: we were all focused on the task at hand.

One day Carli and I talked about 2007. Her theory was that if Greg hadn't fucked up and I hadn't spoken out, nothing might have changed on the team. The bad dynamic might have continued. Out of all that struggle and pain, Carli said, we ended up having a better team. "You helped change that," Carli said.

I didn't know if I had changed it, but things were clearly different now. Nothing underscored that transformation more dramatically than my relationship with Abby. We not only tolerated each other now; we liked each other. Abby had reached out to me with her letter during the Olympics, and that started the healing process. She seemed humbled by her injury and by missing the Olympics. Abby and I were often together on photo shoots or at Nike events, away from the rest of team. We would hang out and have cocktails in the airport bar while we traveled. When we were in a foreign hotel, Abby and I were always first at breakfast, sitting together and reading the paper while drinking four or five cups of coffee. We quietly built our relationship with every camp and every game.

"You know, Hope, we're really pretty much alike," Abby once said.

"We are," I agreed, then laughed, "but we're also pretty different."

We were both crazily competitive and honest. We both demanded excellence and professionalism and would do anything to win. We both liked to party. And I knew I could rely on her. We needed each other. We didn't have to be best friends to be great teammates, and if we were going to win the World Cup, we both had to excel.

II.

After ten days, we left our beautiful alpine spa and boarded a charter flight for Dresden, the site of our first game, against North Korea.

At the airport, we saw the World Cup banners and the mood immediately changed. This was it.

The atmosphere in Germany was exhilarating. A few hours before the game on June 28, I got—as I had for all my other games—a huge shot of Toradol in my ass. I knew what was going to happen next. My arm was going to feel like Gumby—bendable with more range of motion. And after the game, I was going to be in agony from moving my shoulder in ways I shouldn't have been able to. My shoulder was now my source of inspiration. Athletes have to keep finding new forms of motivation. In 2007, I was motivated to play for my father's memory. In 2008, I was playing not only for myself, with a kind of "fuck you" attitude to the world, but also for my mom and Marcus, Grandma and Grandpa, Adrian and Glenn, Lesle and Amy, aunts and uncles—my lifelong team. In 2011 my motivation was the constant pain in my shoulder. I wanted to prove the doubters wrong, to show that I could come back from a devastating injury. And I wanted to earn the right to be called the best goalkeeper in the world.

I reminded myself to lock in every memory. I tried to soak in every moment—standing apart from my team during warm-ups to look at the faces in the crowd, to study my opponents, the vibrant colors in the stadium. Not every athlete gets to experience such a grand event.

Once again—as we had in the previous World Cup—we opened with North Korea. Though the game lacked the dramatics of 2007, it was far from easy. I had to make two difficult saves in a ten-minute span in the first half. There was no score at halftime, but early in the second half, Lauren Cheney headed in a perfect service from Abby. Twenty minutes later, Rachel Buehler gathered up a deflection on a corner and scored. We won 2–0.

WE FLEW TO Frankfurt and then took a bus to Heidelberg, where we practiced in front of a group of American military personnel and their families. I felt so proud to be wearing a USA jersey in that environment. It was thrilling to get that kind of hometown support in a foreign country.

The sold-out crowd at Rhein-Neckar Arena two days later was full of American flags and red-white-and-blue painted fans. We dominated the Colombian team. Heather O'Reilly scored in the first half, and we all ran to one sideline and saluted the fans. (It was the first time I had ever celebrated a goal on the field and I was honored to recognize the service men and women who were in attendance.) In the second half, Megan Rapinoe and Carli added goals. When Megan scored, she ran to the oversize microphone in the corner of the field, picked it up and sang "Born in the USA," as a tribute to all the Americans in the crowd. We were having fun. The 3–0 final assured us of a spot in the quarterfinals, even though we had one more game of group play—against our toughest opponent, Sweden.

The tournament was getting rave reviews. The stadiums were packed, the crowds were electric, and many of the games were thrillingly close. The competition was far more evenly matched than it had ever been before. It was stunning how much women's soccer had progressed around the globe. I could see it starting to happen when I had been playing overseas. Now, teams that had never made an impact before, like France and Japan, were serious threats.

We flew to Wolfsburg, where it was raining. I could tell that Pia, though happy we had advanced, really wanted to beat Sweden, the team she had starred for as a player. But we had bad luck, and Sweden played smart and physical. In the first half, Amy LePeilbet took down my old buddy Lotta Schelin in the penalty box and was given a yellow card. I read the penalty kick correctly and was fully extended, but the ball slipped just past my fingertips. Twenty minutes later, a free kick ricocheted past me into the goal. We were down 2–0.

We had our chances but didn't score until Abby got us on the board in the second half. The 2–1 loss was our first ever in group play and meant we finished second in the group.

I wasn't stressed about that. We had lost in group play in the Olympics to Norway and won the gold medal. We had advanced.

That was all I cared about. But we were taking a difficult path. Our quarterfinal opponent was Brazil.

III.

The match felt epic from the start. The stadium was sold out and the air crackled with the kind of electricity that only comes in big sporting events. The German crowd—disappointed that their team had been stunned the day before by Japan—was rooting for Brazil. Brazil almost always had the crowd on their side: their fans are fun, their soccer is pretty, and Marta was the most famous female soccer player in the world.

A lot was made of the fact that we were playing on the twelfth anniversary of the 1999 World Cup final. Many of the '99ers were in Germany working for ESPN: Brandi, Bri, Mia, and Julie, as well as Tony DiCicco. Those comparisons continued, as did some of the animosity. I heard from friends at home that Bri had criticized me on air for being a bad teammate after the North Korea game. I was so weary of the shadow. What was left unsaid was how much the game had improved in twelve years and how much more skilled our team was. It's simply the evolution of sport.

Lesle and her son Zac, Amy and her husband and their two boys, had all been in Germany for the entire tournament. The rest of my support group arrived in time for the Brazil match: my mom, Marcus and Debbie and little Johnny, my sister Terry, Aunt Susie and her sons and Uncle Frank. Adrian was there too—I wouldn't have to call him in the middle of the night from this tournament. As the national anthem played, I spotted my loved ones in the stands. Unfortunately, my grandma and grandpa weren't there; Grandpa Pete had been diagnosed with dementia, and his health was declining. Grandma Alice didn't want to leave him.

We got on the board almost instantly. Brazilian defender Daiane scored an own goal trying to clear a ball Boxxy had sent in. It was the opposite of what had happened to us in 2007. It was a nice start, but we knew we were in for a long day. We clung to the 1–0 lead at halftime.

In the sixty-fifth minute, Marta came streaking toward me with Rachel Buehler chasing. Rachel made a slide tackle, taking Marta down in the penalty box—a player like Marta is always going to get that call. Rachel was shown a red card and, completely distraught, left the field. Once again we were going to be playing shorthanded against Brazil. Even worse, Cristiane was lining up against me to take the penalty kick. As I made my way into the goal, I was swinging my arms to loosen up my shoulder. The referee—Jacqui Melksham from Australia—pointed at me to get on my line. I jumped up and down, raising my arms a few times, just to let Cristiane know I was there, and then I was set.

Cristiane shot to her right. I read correctly, diving to my left and batting the ball away. I was so fired up—saving a penalty kick takes both luck and skill and can be a huge momentum shifter. I jumped to my feet clapping, and Carli and Boxxy ran up to hug me. But then mass confusion broke out—Melksham had waved off the save, and was awarding Brazil a do-over. She told me I had moved off my line—I was sure I hadn't, I never believed in moving off the line because I didn't feel it gave me any advantage on the save. Melksham showed me a yellow card as I raised my hands in protest. "Are you fucking kidding me?" I shouted, trying to keep my mounting anger in check. That call is still a total mystery to me. On the field, Melksham told me I had moved. But afterward she changed her call to encroachment on Pearcie—she said our captain had moved a step forward before the ball was kicked. It was a ticky-tack call in a critical game. The crowd started to turn right then, booing the referee and booing Brazil for getting an unfair advantage. As boos and whistles rained down on her, Marta stepped up to retake the shot Cristiane had missed. Of course, she made it this time. The game was tied 1–1 and we were shorthanded. Our team gathered to talk about setting the defense without Rachel. Boxxy was going to move back, taking on more defensive responsibilities. I was still in shock over the bad call. As I went back to my line, I raised my hand again in disbelief. The crowd took it as a cue and began to chant "USA! USA!" Brazil had tied the score but lost the home field advantage.

Regulation ended in a tie: we would play two fifteen-minute overtime periods, shorthanded.

Two minutes into overtime, Marta got her left foot on a cross that I thought had come from a player who was offside. Boxxy raised her hand to signal offside but no call was made. Marta lofted the ball toward the far post and into the net. Brazil was ahead 2–1 and had a man advantage. I didn't lose hope, but as the minutes passed and our shots flew wide or high, things were looking grim. I started to worry. As the seconds ticked down, Brazil was stalling, which further incited the crowd. Erika faked an injury and was carried off on a stretcher and then—as soon as she was off the field—she jumped up, suddenly fine. She was given a yellow card for stalling, and two minutes of extra time was added on. The crowd was angry at Brazil's tactics and applauding our gutsy effort. It felt like *Rocky IV*, when everyone came to the fight hostile to the United States but ended up cheering for Rocky by the end. But a happy ending today seemed less and less likely. We were in the 122nd minute of the game. At my end of the field, Pearcie passed the ball to Ali Krieger. Krieger passed to Carli in the defensive end, who then beat two players and passed wide to Megan Rapinoe. She brought the ball down toward Brazil's goal and sent a hopeful thirty-yard cross off her left foot, perfectly placed toward the net. Abby launched herself toward the ball, hit it squarely with her forehead and sent it screaming into the back of the net.

We all went crazy. Abby ran toward the sideline and then slid on her knees; she was instantly dog-piled by our teammates. The fans exploded in a roar of amazement, and I was jumping up and down and wheeling my arms around, alone on my side of the field. I looked into the stands and spotted Adrian beaming with pride.

The whistle blew. We were going to penalty kicks.

IV.

My team was amped up at midfield, full of energy and adrenaline and pulsing with confidence. I walked away from them to compose myself; I didn't need amping up. I needed to be calm and clear-minded, fully focused. I walked over to the corner flag on the side of the field where my loved ones were sitting. They were so close I could almost reach out and touch them. I sat on the grass and took deep breaths and looked up at Marcus. I could see how nervous he was—he looked as though he might faint. My mom and Adrian gave me nods of assurance—I could see the love and confidence in their eyes. I looked at Amy and Lesle in the front row, my soccer believers.

"It just takes one," Amy said. I could see her mouth the words and hold up one finger. I was having my own private moment with the people who meant the most to me, in the midst of a global audience of millions.

"It just takes one," Amy said again.

"OK," I thought to myself. "I've got this."

We had practiced penalty kicks the day before. I had a good feeling.

Boxxy went first for us. Andréia, Brazil's goalkeeper, came so far off her line to block the shot that even Melksham couldn't screw up the call. Boxxy retook the kick, went the same way—to her right—and made it easily.

U.S. 1, Brazil 0.

I stood up and windmilled my arms as I walked to the line. Cristiane was waiting. I didn't get a good read on the ball—she went to her left and made the shot. U.S. 1, Brazil 1.

Carli was up next. She hammered the ball into the left-side netting past a diving Andréia. U.S. 2, Brazil 1.

Marta walked up next as the crowd booed and whistled. The greatest player in the world had turned into the villain. I've always liked Marta—she's a little dirty, but she plays with so much passion and soul. I was a bit surprised to see her shooting second: Brazil was using their best two shooters in the first two spots, putting pressure on the players who would shoot after them. I guessed left, she went to my right.

U.S. 2, Brazil 2.

Abby was next. She never even looked at Andréia. She kept her head down and put the ball in the right corner of the net. U.S. 3, Brazil 2.

Daiane walked up. I watched her line up to shoot. I felt confident.

I got a good read on the ball. I extended completely to my right and extended my hand, pushing the ball safely away. I was already celebrating as I landed; I rolled over and jumped up, my arms extended in the air in triumph. *It just takes one*. And I had one. U.S. 3, Brazil 2.

Rapinoe was next. She shot under a diving Andréia. I liked seeing the calm confidence from our players, many of whom had never been on such a big stage. U.S. 4, Brazil 2.

Franciela was up. She put a shot past my right hand. U.S. 4, Brazil 3.

One more converted kick and we would win, completing the amazing comeback. I went back to my corner to watch.

Ali Krieger stepped up. She kept her head down and didn't look at Andréia, who stood on the line like the Cristo statue in Rio, arms outstretched. Andréia jumped off her line well before Ali shot, but it didn't matter. Ali tapped her shot into the left corner of the net. U.S. 5, Brazil 3.

Ali sprinted toward our bench, where the reserve players and coaches were flooding onto the field, leaping with joy. The players on the field all ran to envelop Ali.

All but one. Abby veered to her right, sprinting straight toward me. I ran to her and leaped into her arms screaming with joy, and we fell to the ground. Together.

CHAPTER TWENTY-ONE

The Silver Lining

Forty-seven thousand fans in Yankee Stadium roared at the big screen as we went to penalty kicks against Brazil. Flights in Denver were delayed until the game ended. Everyone back home, it seemed, had stopped whatever they were doing to watch our game as Sunday morning stretched into Sunday afternoon. Even if they didn't start out watching it, as the game progressed, someone called or tweeted or posted on Facebook about this amazing soccer game, and more and more people tuned in to see what it was all about. And they were captivated.

"I *love* these women!" tweeted Tom Hanks.

LeBron James offered, "Congrats, ladies!"

"Amazing game," Aaron Rodgers tweeted. "Now let's get the cup, ladies!"

I was named the player of the match. That night Abby and I took a car service to the ESPN set in downtown Dresden. "When did you score your goal?" I asked her in the back of the car, while I checked the messages and texts flooding my phone.

"I think in the 120th minute," Abby said.

No, Aaron Heifetz said, it was later than that. It was the latest goal ever scored in the World Cup. The 122nd minute. "Oh my God," we both said.

"I don't get how that just happened," Abby said of the match. "I just kept saying 'One chance.' That's all we need."

On the ESPN set, we finally had a chance to see the highlights, every crazy thing that happened in the game. We couldn't believe the roller coaster we had just been on. "Everything was against us," I told host Bob Ley. "This team has something special. We found a way to win."

It was inevitable that 2007 would come up. How, Ley asked, did we put the divisions behind us? Perhaps, he wondered, there were even tensions between the two of us? We both just smiled. "Pia came in and changed the dynamics of the team," I said. "And to be honest, we grew up. We threw our differences out the window and learned to respect one another off and on the field."

Abby said, "I'd rather have no other person in goal behind me; this woman saves sure goals. Hope's the best goalkeeper in the world. I'd rather have no one else behind me."

AFTER WE LEFT the set, we went to a late dinner with our family and friends, buzzing with excitement. We watched the replays—amazed at Rapinoe's laser-like cross finding Abby's head. We jeered the referee and her double penalty kick.

Late that night, Adrian and I wandered the cobblestone streets of Dresden in the rain. The city glistened. It was the perfect place to celebrate all that Adrian and I had gone through together, and what the team had accomplished. Adrian kept reminding me to enjoy the night—my instinct was to leap forward to the semifinal game, but Adrian wouldn't let me. He told me how much emotion there was in the stands—the fans praying, how he had prayed to his father, held his dad's necklace, asking him to "let Hope have her moment."

"That was one of the greatest sporting events in history," he said, intense and almost in tears. "Don't ever forget that."

The next morning, my teammates and I ate breakfast silently. We knew it was time to turn the page. We had to play France in the semifinal in just two days. But when I made eye contact with Megan Rapinoe, she started laughing and I said, "That was crazy, huh?"

It was crazy. Abby and I were on *Good Morning America* the next day. Some American journalists who hadn't been in Germany flew in to write stories about the most talked about sports team on the planet. Everyone was calling the Brazil game the greatest moment for women's soccer since the 1999 World Cup, and the overnight television ratings were the best since that epic tournament. The comparisons were inevitable, I guess—a thrilling game that ended in penalty kicks, capturing the attention of the country—and having so many of the '99ers in Germany working for ESPN made the connection easy. But we were all weary of the comparisons. "That's all we've ever heard about," I told reporters. "And we all know that they paved the way. But at some point in time you have to let go and build new stories and new names to the game. I think if there's any team to do it, it's this team. . . . We're not here to win because they did it twelve years ago. We're here to win for our country, for our team, for all the work we've put in. So all this stuff about '99—their journey was great—but that was twelve years ago." Though forces kept trying to pull us back, we finally stepped out of the shadow of the past.

II.

Our semifinal game against France was my hundredth cap: one hundred games for the national team since that first one in the spring of 2000, when I played against Iceland as an eighteen-year-old college freshman. Now I was two weeks away from my thirtieth birthday, my shoulder full of scar tissue and metal and pain. I was now a veteran.

Customarily, a player's hundredth cap is a big deal, something to be saluted with a ceremony, but I asked the staff not to even mention it: this game didn't need any personal tributes; it was a World Cup semifinal. We needed to focus completely on France, one of the surprise teams of the tournament. France was coming into the game on an extra day of rest—while we had played an extra hour against Brazil. Our legs were shot. We spent the little time we had in Mönchengladbach trying to rejuvenate our legs and study France, a team we hadn't played in five years.

The night before the game, my goalkeeper coach, Paul, told me he wanted me to go over film with him. To my surprise, after we sat down in front of the screen to watch video, all my teammates entered the room. Paul started the film: it was a compilation he had put together of almost every one of my hundred games. It was hilarious— different uniforms, my hair changing color as the years passed. My teammates applauded and laughed and gave me cards with their handwritten tributes. The compilation ended, of course, with the Brazil game. Everyone cheered. I was touched. It was a beautiful gift. It had taken me eleven long years to get to one hundred—only the second goalkeeper in history, along with Bri, to achieve that mark. It was worth the wait to earn the honor with this team. My team.

It occurred to me later how much had changed in four years. The night before the 2007 semifinal game, I had been exiled. In Germany, I celebrated.

III.

France was all over us on that rainy Wednesday night. We got an early goal on a cross from Lauren Cheney that Heather O'Reilly tapped in, but France was relentless, connecting passes and un-afraid to shoot. Our defense was constantly challenged; Becky Sauerbrunn was in as a replacement for Buehler, who couldn't play because of the red card.

France tied the game in the second half, when I came out for a cross that Sonia Bompastor looped in toward a runner; I was expect-ing a header, but the runner leaped over the ball, and it slipped into the right side of the net. France continued to dominate possession. Alex Morgan came in for Amy Rodriguez immediately after France tied the game, and was aggressive right away. She almost scored but was called offside on the play. Still France kept pushing forward; a berth in the World Cup final was twelve minutes away. And then Abby's forehead came to the rescue again. Lauren Cheney sent a corner to the far post and Abby rose up above everyone—I could see her elevate from my end of the field—and hammered the ball into the net.

Moments later, Alex, our rookie, scored her first World Cup goal, lifting the ball over the French goalkeeper who had slipped to the ground, to give us a 3–1 lead. A few minutes later, the victory was complete. We were in the World Cup final for the first time since 1999.

IV.

We drove by bus to Frankfurt, the site of the final. We tried to recover our legs and relax a little. We goofed around, playing soccer tennis. I did very little in training. The pain in my shoulder was getting worse and worse, and I went through hours of treatment between games. On the practice field, I couldn't dive. I did everything I could to save myself for the competition. And every night I had to take a heavy dose of painkillers to get to sleep. I was taking a series of shots to prepare for games, something that needed to be scheduled and planned: cortisone, Synvisc, Toradol. Every time the long needle plunged deep into my joint there was searing pain followed by brief relief.

We knew Japan well. We had played them three times in 2011. A lot was being made of our 22–0–3 record against them, but we had suffered our first losses to Mexico and to England in recent months, so we knew all streaks eventually end. Japan's history in the World Cup wasn't impressive: they had won only three games, and had escaped group play just once, in 1995. But they finished fourth in the Beijing Olympics after losing to us in the semifinals, and they had continued to improve. They were a speedy, high-energy, ball-possession team—Homare Sawa was a legend in Japan, and they had other smart, dangerous players, including my good friend Aya Miyama.

We also knew that they were playing at an emotional level that we couldn't comprehend. The wounds from the March 9.0 earthquake and devastating tsunami in Japan hadn't even begun to heal: the dead—upward of fifteen thousand—were still being counted, and thousands more were missing. After the disaster, I tried for days to reach Aya, who was from one of the areas that suffered heavy damage. The country had rallied behind their gutsy women's team, which—playing on the other side of the world—was showing a new tenacity. Japan had knocked off Germany, the host, and Sweden on its way to the finals. There was a lot of talk in the press about how much adversity our U.S. team had fought through on the way to the final, that we seemed to be a team of destiny. But there was another team in the final that had a much stronger claim to such stirring descriptions.

The night before the final, I received an e-mail from Aya, wishing me luck. Normally, I would never respond to a message from an opponent, but I knew these were moments we would never get back. It felt right to honor a person I respected so much, who competed so hard.

Aya,
Let's enjoy this moment no matter what happens.

Hope.

Later that night, my phone buzzed. I had a text from my brother David. He wished me luck. He said he missed me. "I will be a better brother," he wrote.

I hadn't seen David in almost two years. We talked on the phone once or twice a year. His text meant a lot to me—one more part of my support team falling in place. I could feel my dad's spirit inside of me. And now my oldest brother was texting me.

"And I will be a better sister," I texted back. "I love you."

V.

Inside the stadium, fifty thousand people greeted us, many of them holding signs and waving American flags. There were several *Star Wars*-inspired tributes to me—HANDS SOLO and THE FORCE IS WITH YOU, SOLO. Another sign read: MARRY ME HOPE, I'M SOLO. Eight fans held aloft giant letters spelling out my name. Some people wore replicas of my big white goalie gloves. Even President Barack Obama sent out a tweet to our team that morning: "Sorry I can't be there to see you play, but I'll be cheering you on from here. Let's go."

It felt like our day from the start. I had little to do early on and watched my teammates get chance after chance: Lauren Cheney, Rapinoe, Carli, Abby. But the shots went wide. They went high. Rapinoe hit the post. Abby hit the crossbar. We were dominating possession, but nothing was going in, and we were tied at halftime. Finally, in the sixty-ninth minute, Alex Morgan broke the drought. We were twenty minutes away from winning the World Cup. We needed to stay strong. But falling behind seemed to energize Japan. When one of our defenders slipped attempting to clear the ball, my old pal Aya made us pay, banging a shot past me to tie the game in the eightieth minute.

Nothing came easy in this World Cup. So of course regulation ended in a tie, and we headed to overtime. In the 104th minute, Alex sent a cross directly to Abby's forehead, and she slammed the ball in. We had a 2–1 lead in overtime with the World Cup on the line. But who knew better than us that teams can come back in overtime? Early in the second extra-time period, I collided with Yukari Kinga and cut my knee badly. I knew my knee was messed up and I lay on the ground, while our trainer ran out on the field to make sure that I was okay. As I lay there, it occurred to me that I could stay down awhile and waste some time, but as soon as the thought entered my mind, I pushed it away. I wanted to keep fighting, to close out the victory, right away. I didn't want to resort to a Brazilian-type tactic to kill the clock. I had too much respect for Japan to do that. I could tough it out.

We cleared the ball behind our goal setting up a corner. I was down for a few minutes and felt the air going out of the team. I didn't have time to organize the defense for the corner kick. Thirty-two-year-old Sawa redirected the kick, which glanced off of Abby and into the net. Tied again. Twice Japan had fallen behind and faced defeat and twice the team had rallied back. The momentum had shifted. Destiny seemed to have switched sides.

The game went to penalty kicks. Our long World Cup road was almost at an end. I knew how psychologically hard it was for a team to win two games in one tournament on PKs. Japan had already seen us take kicks against Brazil just a week earlier; they had film to study. We didn't have such an advantage.

It didn't go well from the start. Boxxy shot first but Japan's goalkeeper, Ayumi Kaihori, made a kick save.

Aya made her penalty kick to put Japan up 1–0.

Carli sent her shot high over the crossbar.

I made a save on Yuki Nagasato, diving to my right.

Tobin Heath's shot was saved by Kaihori. We still hadn't converted a penalty kick.

Mizuho Sakaguchi made her shot, and Japan had a 2–0 lead. One more converted penalty kick by Japan, and the game would be over.

Abby made her penalty kick to cut it to 2–1.

When Saki Kumagai sent the ball high over my right shoulder, above my outstretched hand, Japan had won the World Cup. They ran to each other as we watched in shock. They jumped and cried, and confetti poured from the rafters. They unfurled a sign, To Our Friends Around the World—Thank You for Your Support. I walked over to the stands, as I always do, to where my friends and family sat. I wanted to thank them for supporting me and to see the love in their faces. We had done everything we could and played in an unforgettable World Cup. The feeling after the loss was so different than it had been in 2007; it was painful but we weren't crushed. It was pain that came with an honest, honorable defeat. Aya came up to me on the field. She wasn't celebrating. "I don't want to celebrate while you are hurting," she told me.

"Aya," I said, hugging her, "please celebrate. You just won the World Cup."

I was stopped for an interview by ESPN. "As much as I've always wanted this," I said, my voice cracking, "if there was any other team I could give this to it would have to be Japan."

It hurt not to win the World Cup. That might have been—for all I know—as close as I would ever get to winning a World Cup. But for the first time in my soccer career, I could see the bigger picture. I had always been so focused on winning, but finally—just shy of my thirtieth birthday—I appreciated the moment, and I could make peace with the loss. Japan was playing for something bigger than just soccer. The outcome felt like fate.

In a ceremony following the game, I stepped up to receive the Golden Glove, the honor of being named goalkeeper of the tournament. It was the award I had always sought—validation that I was the best goalkeeper in the world—but as I stood there, I realized that I had never expected to win it like this, alone, without a winning team celebrating around me. It was a bittersweet moment.

Despite our loss, I knew that what had happened was good for women's soccer. We had built up the game. We had rebuilt our team. I was so proud of everything that we had accomplished together, how far we had come together. We played with fight and we won and lost with class. We could be proud of each other, and our country could be proud of us.

During the medal ceremony, I stood with my teammates on the second-highest podium and felt the silver medal slip over my neck. I kept it on all night.

CHAPTER TWENTY-TWO

Bare-Ass Naked on a Lawn

I ripped off my wig—it was like having a toy poodle clamped onto my scalp. I pulled off one pair of fake eyelashes and then another. I scrubbed off the thick coating of makeup that had been spackled over my face, then stepped into the shower and watched the spray-painted tan bleed off my skin, a steady stream of dirty water washing down the drain. And I thought, *How did someone who loathes all things fake end up here in the land of phony? In Hollywood on* Dancing with the Stars, *partnered with a dancer who was far from the world's best teammate?*

One of the phone calls my agent had fielded while he was riding the bus to World Cup games in Germany was from a producer with *DWTS*, which I loved to watch. Was I interested in being one of the celebrity contestants on the show? "Sure, that sounds fun," I told Rich with a laugh, knowing full well that my soccer schedule would never allow for such a commitment.

I didn't know what lay ahead for me after the World Cup, but I knew one thing: I wasn't going back to the MagicJack. After pushing my shoulder so hard—ten months of grueling rehab and competition—I needed to take a long break from soccer. My goal for the 2012 Olympics was to be healthy and no longer reliant on the pain medication I had been taking for so many months. I had killed myself, but had achieved my goal: I had played in the World Cup, every minute from the first game through to the penalty-kick ending of the final. I was voted goalkeeper of the tournament. Despite all the doubts, I had prevailed.

When the team arrived in New York on the Monday after the final, we were greeted by television cameras, media requests, and a huge throng of enthusiastic fans waiting for us in Times Square. We appeared as a team on the *Today* show, where we were told that our final game broke a world record for "tweets per second,"—surpassing even the royal wedding. We were overwhelmed by our new celebrity status and a bit confused. Only Pearcie—the last of the '99ers—had ever experienced anything like this. But that team had won the World Cup. We had played well, but we had lost.

That made the enthusiastic response even more moving: it was all about the game. The outpouring wasn't a knee-jerk bandwagon response to a winner. Everyone was talking about women's soccer. Even the idiotic commentary suggesting that we choked away the final wasn't, I had to concede, necessarily a bad thing. People were talking about a women's sporting event the way they talked about guys' sports. That's progress.

Abby and I went on the David Letterman show to talk about the game. Letterman didn't know anything about soccer—and made that quite clear. He asked us to go out on Broadway and kick soccer balls through the open door of a cab. I nailed a shot right into a yellow cab. I was on the cover of that week's *Sports Illustrated*. A few days later, in Burbank, I went on the George Lopez show and dunked him in a water tank by kicking a ball to a target that released his platform. "You're badass," Lopez said.

That was generally the response. We were tough, we were gritty, we were badass, and we'd made our country proud.

While I was in Southern California, there were more conversations with the *Dancing with the Stars* producers, and I studied my schedule. The national team had only two games scheduled in a celebration tour. There might be one more friendly scheduled in the fall. But our run-up to Olympic qualifying wasn't going to get serious for a couple of months. I gulped. Turns out I *could* do *Dancing with the Stars*. A grubby kid from Richland all dressed up in sparkles in Hollywood, like Cinderella at the ball. "It'll be a great showcase for women's soccer," everyone said.

That was true. NFL players and other Olympic athletes had received huge crossover exposure on the show. Why not a female soccer player? Why not me? Besides, I'd always wanted to learn to dance.

II.

Little girls were pushing up against the railing for autographs. A few months earlier, the MagicJack had played in front of a handful of people scattered across vast expanses of empty bleachers. Now we had a packed house and a frenzied crowd. Kids leapt over barricades and rushed onto the field as soon as the game ended, and players from both teams were sequestered in the locker room for more than an hour because the crush was so intense that we couldn't leave. Abby—who was now the MagicJack player-coach—couldn't address the media after the game because she couldn't get to them. I was there just to make an appearance—speak at halftime and sign some autographs. I was mobbed and at one point had five security escorts trying to get me out of the stadium and into a van with tinted windows. It was pandemonium.

But the enthusiasm couldn't sustain the beleaguered league. While we had been busy with the World Cup, a war was brewing between our owner, Dan Borislow, and league officials. The league told Dan it was considering terminating his ownership rights. Dan countered by filing a lawsuit to prevent that. It was a mess. Meanwhile, the league was asking some players to play for just a couple of hundred bucks a game, without health insurance. After the positive experience of the World Cup, the WPS felt like a black hole of negative energy.

I wasn't playing soccer, but I wasn't exactly resting. Gatorade signed me to a contract, I agreed to be involved in the Chicago Marathon and I drove the pace car at the Brickyard 400. I moved some of my belongings into a condo near the Grove in West Hollywood, which would be my base for *Dancing with the Stars*. But that August, I really felt that my home was seat 5A on a 727 crossing the country.

My partner in my travels was Whitney Unruh, Rich's assistant. She was a godsend, not only keeping my schedule and appearances organized, but also becoming a close friend. On my thirtieth birthday, I celebrated in Indianapolis—the Brickyard 400 was the next day—with Whitney and Adrian. We toasted the future: thirty is a significant milestone for anyone, but especially for a professional athlete. I was pretty confident—with my repaired shoulder and wisdom gained over the years—that I had several more years left.

There was one weekend that I kept free of commitments. Cheryl and her longtime boyfriend, Galen, were getting married on the water in Port Ludlow, Washington. I was so happy for Cheryl, but I was also wounded. She hadn't asked me to be her maid of honor, a decision that hurt me. I understood, of course, that Megan was the right choice. I had been committed to the World Cup for the last several months; there was no way I would have been able to organize everything or fulfill all those duties that a maid of honor has. But it stung. We had been like sisters for twenty-two years.

The day before the wedding, Cheryl and I finally spoke about the pain we'd caused each other. I told her how hurt I was to not have a special place in her wedding; she said she and our other college friends had been hurt by my inability to stay in regular touch and participate in their big moments. They didn't seem to understand my life and the commitments I had. I couldn't just walk away from a national-team camp in order to make a social engagement. It was a hard conversation but long overdue. When I get married, I don't think I'll even have a maid of honor; I'll include all my friends equally—Cheryl, Tina, Malia, Terry, Debbie, Sofia, Whitney. That might not be conventional, but I've never been very interested in "conventional" anything.

Not that anyone should need further proof of that, but one day in the weeks after the World Cup, I was standing bare-ass naked on a lawn on the Warner Bros. studio lot in Burbank. *ESPN* magazine was shooting its Body issue, and I was going to be on the cover. I was excited—I loved powerful images of the human body. In 1999 Brandi Chastain was criticized for her nude photo—crouched over a soccer ball—on the cover of *Gear* magazine, but I loved that shot—it showed strength and beauty.

But admiring such a photo and preparing for one are two different things. "Do you want to start out wearing underwear?" the director asked. "To ease into it?"

"What's the point? Won't that just prolong it?"

I've never been a prude, but I was extremely nervous. I figured it was best to just get it over with, so I dropped my robe, stepped out of the tent, and was quickly surrounded by about eight strangers—makeup artists, photographers, and their assistants. We were out there for almost six hours, shooting on the same neighborhood set where *Bewitched* was filmed. It's funny how quickly I got used to it—just another job. Soon, I was sprinting down the empty street—I'd always wanted to run naked outside. It felt liberating.

Because I was going to be on the cover in an athletic action pose, they needed some different shots of me for the inside pages. At one point, the photographer handed me a garden hose and asked me to hold it in front of me and spray. The imagery was obvious and distasteful. After a minute—during which Whitney and a few other people, including an ESPN representative, expressed their displeasure with the shot—I dropped the hose. "Let's do something else," I said.

When I was in the trailer after the shoot, the photographer came in and showed us his work. I loved all of the images except one. "I don't like that," I said of the hose shot. "You won't use that, will you?"

We were verbally assured that the hose shot wouldn't run in the magazine, that at worst it would be online with an album of other photos. I was putting myself out there with ESPN, pushing outside my comfort zone. Standing naked in front of photographers was difficult and scary. But it was relatively easy compared to what I was facing next—dancing in front of millions of people.

III.

I sat in a car next to a soccer field in Westchester, not far from the Los Angeles Airport. The cameras were all set to capture the moment I met my *DWTS* partner, the pro I would rely on. I suspected that my partner was going to be Maksim Chmerkovskiy—the handsome "bad boy" of the show, who liked to keep his shirt unbuttoned. He also was the only pro dancer tall enough to pair with me.

A red Rolls-Royce pulled up to the soccer field and Maks got out. I started laughing—what a Hollywood entrance. As my producers requested, I got out of my car and began warming up in goal, and they shot Maks walking across the field to meet me. It was so staged and awkward. I tried to keep it real and cut the ice—I started giving Maks a hard time. "Wow, those are some tight jeans you're wearing," I said. And, "Are dancers even real athletes?"

I could tell Maks was a little surprised. He's used to women fawning all over him, but I figured I should put us on even ground while I could. The producers were encouraging me to stand up to him. I figured Maks knew what was going on.

When he assured me that he was very athletic, I said, "Come on Maks—let's see how good you are at my profession. Block some of my shots."

I started shooting balls at him and he shuffled back and forth in front of the goal as best he could in his tight jeans, while I drilled balls past him.

Later that day, we had our first rehearsal. I found Maks personable and refreshingly honest about the show—dishing dirt on everyone and filling me in on what to expect. I knew he was considered moody and high-maintenance, but he was going to be my coach and teammate for the next several weeks—however long we lasted in this crazy competition—so we were going to have to get along.

IV.

I was sitting in the makeup room with the other "stars." The cast was going to be revealed on *Bachelor Pad*. It was the first time I had met most of them: Rob Kardashian, David Arquette, Kristin Cavallari. Everyone was feeling each other out; everyone seemed nervous.

When the makeup crew was finally done with me, I almost cried when I saw what was looking back at me in the mirror. I looked freakish. My long hair was huge, poofed up and hair-sprayed. "Oh my God," I said.

"Get used to it, honey," laughed one makeup artist. "This is just a fraction of what you'll go through when the show starts."

Maks and I went to work, with long hard rehearsals. I'm an athlete, I'm competitive, and I'm confident that I can excel at any physical activity, but dancing was harder than I expected. It felt unnatural—my body refused to contort into unfamiliar positions, my neck was always sore. I rarely wear high heels, but now I was being asked to dance—backwards—in them. My feet were covered with blisters after the first couple of rehearsals.

The first show was September 19. On September 17, I started for the national team in a "celebration tour" game in Kansas City. Maks came with me—we had to find a dance studio near the hotel so we could practice. Though the scheduling was insane, it was great to be back on the field with my teammates. The normal routine helped ease my nerves and distracted me from what was looming in just a matter of hours.

The night of the first *DWTS* show, I was so scared I thought I might be sick. My support crew was there: Adrian, Terry, and Tina had all flown in. Rich and Whitney drove over from their L.A. office. When I walked into the trailer that served as my home on the lot, after hair and makeup, they were shocked. "Hope, you've never looked so girly!" Tina said.

I was wearing a sparkling pink dress with flowing sleeves, long dangling earrings and a necklace that could have doubled as Liberace's candelabra. I downed a glass of white wine to calm my nerves. "You're beautiful, babe. You're going to be incredible," Adrian whispered in my ear as I left the trailer.

Maks and I waltzed to Dave Matthews's "Satellite." The good news: I didn't fall down; I didn't make any major mistakes. When the song ended, I was exhilarated. I looked over at my section—my support group was giving me a standing ovation. And then the judges spoke. Though they were complimentary, each one mentioned my "strength" or my "muscles." I was told I needed to be more feminine, as though having muscles and being strong wasn't feminine. I smiled. I was relieved it was over, but I wasn't sure what they wanted from me.

The morning after the first results show—where I learned I would be back for another week—Maks and I flew to Portland. I had another soccer game to play. Two days later, I started in goal against Canada in a game that was a celebration of my hundredth cap, which had come in the semifinals against France. My family and friends were in the stands—my grandma was there in her Solo jersey. *This* was the kind of stage I understood. The next day we flew back to L.A., where Maks and I continued rehearsing the jive.

That second week, we had to dance first: our soccer-themed dance was a hit with the audience, but the judges scolded me for not putting in enough rehearsal time, even though I had spent many hours in rehearsal. The most difficult thing for me was memorizing the choreography; in each step my arms and body and posture were different. But the judges didn't know how hard I'd been busting my ass, keeping up with my team on the road while the others rehearsed.

V.

We settled into a routine. Sundays were long days with camera blocking and rehearsal. By the time I dragged myself back to my apartment, Adrian was there waiting for me. On Mondays I had a 7 a.m. "call time" and was in dress rehearsal all day. In the afternoon my core support group would arrive. When I had a break we ate cheese and crackers and drank wine to relax. Then my other guests arrived. While everyone found their seats, Adrian and Whitney stayed behind. Whitney helped me with my costume. Adrian had strong words of encouragement. It was like preparing for competition.

It was starting to get strange to be in restaurants or other public places. The paparazzi started following me. People stood up and clapped when I walked into restaurants. Drinks were sent to the table. I appreciated the support, but it was unnerving.

There were many rules and traditions that we had to follow. The celebrities gave each other gifts: lotion, perfume, accessories. I wanted to get everyone in the cast a pair of cool Nikes, so I took everyone's shoe size and went to Niketown in Beverly Hills to buy the shoes. When they were passed out—to both pro dancers and celebrities—one of the dancers told me that I was the first person to include the dancers in a cast gift. That seemed weird—weren't we all working together?

The best part was all the support I got from my friends and family. Terry was so loving and involved—my sister, who used to love to dress me up and do my hair, was there for the ultimate game of dress-up. One week we danced the foxtrot to "You've Got a Friend in Me," from *Toy Story*, with Maks and I dressed up as Woody and Jessie. That week Grandma Alice and Marcus came and brought Johnny, who was wearing his Buzz Lightyear Halloween costume. My mom and Aunt Susie came the week I danced the rumba to "Seasons of Love," from *Rent*. They didn't go Hollywood with designer clothes—they wore their SOLO No. 1 jerseys.

During this crazy, hectic period, my relationship with Adrian was growing stronger every week. He came down from Seattle every Sunday and stayed until Thursday. He shopped and cooked for us and bolstered my confidence. I realized that for so many years, we had been performing our own strange dance—back and forth, pushing away and pulling back. But we finally seemed to be in synch.

In the middle of all this insanity, the *ESPN* Body issue came out, which meant a round of publicity and a trip to New York for the preview party. I brought Maks with me. I was happy with the cover but upset that the hose photo was included inside. There wasn't much we could do about it but ask that they refuse to release it to news outlets as a publicity shot.

Every week, I thought I would be eliminated from *DWTS*, because we were often in the bottom two of the results. I was frustrated, but then I started to hear from some of the more veteran *DWTS* crew, who told me that being among the last couples to find out our results didn't necessarily mean we were in the bottom two of voting. They even say before the announcement, "While not necessarily the bottom two, one of these couples will be eliminated." I was told I kept being placed there because I was good for ratings. The producers were dragging out the drama.

The lack of transparency on the show was frustrating. I started out thinking I was in a competition, but the longer I lasted, the more I realized that it wasn't really a competition—it was an orchestrated reality show with a preconceived plot line. Maks wasn't my coach or teammate—he and I were just characters on a television show. But

I wasn't sticking to the script—I said what I thought and showed my emotions on camera. I was in tears several times, frustrated and tired.

It was obvious that Maks and I were put together so that we would butt heads. Right from the start, the casting producer wanted to see me hold my own against Maks, thinking that would make a good storyline. As the weeks wore on, the compilation footage of our rehearsals that was shown on the show grew more and more negative. Everything we did was on film, and the producers had hours and hours of footage every week—much of it with us laughing and getting along—but they chose to only show us bickering. In the footage, Maks looked like an arrogant ass; I looked like a drama queen. I guess it made for good TV. But there were some things even *DWTS* wouldn't show.

VI.

The week we did our rumba, Maks argued with the judges, who hadn't liked our performance. When one judge, Len Goodman, said he'd been in this business for fifty years, Maks snapped, "Maybe it's time to get out."

Another judge, Carrie Ann Inaba, scolded Maks. "Don't be disrespectful."

When it was time for our scores that week, Maks made things worse by declaring on camera, "This is my show." I didn't know what to say. I was caught in some ongoing *DWTS* feud that had started long before I signed on.

Maks later told me that he had argued with the judges because he had been told we were going to be eliminated, that there was some secret memo going around that said who would be ousted each week. He explained that he wanted to cause some drama on the live portion of the show so that they wouldn't be able to resist keeping us around, hoping for more fireworks. It seems to have worked—we weren't eliminated that week.

Maks was hard on me in many ways, and our contentious relationship wasn't just a producer's idea of good TV. He was often nasty, swearing at me and being harshly critical, telling me that I looked like a dude and walked as though I had balls between my legs. I didn't like being treated like that, but I could take it.

He manhandled me in rehearsals from the start, pushing me, whacking my stomach, bending my arms roughly. I thought that was just how it went—how dancers worked with each other. I was tough; I could take it.

But it kept getting worse. One day, Maks was trying to put me in a certain position and hit my stomach so hard with his open palm that I had a red handprint there for the rest of the day. When I told Adrian, he was livid. Adrian had seen his mother abused when he was a child, and men being physically violent with women was something he couldn't tolerate. But I felt so reliant on Maks that I defended him and minimized his behavior. I viewed him as my coach, and I'd had asshole coaches before. I could tough it out.

The day after Maks's outburst supposedly saved us for another week, we had a team rehearsal: there were six couples left, and we were split into two teams. Maks and I were teamed with Ricki Lake and Derek Hough and Rob Kardashian and Cheryl Burke. In rehearsal, Maks was rough and mean with me, flinging and pushing me around. I could see the shocked looks on the faces of the other dancers. So maybe this *isn't* normal behavior, I thought. Maks could also see their concern—he stormed out, while I tried to hold it together. Derek stepped in and worked with me the rest of the day.

We kept rehearsing our solo dance for the Halloween show: the samba to Warren Zevon's "Werewolves of London." Maks had injured his toe and was in pain, so another pro, Teddy, came in to work with me. We had fun together, and I enjoyed working with someone who kept things light; but our playfulness seemed to irritate Maks. By the end of the week, he was able to dance, but his mood hadn't improved. Late on a Friday night, he was getting angrier and angrier about one particular move that I was struggling with.

He wanted my head in a specific position. To achieve that, he slapped me across the face. Hard. My huge dangling earring whipped into my face. I knew the camera was rolling, so I checked my impulse to fight back: I knew if I stood up for myself, it would end up on the show, making me look like a villain again, yelling at "poor Maks." I walked out of the room, away from the camera, and took off my mike. Maks followed me and took his mike off.

"Don't you ever fucking put your hand on me again," I said.

He was extremely apologetic. I didn't care. My ear was ringing as I walked out, shaking. I had just been hit, and I had been worried about how *I* would come off looking on television. This was a twisted world. I just wanted to get through the damn show. I didn't want any more drama. I didn't want to be the villain on a hugely popular TV show. I didn't want to get hit by my partner. I had just wanted to learn to dance.

That Sunday, I was called into a meeting with the executive producer and some other ABC officials. They told me they wouldn't stand for violence and I could get a new partner and Maks would be off the show. I felt the way I felt back when Greg Ryan had asked me about goalkeeper coaches—I was being asked to make a decision that would affect someone else's livelihood. I didn't want to end Maks's career. And I knew that if I asked for a change, it would be spun in the tabloids and on the show that I was a prima donna. It was another lose-lose situation.

I decided that I was in this with Maks—we'd come this far together despite his obnoxious behavior. I told the producers I didn't want to change.

The next night, before the show, Maks was shown the video of him hitting me. We then met in my trailer and talked and decided to move on and put the incident behind us. (Later, when Whitney asked to see the video, she was told it didn't exist.) That night, after the show, one of the producers brought an envelope to my trailer. Inside was a letter from the producers on BBC Worldwide Productions letterhead, detailing our meeting and copying in their legal counsel.

The letter noted that "following our review of the recorded training sessions" the producers had come to me to let me know that BBCWP didn't approve of "Maks' physically aggressive training methods." They let me know that BBCWP had told Maks to stop any "unnecessarily forceful contact." They noted that they offered me the option of changing partners and that I told them I preferred to remain with Maks. They wanted me to let them know if I had any further concerns.

It was all in writing. The show had covered its collective butt, and I was with Maks the rest of the way.

VII.

Maks knew he'd almost been fired, and he backed off. The next week, we did the quickstep and a jive, and everyone, from the judges to the other dancers, talked about the "kinder and gentler" Maks. We made it through to week nine. I was in the final four—something I never expected when I signed the contract. I felt really good about my accomplishment. The competitive athlete in me wanted to win, but I knew that wasn't realistic. The script seemed to have been written: J. R. Martinez, the Iraq veteran who was a very good dancer, was going to win. Ricki Lake—who was dancing with Derek, the most popular pro—was going to be close to the top. And Rob Kardashian kept improving—plus, he brought half the cast from his family's reality show to the audience every week. The producers gushed all over Kris Kardashian and Bruce Jenner during every commercial break. I was just an athlete, and I was paired with Maks—a dancer who had never been paired with a winner and who riled the producers and judges despite the ratings he brought to the show.

On that last Monday night, the audience fluffer had them all up out of their seats giving Rob a standing ovation before he'd even danced. We had to perform three dances that night. One was a difficult Argentine tango— it was physically taxing and full of lifts. We were the only dancers athletic enough to perform such a demanding routine. We knew it was one of our best. Of course, the judges were critical and sounded as though they were saying goodbye. "I really admired you for coming this far," Carrie Ann said.

When I heard that, I knew the next night would be our last.

Before the show started I was in the audience with Tina, Whitney, and Adrian. Before every show the audience is invited on stage to dance. But the cast doesn't usually join in. That night, however, I jumped in with my support group—nearby dancers circled around me as I cut loose. I'd come a long way. I had nothing to lose.

It was a rough evening. The producers had put together a compilation of footage from the night before that painted us in the worst light: when we got our scores, I had said, "Kiss my booty" and "Give us your little eights." I was tired of the game. Backstage before the tango, Maks had given me a pep talk telling me, "Fuck the judges. Dance for yourself; be proud—no matter what—of this tango. No other dancers can do what we're about to do." He had already told me that the judges would crush us. I mimicked him in a kind of joking pregame get-fired-up chant "Fuck 'em." But the producers edited it to look as though we'd said "Fuck the judges" as soon as we finished dancing. We went out as the villains.

When we were eliminated, the show didn't play a montage of my highlights, as they had for other contestants. I was told I wasn't going to New York for *The View*—a trip the eliminated celebrity contestant normally makes—or to the Jimmy Kimmel show that night. I went through the press line alone—ABC told Maks he wasn't allowed to do press this time. I did one interview with Tony Dovolani, who was one of the dancers on the show, working for *Extra*. He had become my friend, and he said some beautiful things to me when I came over for an interview: that I was his role model and he wanted his daughters to be like me. It hit me right then how far I had come—I had just wanted a challenge and to give women's soccer some exposure, yet I had made it to the final four on *Dancing with the Stars*. I got very emotional when I answered his questions. Because of that, my PR person thought it was best if I didn't do any more interviews.

The next day, all the gossip rags claimed that I was a sore loser who refused to talk to the press. *DWTS* never disputed those reports, which made me feel they were fine with having me portrayed as a bad sport.

My time as Cinderella was over. My trailer was turning into a pumpkin. We packed up, and the next day I flew home to Seattle, wearing my Nikes and my real eyelashes.

VIII.

Grandpa Pete passed away in December, and my family gathered in Richland to say good-bye. He was our patriarch, the one who had moved us to eastern Washington and set my family on its journey. He had been my staunchest supporter, traveling the world to see me play and always encouraging me to be the best I could be. He could always make me laugh; when things got too serious or scary in my life, Grandpa Pete would crack a joke.

After the funeral, we released doves into the cold wind blowing off the Columbia River. I looked around at my family: my grandma Alice, her faith calming her grief; my mother, who was dealing with her husband's serious illness but remained strong; and my brother Marcus, the abandoned son who was now a loving father to Johnny.

I LOOKED AT Adrian. I had always thought my grandpa might walk me down the aisle. He wouldn't be there to do that now, but I felt I had finally found the person I was going to make my life with; the person who had been right there for so many years.

Two weeks later, Glenn had to be admitted to the hospital on New Year's Eve. It was my mother's birthday; she was worried about her husband, exhausted from trying to care for him while he'd been at home. Adrian and I told her to go home; we'd sit by Glenn's bedside. As we sat there, Glenn drifted off to sleep. At about eleven thirty, my phone rang. It was Grandma Alice. "This is the first time in my entire eighty-four years that I've rung in the New Year by myself," she said.

When I told Adrian what she'd said, he jumped up. "Come on," he said.

We rushed to the house on Hoxie and gathered up Marcus, Johnny, Mom, and the ice cream pie I had gotten for her birthday; then we hurried the four blocks to Grandma's house. We stepped over the doormat that read GRANDCHILDREN WELCOME, and found Grandma in the bedroom she had shared for so many years with Grandpa Pete. There was only a minute to spare in the old year. We sang "Happy Birthday" to my mother, and then with Champagne, Clamato, and ice cream pie, we toasted another new year.

We stayed in Grandma's warm home playing Cranium until two a.m., Adrian and Marcus against me and Grandma, who kept trying to cheat. My mother held Johnny, asleep in her arms, and laughed at our crazy antics. Outside the wind blew off the Columbia, the river that flowed through our lives, its waters rushing past us and out into the sea.

Grandma Alice looked out the window into the dark night.

"God's second paradise," she said with a smile.

Closing Ceremonies, 2012

H ope," Pia said without a trace of a smile while we sat in her Los Angeles hotel room last December. "I can assure you it would be easy to leave you off the team."

Wait, what? It was less than six months after I had won the Golden Glove at the World Cup. Less than six hours after she had told a reporter that I was the best goalkeeper in the world. And now she was raising the possibility that I would be excluded from the Olympic team? What was my transgression?

This book. It was originally scheduled to hit the shelves just days before the 2012 Olympics began. I knew that not everyone within the U.S. women's national team would be thrilled with my side of the 2007 controversy (when Greg Ryan had benched me before our World Cup final defeat and I'd said publicly what I thought about his decision and the four goals we allowed). I'm sure they were worried about what else I might say.

But sports figures write books all the time: Tim Tebow published *Through My Eyes* as soon as he was drafted. Victor Cruz, Josh Hamilton, R. A. Dickey, LeBron James: no one interfered with *their* publication plans.

It felt like a double standard: just another indignity that prominent female athletes have to face. I explained to Pia that I'd always planned to tell my story. *Solo* is about a lot of things: my dad and my childhood, not just about 2007. She wasn't interested.

"This will have a negative effect on the team," she insisted. "You're putting me in a position where you're ruining our journey to the Olympics. They'll take a quote out of the book from 2007 and ask me what I think about it."

"Pia," I said. "It's not like some big secret. We talk about 2007 all the time. Plus, with the growth in our game come opportunities, the same opportunities that are in men's sports."

"I think that's the problem with men's sports," Pia snapped. Pia was adamant.

I walked out of our meeting and called my agent, Rich. I couldn't believe what had just happened. We were just seven months away from the Olympics, and I was having another conflict with my coach. I felt a little better when I spoke to my goalkeeper coach, Paul Rogers, about it; he just rolled his eyes and laughed it off.

Nobody was up for a battle. We decided to push the release date back to a few days after the Olympic gold-medal game. I can't imagine anyone asking Michael Phelps or Kobe Bryant to accept such an ultimatum, but—obviously—I wanted to play.

II.

After the whirlwind of the World Cup and *Dancing with the Stars*, I didn't know if life could get any more hectic. But it did. The months leading up to the Olympics were unrelenting and demanding but also threaded with heartbreak.

First, my grandpa died. His passing wasn't unexpected, but it was very difficult for all of us, especially Grandma Alice. Despite her sadness, her outlook on life remained as optimistic as ever, buoyed by her faith.

"Well, at least we know where he is," she said to those who

offered sympathy for her loss. She meant that my grandpa was in heaven, watching out for all of us. We all felt that way.

It was a rough time. Grandma Burnett, mother of my stepfather, Glenn, had died in November. So had a family dog that Glenn had gotten for us. And my mother was coping with the declining health of her husband. Glenn had been in and out of the hospital for almost two years, originally with breathing problems. He was shuttled between a rehab facility and a hospital near Richland, and Mom kept waiting for him to come home. He did, but only for a short time, confined to the same hospital bed my grandfather had lain in before he died. We quickly learned that Glenn needed more care than we could provide, and after yet another frightening trip to the emergency room, he had to go back to the hospital.

As the march to the Olympics progressed, I worried about Glenn. Our qualifying tournament took place in Vancouver, British Columbia, which meant we were close enough for me to see him before and after.

But the travel became more intense. We left for several weeks in Portugal, followed by a trip to Japan. In the few days I was home, I became seriously concerned about the level of care Glenn was receiving and with Adrian's help began to investigate other hospitals where he might get better treatment. Before we headed to Japan, we were able to move him to a high-quality facility on the other side of the mountains in Bellevue, Washington. My mother was able to stay at my house in Seattle. She was worried only about Glenn's comfort, but I was concerned about her mounting medical bills and the complicated logistics. I was reluctant to leave the country again.

I didn't have a choice. I had committed to a goodwill tour in Japan that took me to areas of the country that suffered the most devastation in the earthquake. Adrian went to the hospital in my place and sat by Glenn's bedside every day, which made me feel a little better.

"Did you ever think it would be me, Glenn?" Adrian asked him one day. "Sitting here with you?"

Glenn laughed. They had never really given each other much of a chance, but here—at the end—they were bonding.

Adrian was beyond committed, a steady support system for me through these difficult times. Somewhere in the past year, there had been a significant shift in our relationship, and our full commitment to each other became clear and ironclad. We decided to start looking for a home, one where we could build our life together. We found it near Seattle.

I was leaving behind my little cabin—my "temporary" home where I had lived for more than six years. The new house is big—too big for just the two of us. But with the changes happening in my family, I realized I needed a place with room for my mother, Adrian's mother, my grandmother, and other family members. It makes me proud to take care of my family and excited to put down roots where I've always felt I belonged.

The team finally returned home from Japan, and I went straight to Glenn. All those hours of sitting by his bedside gave me time to reflect on our relationship and the part he had played in my life. Although Marcus and I had rebelled against him as kids, I know he was always trying to do the right thing—trying to provide a stable home and help us grow up. As I grew older, I saw how his love was manifested: how he went down to the school and fought for me when I was kicked off the basketball team, how he worried when I had a stalker and then made sure that I knew how to protect myself. For a girl who had spent much of her youth searching for her dad, I realized that I was lucky. I had had three father figures: my grandfather, my father, and Glenn. And they all loved me very much.

We had a training camp in Florida and then another in Princeton, New Jersey, in May. I was in constant touch with my mother. The prognosis for Glenn was grim, then encouraging, then grim again. We were teetering on the brink of grief. My mom held on to her faith that he would get better and come home soon.

Things took a serious turn for the worse while I was at training camp in Princeton. I knew I had to go home and say my good-byes.

Glenn had been hospitalized for the better part of two years when he passed away, on May 19, 2012. Knowing how much he suffered carved me up inside. I put my arms around my poor mother and held her close. Glenn had given her so much—her strength, her home—and all I could think was whether better care earlier could have spared her losing another husband.

III.

I was sitting in a store copying my passport and other documents that needed to be in order for the Olympics. I looked down at my phone and saw I had two missed calls from unfamiliar numbers. I signed on to my e-mail and my stomach dropped.

There was an e-mail from USADA—the U.S. Anti-Doping Agency, a governmental body that oversees the antidoping programs for Olympic sports. Travis Tygart, the head of the organization, was trying to reach me. I called back the missed number, which was Travis's cell phone. Travis answered and suggested I call him at his office.

Why? Did he want to record our conversation? I was shaking. In an instant, I was living every athlete's worst nightmare. I knew I had done nothing wrong, but I also knew that there was probably only one reason USADA would be calling me. And it wasn't good news.

Travis had a reputation as a hard-ass: USADA was currently after Lance Armstrong, and Travis was all over the news. Why did he want to talk personally to me? With trembling fingers, I punched in his office number.

He explained to me what had happened. A substance called canrenone had shown up in a routine drug test I took on June 14 after a game we played in Sweden. It is on the banned substance list as a diuretic. But Travis was almost apologetic. He told me that I shouldn't say anything until I talked to my representatives. I felt that he had left a small window open for the possibility that something could be done and my Olympics wouldn't be ruined. But he also told me that he had to inform U.S. Soccer, the U.S. Olympic Committee, and the International Olympic Committee.

We hung up. Still shaking, I grabbed my papers and went out to my car, where I immediately called my agent. I knew Rich would know what to do and would give me his support. Although it was the Fourth of July weekend, Rich leaped into overdrive and started working day and night to figure out what my options were.

I was stunned, but I knew I was innocent. There was nothing I could do but wait for the process to unfold. I knew where the positive result had come from: I was taking a prescription medicine for premenstrual purposes, the only medication that I take on a semiregular basis. My doctor in Seattle had prescribed it, and I had been taking it for more than a year and had never once registered a positive drug test.

But when I left training camp to be with Glenn, I had skipped a mandatory test that needed to be made up. So I made up the test in Sweden after our game there in June. The European laboratory may have had different standards, which is why it showed up then, even though it hadn't before. Still, the burden of proof fell on me. Part of being a world-class athlete is keeping aware of everything that enters one's body. I understood I needed to file a TUE—a therapeutic use exemption. I knew all the rules; I just hadn't known there was anything in the drug that I needed to worry about. I couldn't believe that my Olympic dreams could be ruined because of a medication I'd been taking for more than a year. But I also knew that USADA was intent on maintaining its reputation and wasn't going to be giving anyone a break.

The last female player who had tested positive for the drug was given a two-month suspension. That would take me through August 14—and the gold-medal game was scheduled for August 9.

U.S. Soccer was supportive, and Rich worked tirelessly. But for almost a week in early July, I had no idea whether or not I would be able to compete for a gold medal. It was agonizing. I tried to stay focused and quell the panic.

Finally, the decision came down. I wouldn't be suspended—it was clearly an honest mistake—but I would give up my right to privacy. I would receive an official warning from USADA, and that warning would be made public. I knew that wasn't good for my image (or my endorsement deals), but what the hell—I'd had image issues my entire career.

The upshot was that I got to play in the Olympics, in every game. I took a deep breath, flooded by relief. I could concentrate again.

Except that another shitstorm had descended. After we left for the United Kingdom, a story ran in *ESPN* magazine about sex at the Olympics. The reporter who wrote it had come to me with an obvious angle, asking me question after question about hooking up in the village. I played along, saying that I'd heard stories but that his gossipy anecdotes included things I'd never heard before. Some of my quotes were pulled out and put together with stuff from other athletes in an absurd attempt to make me sound like a slutty drunk who had spent all of Beijing partying my ass off.

The backlash I had expected over my drug test hadn't materialized. Instead, this half-baked story about sex and partying was picked up around the world. Once again, I was portrayed as a loose cannon, flouting the rules. I was getting all the negative feedback while we were in Darlington, England, for our pre-Olympic training camp. It was too much. I thought, *No wonder I had wanted to write my own story in the first place.*

I was able to keep my focus in training, which was going very well, but off the field, it was too much. One night, I broke down in tears. But after that I adopted my old attitude: fuck it. I'm not here to please people. People are going to think what they want to think about me. I've given my life to this sport, and I am going to work hard with my team and enjoy this incredible moment. I was not going to let the devil steal my joy.

When we arrived at London's Heathrow Airport, I couldn't help but notice a book prominently displayed in the airport newsstand: Kelly Smith, the British team's star, had had the audacity to publish her memoir, *Footballer*, before the games even began.

IV.

We were down two goals in our first Olympic match. It was a familiar feeling. Back in 2008, we had lost our first game of the Olympics to Norway after giving up two goals in the first five minutes.

Now, at Hampden Park in Glasgow, France had scored two goals on us in the first sixteen minutes. The first, at the fourteen-minute mark, was a long shot from Gaëtane Thiney. I stretched for the ball, but it grazed my fingertips and went into the net. France was fired up and kept attacking. Two minutes later, Marie-Laure Delie buried a shot from six yards out. Then Boxxy went off with an injury. Nothing seemed to be going right.

Maybe our nerves hadn't completely settled. We were the very first American team to play on the very first day of competition, two full days before the opening ceremonies.

But there was a different, more cohesive feeling with this team than in 2008. There was no panic or worry in anyone's eyes. Despite falling behind, we kept our cool and remained completely confident.

Carli came on to replace Boxxy. She had lost her starting job in June but handled the situation with immense grace and composure and kept working hard every day. I knew she was ready.

Within fifteen minutes, we were even again. Abby headed in a corner from Megan Rapinoe, and Alex Morgan got on the end of a kick that I had sent about sixty yards. I got an assist on that one—the first of my national team career.

In the second half, Carli put us ahead for good with one of her trademark long-range blasts. She had scored the winning goal in our last Olympic game, the gold-medal match in Beijing, and here she was with the go-ahead goal in our first match of the London Olympics.

We knew France was good. But we knew we were better. Alex, with her lightning speed, kept getting behind France's defense. She got her second goal late in the game on a tap-in. We won 4–2, beating the best team in our preliminary group.

I was kind of pissed after the game when Pia told reporters that the sun had been in my eyes on the first goal. Sure, there was glare. But I would never use the conditions as an excuse.

More annoying was the feedback I heard from home and from fans on Twitter about the way the game was being broadcast on television. NBC had hired Brandi Chastain to do the color commentary on our games. She had been relentlessly negative during our qualifying matches, nitpicking little details and criticizing Pia's strategy. I had tweeted back in January, "Hey brandi did you find anything positive in our game? Curious minds over here . . ."

I'm not looking for a cheerleader—far from it. We're all soccer junkies, and we hear a lot of expert commentary while we travel the world. I want the best of the best for our games, and I just don't feel that Brandi is very good at articulating the game. I love that ESPN added Ian Darke to their team for our World Cup, and I like Arlo White on NBC, but I feel that our networks too often take the easy way out: "Oh, let's hire Brandi. She's a world champion who took off her shirt, and people know her name. It doesn't really matter if she's a good analyst or not."

Everything Brandi says seems to have a direct correlation to her playing days, so many years ago. "When I played with Carla Overbeck . . ." she will say again and again. I'm not sure that many of our new fans have any idea who Carla Overbeck was. It seems to be a continuation on that long-running theme: the '99 team would never give us our due or recognize how far the game had advanced or how much more athletically skilled our team was than theirs. They were clinging to their glory days and unwilling to recognize that times have changed. Most of us were sick of it.

Brandi kept up her negative posture in the days before the games began. She gave an interview to a blog called *Larry Brown Sports*, claiming my positive drug test was a distraction to the team. She said, "I was disappointed . . . for as careful as I think everybody is, I think we could all go without some medication for a short amount of time and not suffer too greatly."

Huh? She didn't know what the hell she was talking about. Did she think I *knew* there was something in my medication that would turn up positive, even though I had been taking it for many months? Had I "disappointed" the great Brandi Chastain?

We watched the opening ceremonies on television at our Glasgow hotel, getting ready for our next match against Colombia. The game was a struggle. Colombia just wanted to disrupt our flow, and one player, Lady Andrade, even resorted to sucker-punching Abby in the face. Still, we won, scoring three goals—by Megan, Abby, and Carli—and I didn't face many challenges. With the win, we were assured a berth in the quarterfinals.

So it was disappointing when we got on the bus, checked our phones, and got another onslaught of feedback about how negative Brandi had been on the broadcast. She was killing our defense, singling out Rachel Buehler in particular. Buehler was upset, and I didn't blame her. There wasn't much to criticize in the way we were playing, but somehow Brandi had decided Rachel was the weak link.

Rachel was quiet on the bus. I felt bad for her; I know the feeling of being singled out, set apart from my team. A lot of us were frustrated by the sense that our accomplishment was being picked apart.

I got out my phone and logged on to Twitter.

2 bad we cant have commentators who better represent the team & know more about the game @brandichastain!

Lay off commentating about defending and gking until you get more educated @brandichastain. the game has changed from a decade ago.

Its important 2 our fans 2 enjoy the spirit of the olympics. Its not possible when sum1 on air is saying that a player is the worst defender.

I feel bad 4 our fans that have 2 push mute, especially bc @arlowhite is fantastic. @brandichastain should be helping 2 grow the sport.

I knew that would get a reaction, but I felt that someone needed to stand up to Brandi. She had a microphone and an international platform. Why couldn't I voice my opinion? That's the beauty of social media.

When the tweets came across everyone's Twitter feed, the bus erupted with cheers.

"Hell yeah, Hope," my teammates cried. Pearcie and Abby and others offered up high fives. "Somebody finally said it," they said. It was a bonding moment for our team.

Within minutes my comments were retweeted around the world. And within the hour, blogs were filled with opinions about me. How could I take on a legend? There's Solo going solo again. How could Solo not acknowledge what Brandi has done to grow the sport?

I know what Brandi and the other '99ers did for the sport. Believe me, you can't escape it. But I also know what *we're* doing for the sport—something the old guard doesn't seem to want to recognize. We're a new generation, claiming our own mantle and doing as much for the sport as they did.

The uproar echoed online for a couple of days. It was early in the Olympics; I guess there wasn't that much else to talk about yet. Brandi had built up twenty years of goodwill with a lot of reporters, and they weighed in on her side. Julie Foudy fell in line, saying she was sad about the incident. A few emotional tweets had grown to ridiculous proportions.

When Pia met with reporters later, on Sunday, after meeting with me and the captains, she was asked if I was going to be disciplined or if I had been reprimanded. That made me laugh. Our meeting was about what we were doing in training. Pia told me that she, in fact, *did* press mute when she watched the games of ours that Brandi worked from the booth. My teammates shared the opinions that I had voiced on Twitter. We were tighter than ever.

My birthday was on Monday, July 30, and my teammates presented me with two beautiful cakes. They also decided that if we scored a goal the next day at Old Trafford in Manchester, I had to be a part of the celebration.

They'd tried to get me involved before, but I always balked. Was I going to run all the way upfield and then sprint back for the kickoff? Abby is usually the one choreographing an elaborate goal-scoring dance. My teammates thought it was cool that I could do the worm—that old-school break-dance move. Pearcie said she would do it with me. So they came up with a celebration in which the rest of the team would do a move, then turn toward us, and we would do the worm near midfield. I couldn't believe I was agreeing to it—it was so corny!—but I could tell that the team really wanted to involve me. It was a way of broadcasting to the world that no matter what might be written or said outside of our locker room, we stood strong together.

V.

Oh, great. Canada.

We had beaten New Zealand in the quarterfinals at St. James Park in Newcastle, 2–0. Abby scored and then Sydney Leroux added an insurance goal in the eighty-seventh minute. I was so happy for Syd, the baby on our team. Her raw joy at scoring made us all a little emotional. She's going to be so important to our future.

We'd made it to the semifinal, and our opponent would be Canada. I had been hoping for Kelly Smith and Great Britain. It would have been exciting to play the host country at Old Trafford, one of the world's legendary football stadiums. Besides, we play Canada all the time. We had beaten them 4–0 in qualifying in their home country and had just beaten them in a friendly in Utah, our last game before heading to the United Kingdom. We hadn't lost to them since the 2001 Algarve Cup, when we took an incredibly young team to Portugal. In that game, I was making just the fourth start of my career and gave up three goals, one to my collegiate nemesis, Christine Sinclair, who was just a kid then. Now she was one of the best players in the world. She and Abby were in a race to see who would surpass Mia Hamm as the all-time leading goal scorer.

We knew how Canada would play us: physical. It wasn't going to be pretty soccer. So I laughed when their coach, John Herdman, said the day before the game that we used "highly illegal tactics" on set pieces, singling out Abby. He was trying to get any advantage that he could. His gamesmanship was an attempt to influence the referee and get in our heads.

We fell behind 1–0 in the twenty-third minute. Our back line had a lapse, and Christine Sinclair came through the six-yard box. I was a sitting duck—she could beat me to my left or to my right. She went right. It was a well-deserved goal.

Canada wanted to turn the game into a rugby match. Every time Abby turned around, she was taken out. The referee called a lot of penalties, giving us plenty of dead-ball chances, but we couldn't convert. The Canadians, who had come in complaining about our tactics, seemed intent on continuing to push the edge physically.

Early in the second half, we finally broke through to tie the game. Megan Rapinoe's corner kick curled in without being touched. We were even, but the tie didn't last long. There was a wild six-minute span with three goals scored. Sinclair punched in a header in the sixty-seventh minute, then Megan scored again on a beautiful strike from distance that ricocheted off the post and in, and then in the seventy-third minute, Sinclair scored again on another header.

It was a frustrating game. Our team is known as the best in the world in the air, at winning headers on set pieces. Flicked headers are trouble for goalkeepers: you don't know where they're going. It's not like reading a shot from the ground, watching the feet and hips. But for some reason, we were off our game against Canada.

However, we still had seventeen minutes of regulation play. We were pretty calm. We'd already come back twice, why not one more time? We knew we were the superior team. There was no way we could lose to Canada in the semifinals.

Canada tried to stall, and the referee warned their goalkeeper, Erin McLeod, about taking too long on dropkicks. Abby took to counting loudly on the field—the keeper is supposed to get the ball away within six seconds, but Abby counted as high as ten on a couple of occasions.

Finally, in the eightieth minute, while Abby was counting again, the referee blew her whistle and called the six-second violation on McLeod. I'll admit—as a goalkeeper, I was surprised. But then again, you frequently see unusual calls in big games. Shit happens. It has to us, anyway, plenty of times (like when the referee nullified my save on a penalty kick and allowed Brazil to retake the PK in the World Cup).

We were awarded an indirect free kick. Carli took the kick, and it hit a Canadian player's arm—handball. The ref pointed to the spot and gave us a penalty kick, which Abby buried. We were tied again, and Canada was apoplectic. Their players were screaming in fury.

I didn't care. We were even, and I was damned if I was going to let in another goal. In the eighty-ninth minute, a Canadian player had an open shot, which I dropped to my knees and blocked.

We were going to overtime. We had dominated the run of play but couldn't score. The minutes ticked off. Canada was still intent on turning the game into a bloodbath. At one point, Melissa Tancredi stepped backward and deliberately stomped on Carli's head as she lay on the ground. I worried about our field players' legs. This was the fifth game of the tournament; they were giving everything they had, and now we were in overtime. Syd had come in earlier in the game, to give us three forwards up top. In overtime, Heather O'Reilly subbed for Lauren Cheney, who had injured her ankle, and Becky Sauerbrunn came in for Buehler. We were out of subs.

At the end of 120 minutes, 3 minutes of overtime were added. The seconds ticked off. I walked back to my line and took a hard look at the penalty spot, trying to get a feel for it. Were we really going to go into PKs against Canada?

And then Carli passed wide to Heather, who gathered up the ball in the corner and launched a cross toward the box. From my vantage point in front of our goal, I could see Alex Morgan rise up and get her head on the ball. She launched it high over McLeod and into the net. The crowd roared; the moment crackled with electricity. For the first time all night, we had the lead.

Pearcie ran back to me. "OK, let's hold it down," she said.

We locked eyes.

I replied: "Hold. It. Down."

The final thirty seconds ticked off, and we were able to collapse in celebration.

We were going to London.

Inside the locker room, we laughed and shook our heads in amazement.

"Why do we do this to ourselves?" we cried. I don't know why we seem intent on making it so hard on ourselves. But all those stressful games—like the one we had just played and the ones against Brazil and Japan the summer before in the World Cup—were also exciting, wildly entertaining matches that delighted the fans, and back home in the States our team once again was blowing up. Everyone was talking about women's soccer.

The Canadians were bitter and ungracious afterward. They claimed to have outplayed us the entire game—ridiculous. Melissa Tancredi told the referee she should have been wearing an American jersey. Christine Sinclair said she believed the referee had decided the outcome of the game before it even started. Oh well.

We were in the gold-medal match at Wembley Stadium. And of course we would play Japan.

VI.

The next morning, before we got on the bus, Pia called a team meeting.

"We need to focus for two more days," she said. "Let's put this game behind us. Take care of your bodies. Get your rest. Don't get caught up in the excitement of the village."

Pearcie, our captain, reminded us how we had refocused after the Brazil match at the World Cup. The Canada game had been so emotionally and physically draining that it would be easy to keep replaying it in our heads, but we had to put it behind us and move on.

Keeping our concentration was even more challenging than it had been during the World Cup. For weeks we had been in our own protected bubble, living in hotels with everything we needed right there in the same building—our meals, our physical therapy, our trainers. There was no bustle or excitement or any influences creeping in from the outside world.

Now we were going to London—finally, the *actual* Olympics. We were moving into the village, where other athletes had been living for two weeks. We had a lot of young players who had never been through this drill before, and we needed to keep our focus. We had the rematch we'd been aiming for all year—a chance at redemption against the team that defeated us in the 2011 World Cup, a chance at another gold medal.

It was great to move into the village and see the other athletes. Everyone we ran into offered enthusiastic congratulations and told us how excited they had been watching our game. We finally felt part of Team USA.

And we saw the Japanese team at the village. We could tell how excited they were to play us. We have so much love and respect for those players.

The day before our game, there was a huge press conference in the main press center of Olympic Park. Abby, Carli, Alex, Megan, and Pearcie all went. I wasn't asked to go. I didn't even know it was taking place until they got back. Some reporters asked where I was. They thought it was strange that the team wouldn't make me available for our only interaction with all the reporters who were based in London and hadn't traveled to our games. There was speculation in print and on Twitter that U.S. Soccer officials were trying to muzzle me. I guess they were.

On August 9, we boarded the bus for Wembley. I put on my headphones and turned on my music. I felt incredibly relaxed. I knew this one hour bus ride was the last leg of our long, long journey, the one that had begun with World Cup qualifying so long ago. The cycle was almost over. Careers would end. Pearcie, our thirty-seven-year-old captain, might not be playing in the next Olympics. Neither would some of my other longtime teammates.

I looked over at Heather Mitts, who was sitting across from me, and my eyes welled with tears as I realized that this was probably my last bus ride with her. She would be retiring, and I was so happy that she was going to go out on her own terms: healthy, still strong and talented. She had kept fighting over the years and had made our team, proving a lot of people wrong. I sent her a text telling her how happy I was for her and how much she had meant to me through the years. I hoped that someday I would be able to retire with as much grace and respect. I looked over at Heather and saw she had tears running down her face as she read my message.

As we got close to the stadium, I looked back toward Carli, and we smiled at each other. Four years earlier, we had looked at each other on the bus in Beijing with complete confidence. I felt sure something good was going to happen tonight too.

We pulled up outside the huge edifice of Wembley. We hadn't been able to practice there the day before, so it was our first chance to see the fabled stadium, home of England's national soccer team and the site of so many famous soccer matches.

When we went out on the field for our national anthems, I looked around the sacred ground. It was almost completely full, all the way up to the highest seats in the top row. The crowd would be announced at 80,203—the largest crowd I'd ever played in front of and the largest crowd to watch women's soccer since the 1999 World Cup final at the Rose Bowl. It was historic: in football-crazy Great Britain, in their national stadium, we had a full house for a women's game.

We jumped out to an early lead. In the eighth minute, Tobin Heath crossed the ball to Alex, whose first touch took her deep toward the end line. She turned and crossed the ball back toward Abby, who leaped high to try to get her foot on it. But diving in low was Carli, who got her head on the ball and punched it in. Carli—benched to start the tournament—was playing out of her mind. I almost laughed. I couldn't believe she'd done it again.

But a 1–0 lead was never going to be enough against dangerous Japan. And Japan started to control possession for long stretches. Pearcie stepped in to knock away a shot that got past me. A minute later, Yuki Ogimi took a shot that I leaped to push over the crossbar.

I hadn't seen much action the entire tournament, but the gold-medal game was going to be different: I was going to have to make a difference. The game was coming to me. In the first half, I had to make three difficult saves, including a shot I stopped on the ground and another leaping save over the crossbar.

We caught a break in the twenty-sixth minute when a free kick hit Tobin Heath's arm. There was no call for a handball and play continued.

Early in the second half, Carli brought the ball about twenty-five yards upfield, dribbling through the Japanese team, and then unleashed a twenty-yard blast off her right foot that seared the back of the net. We were up 2–0, and I felt overcome with emotion for my friend. Carli had scored the game winner in Beijing in over-time. She had scored the game winner in our first game of these Olympics. And now she had two goals in the gold-medal game.

She was focused and confident. She had been so angry when she lost her starting job, but the setback made her work harder. She is the most professional player on our team, taking care of her body and staying mentally strong. Her reward was her play, a thing of pure beauty.

Japan's pressure continued to be relentless. In the sixty-third minute, Japan put together three quick passes in front of the goal, Ohnu to Sawa to Ogimi, who shot the ball past me. It was 2–1.

The crowd was roaring, enthralled by such beautiful soccer and tense competition. There were chants of "USA, USA" and "Nippon, Nip-pon." It was an incredible atmosphere, and I didn't try to block it out. I wanted to soak it all in, feel the energy of the crowd. It was beautiful.

In the eighty-third minute, we had a breakdown in front of our goal. Pearcie didn't see Iwabuchi coming and was stripped of the ball. I knew I had to find a way to make the save. I was confident in my angle, but if Iwabuchi passed the ball to a teammate running through the box, it was going to be bad news. Becky Sauerbrunn, who had come into the game three minutes earlier for Buehler, stepped up on the back post, forcing Iwabuchi to take the shot.

She shot. I dove, stretched out completely to my left, punching the ball safely away.

We had practiced that very situation in our pre-Olympic camp. One day, our defensive coach, Tony Gustafsson, had pulled me out of shooting drills with the forwards to work with the defenders over and over again on a similar type of play. They played the ball out wide, I cut off the angle, and the defender marked up on the back post, cutting off a pass and forcing the shot. For Becky to step into the game and process that scenario in the two seconds she had to react showed her level of sophistication. She's going to be a great, great defender for years to come.

The last seven minutes plus two minutes of extra time seemed to take forever. The crowd was roaring. Japan was pushing forward.

But finally the whistle blew. I hugged Pearcie, my awesome captain. And we were surrounded in a group hug. Abby embraced me, telling me, "Big-time players show up in big games."

I jumped into Paul Rogers's arms when he came out on the field. We were handed Nike T-shirts that said, GREATNESS HAS BEEN FOUND. I twirled mine around my head in celebration. It was such a fulfilling feeling to complete our journey with a victory.

We congratulated the Japanese players on a wonderful game. My dear friend Aya Sameshima was so complimentary and respectful. All the players were lovely and gracious. Not one complained about the fact that no handball had been called.

We waved to our fans. I spotted Adrian and my Mom in the crowd. Carli and I grabbed either side of an American flag and ran around the field, thinking of all the things we had been through together, from the 2007 World Cup to our second gold medal together. What a moment.

Back in our locker room, we sprayed champagne and beer. I looked around at our team and felt so proud, so fulfilled. We had won all six games—the first time our team had ever done that in a major tournament, with the exception of the very first Women's World Cup, way back in 1991.

And we had won the gold medal with the most complete team I had ever played on. Every single one of my teammates—numbers 1 through 18 and all four alternates—was capable of stepping in and making a contribution. Every single person had made an impact. I couldn't remember any other team with such camaraderie and such depth.

We took the field for the medal ceremony. The Canadians were there to receive their bronze medal; they didn't even shake our hands on the podium, as teams usually do. Maybe they didn't know the protocol. The Japanese players shook our hands and cheered us. They danced on the podium, delighted with silver. Then it was our turn. I was the first to bow my head and feel my medal slip around my neck. It was huge and heavy. It felt wonderful.

After we dressed, I headed out to the mixed zone to do interviews. I was asked over and over about the save in the eighty-third minute.

"I think I play well under pressure," I said.

"Hope," someone shouted from the back, "do you like proving Brandi wrong?"

I smiled. "I like proving everybody wrong," I said.

VII.

We drank champagne in the car on the way to see Bob Costas—me and Abby and Alex and Carli. Our media director, Aaron Heifetz, tried to get us to stop, probably remembering that story about being drunk on the *Today* show.

"We can handle it," we told him. "We just won the gold medal. We're going to celebrate."

And we did. All night. When we got back to the posh hotel in Mayfair where our postgame party was, the music was pounding. The drinks were flowing. It was a sea of red, white, and blue and smiling faces. Our families were all there—my mom and Adrian were there for me. Some NBA players who were staying there— Kevin Durant, Carmelo Anthony, Dwayne Wade—came downstairs to offer congratulations. Actor Tim Robbins dropped by. President Obama gave us a shout-out on Twitter.

Dan Flynn, the CEO of U.S. Soccer, wrapped me in a big hug.

"I'm sorry, Dan," I said to him. "I know I make it hard for you guys sometimes. I know it's never easy with me."

Dan just laughed. "That's why we love you, Hope," he said. "You are who you are."

I knew the questions would start tomorrow. What would happen for the next three years before the 2015 World Cup? Would there be an attempt at another league? Who would retire at the end of our ten-game victory tour? What were my plans for the future?

I didn't want to think about any of that. I wanted to live in the moment and celebrate what we had accomplished. The beautiful soccer we had played. The thrills we had given fans. The love we shared on our team.

In the wee hours of Friday morning, the hotel shut down and the bartenders told us the party was over. We had to be on the *Today* show in just a few hours, but we needed to get back to the village. Like foamy champagne, we all poured out of the hotel and onto the London sidewalk.

Someone hailed a black cab, the kind that can seat six passengers.

"Come on, Hope," someone yelled.

I piled into the cab with my teammates and headed east, toward the new day.

ACKNOWLEDGMENTS

Writing an honest book means that family secrets and private moments are exposed for the world to see. So first and foremost I want to thank my family, who have been unconditionally loving and supportive through both the good times and the rough spots. The process of bringing my story to print required unearthing some painful memories, but I share them here in the hope that something constructive might come from them. My family's courage and faith know no bounds, and I thank them for providing the foundation for my own path to happiness. Reality has tested us, but love has saved us. Here's to our beautiful struggle—Judy and Glenn Burnett; Marcus and Debbie Solo and their son, Johnny; David Solo; Terry and Christian Obert; Grandma Alice and my late Grandpa Pete.

And to my dad, who taught me to never give up.

Life has blessed me with many teachers and guiding influences who have, in their own ways, each contributed to the writing of this book.

To my family and friends, who have enriched my life in more ways than I can express: Mary and Dick Gies, Cheryl Hirss, Liz and Nan Duncan. Aunt Susie, Uncle Frank, and all of my cousins. Anita and Bob Galaviz, Uncle Raul, Jeff Obert, Carli Lloyd, Sofia

Palmqvist, James Galanis, Tina, Mya, and MacKenzie Ellertson. My St. Louis family—the Owenses, Tim Owens, Tony Hubert and Jeff Cooper. Malia Arrant. Lesle Gallimore and Amy Griffin. And to other friends who I may have failed to mention here by name but who I hold in my heart with continued love, gratitude, and respect.

To my soccer family: my youth coaches Tim Atencio and Carl Wheeler. Pia Sundhage, Cheryl Bailey, Paul Rogers, April Heinrichs, Phil Wheddon, Sunil Gulati, Dan Flynn, and my teammates past and present.

Without the help of an unbelievable medical team, I couldn't have gotten back on the field to experience the fulfillment of a World Cup and the thrill of another Olympic Games. Thanks to Dr. James Andrews and his medical team (Butch Buchanan, Luke Miller, and Harrison Reich) led by Kevin Wilke.

And to my rock Bruce Snell, Dave "Supe" Andrews, Ivan Pierra, and, of course, Hughie O'Malley.

To all my sponsors who have helped me in immeasurable ways, and, in particular, to Joe Elsmore and all my friends at Nike for their continued support.

To Richard Motzkin, for his longtime guidance and support, and to the indefatigable Whitney Unruh, for her friendship and for always knowing how to get the best out of me. She read me as closely as she read this book and was my rock solid. Rich and Whitney's dedication and hard work go beyond the call of duty, and I owe them a special debt of gratitude.

Completing the book is a testament to the talents and involvement of a great many people. This book would not exist without the unwavering support and enthusiasm of my editor, David Hirshey, who understands the importance of both soccer and women's sports and does his part in building the game by writing about it for ESPN and coaching his HC team to one championship after another (as well as one pitcher of beer after another!). Thank you, David, for challenging me to dig deep and trust my voice. Thanks also to associate editor Barry Harbaugh, for his grace under pressure in the home stretch, and to all the staff at HarperCollins, for their support and patience.

Thank you to Ann Killion for helping me tell my story and never being judgmental about the more fragile parts of my life. In essence, you became the counselor I always fought against having. Your dedication, reliability, intelligence, and efficiency will never be forgotten. You have the rare talent to see through the glitz and glamour of women's sports and write about them in an honest and enlightening way.

To Adrian, a blessing in my life. Thank you for strengthening my confidence in myself and for encouraging me to remain true to who I am at all costs. You have believed in me in ways that nobody else ever has. Our love is a love that builds a deep and unbreakable bond, no matter what challenges and heartache come our way. Some things were never possible without you by my side. We can do anything together. I love you.